RASPUTIN

RASPUTIN

R. J. Minney

CASSELL · LONDON

CASSELL & COMPANY LTD
35 Red Lion Square, London WC1R 4SG
Sydney, Auckland
Toronto, Johannesburg

First published 1972

I.S.B.N. 0 304 93893 9

F.1072

Printed in Great Britain by
The Camelot Press Ltd, London and Southampton

FOR PRIMROSE

Foreword

It is not my purpose to try to prove that Rasputin was a saint or a sinner, a profligate monk or the Devil incarnate, a man of gentleness and consideration who would go out of his way to help others or a man who grabbed all he could get. As the story unfolds you will be able to judge which of these alternatives is applicable.

When he was murdered in December 1916 thousands rejoiced in Petrograd and the columns of the newspapers were filled with the wildest abuse. It was these extravagant, unchecked Press accounts that inspired the earliest books about him, some of them rushed out within weeks of his death. That black, vicious, horrifying portrait of a monster who brought misery to millions has survived for more than half a century: we have seen the beast in the cinema and on television, and though the fleeting vision lasts barely an hour on the screen, its most evil aspects linger in the memory for ever.

His life, simple but at times dramatic, is basically a simple study, for the path he chose and tried to follow was the essence of simplicity. He was taught the Scriptures by his father long before he could read, and faith in God was always the strongest strand in his attitude to life. He never denied that he sinned; he insisted that all men, even monks and priests, sin. His reasoning told him that every living man and woman lives in the body as well as the spirit: each has its own functions. If some bodily actions are looked on as sinful, then one must seek redemption.

You will see how his life shaped. Many writers insist that he was 'all villain, the pure quintessence of wickedness, a monster . . .'. 'Nothing is good about him,' Alan Moorehead commented, dismissing the sweeping condemnation which clings to our memory of him. Rasputin certainly had the gift of healing and of prophecy, vouched for by many witnesses. Did he use these gifts to help others, or did he use them for his own advancement and profit? Did he seek fame or did he disregard what others said of him? Some, especially in the grand ducal palaces and in the drawing-rooms of society, regarded him as the evil genius of Russia. Ten attempts were made to murder him. The first, an attack with a knife a few weeks before the First World War, was so gravely serious that it seemed unlikely he would live. The tenth attempt, two and a half years later, succeeded: there are three versions of what really happened then; I draw on all three.

As you read these pages you will be able to decide which was the real Rasputin. Whichever way you look at it he was an outstanding figure in modern history, larger than life even in the shadow cast by him across the years.

Contents

Illustrations

Acknowledgements

I am indebted to a number of people for their help with this book—some in America, Britain, France, Germany, Russia including Siberia, and Africa, others no longer with us: they gave me hours of their time, talking, telephoning, writing long, interesting letters, advising, arguing. I have tried to separate the strong prejudice against Rasputin (so much of which has survived) from the facts available in records that can be examined and analysed.

And I owe much to the large number of books about him, published in Russia, Germany, France, Britain and the United States of America, at times accurate, at times not. I have drawn on *The Fall of the Russian Monarchy* by Sir Bernard Pares; the *Letters of the Tsaritsa to the Tsar*; of the *Tsar to the Tsaritsa*; the *Letters of the Tsar to his Mother the Dowager Empress Marie*; the *Tsar's Diary*; and the intimate narratives of Lili Dehn, Anna Vyroubova, both of whom knew Rasputin well, and the two books written by Maria Rasputin about her father and their family life in their home in Siberia and in his apartment in St Petersburg; and also the equally intimate and frank biography of the last Tsar's sister, the Grand Duchess Olga.

Among those with whom I discussed Rasputin were Sir Paul Dukes, a member of the Anglo-Russian Commission 1915–19 and in the Intelligence Service in Soviet Russia 1918–20; Sir Robert Bruce Lockhart, Acting Consul-General in Moscow 1915–17 and sent to Petrograd and Moscow as Head of Special Mission to the Soviet Government in January 1918; Baroness Moura Budberg; Sir Osbert Sitwell; Mr Joann Simanovich; Mr Nicholas Katkoff, a close friend of Prince Felix Yussupov; Mrs Zina Louie; Mrs Mariamna Fortunato; Mr John Stuart, who has made a study of ikons; and others who prefer not to be named.

Indebtedness must also be gratefully recorded for the guidance given me by Mr Douglas Matthews, Deputy Librarian, London Library; Miss Joan Bailey, London Library; Miss Jean Mauldon, Tunbridge Wells Public Library; the Library of the Society for Cultural Relations with the U.S.S.R.; and especially Mr Julian Bach, for his unfailing advice and guidance.

Siberian Childhood

In the remote Siberian village of Pokrovskoe, about 200 miles east of the Ural mountains and six to eight days by railway, river steamer and cart from St Petersburg, the capital of the Russian Empire, Grigori Efimovich Rasputin was born in June 1872.

The river Tura, covered with ice in the winter, swift in the summer and at times turbulent, rushes past the village and some miles to the north joins the Tobol, then merges into the river Irtysh which, having come 2,300 miles from China, takes the new name of Ob and empties into the northern Arctic waters.

Around Pokrovskoe the land is flat and limitless, parched by the scorching sun in summer with fierce storms roaring round the small wooden houses in the early Spring and sprinkling the land with swamps and bogs. Slowly the landscape, frozen white for half the year, with silver birch trees beautified by a filigree of snow, begins to awaken and the delightful tinkle of sleigh bells have to wait for the return of winter. The steppes are beautiful in the Spring: there are wild flowers in abundance everywhere—irises, forget-me-nots, ranunculi—the birds sing gaily in the trees and as summer approaches one's nostrils are filled with the fragrance of the pines. Here and there one sees a slight rise in the land and further on some small lakes.

The village of Pokrovskoe, even a century ago, was neither small nor sleepy. In the summer the steamships brought passengers and freight from the provincial capital Tobolsk, 120 miles to the north, and conveyed them to Tyumen, the nearest town, sixty miles to the west. In the winter the carts or *troika* sledges conveyed the passengers and goods across the frozen rivers. Pokrovskoe was one of the staging posts on the route and all mail carts and waggons pulled up there in front of the Rasputin house to change horses.

The quay swarmed with people in the summer: the villagers, the women in orange, vermilion and blue cotton dresses, the men in long belted blouses hanging outside their trousers, rushed out of their houses on hearing the steamship's blast, to see who were arriving and who leaving. On the crowded deck, equally curious, were gathered lumbermen, pilgrims, beggars, traders, soldiers, priests, women with black shawls over their heads, and little children running, falling, screaming. It provided the village with a varied, fleeting panorama of a wider world that most of them would never see.

Pokrovskoe was not without diversions of its own. Near the white-steepled church was the village hall where the people gathered in the evenings, gossiped, drank vodka or madeira, danced and sang. The girls wore their *sarafanes* (embroidered dresses) and sat on wooden benches ranged along the wall, exclaiming, laughing until the boys grabbed and whirled them round to the music of the *galmotchka*, the Russian accordion, and the *balalaika*. Even the old people danced, for music if played rousingly will drag every Russian out of his seat.

A much milder but inescapable diversion, especially for the girls, was to sneak into the house of Groucha, the village fortune-teller, to ask when they would marry and whom they would marry. Another was to see the mail coach arrive. The people gathered outside Rasputin's house to stare at the passengers and watch the village wheelwright Dyck Stepanovich test the road-worthiness of the coach wheels, and they would nudge each other to draw attention to the magistrate's clerk as he came up to see that all regulations were being fully observed: he was stout, wobbled as he walked and always smelt of brandy.

Most of the *isbas*, the homes of the peasants, were larger and better than the normal peasant dwellings in Siberia, or Russia for that matter. The house in which Grigori was born was spacious, but not particularly comfortable. His father Efim Andreievich Rasputin had an extensive farm with twelve cows and eighteen small, sturdy Siberian horses. He was headman of the village, deeply religious and read the Bible to his family every evening. Grigori's mother, Anna Egorovna, tall, slim with pleasant smiling eyes, a Samoyed, it is said, of Mongolian origin from near Tobolsk, shouldered the domestic duties, kept the house meticulously clean and also helped her husband on the farm. They were well-to-do but by no means rich.

Their ancestors were not serfs, nor were they descended from the criminals or the political prisoners deported to Siberia. Grigori's grandfather used to say: 'When Yermak* sent his ships along the Tura in the sixteenth century we were already Rasputins.' The exiles were sent to the remote eastern regions to prevent their escaping and returning to

---

* Yermak was the Cossack leader who defeated the Tartars and captured Sibir, their Siberian capital.

Russia. In the western regions of Siberia people who wanted to farm were allowed to take any uncultivated land they were capable of ploughing and cultivating, but they were not allowed to take land that belonged to another.

Siberia, which Yermak handed over to Ivan the Terrible in 1582, was too far away for the serf system, introduced by Boris Godounov a century later, to be extended across this vast stretch of nearly 4,000 miles beyond the Ural mountains. In Russia there were three categories of serfs—the *Pomestichikii*, owned by the nobles, who treated them harshly, at times tyrannously; the *Darstvenny-Kristiane*, State-owned serfs; and the *Udelnyi*, serfs of the Imperial family. In Siberia there were practically no nobles, so there were no serfs of that category; the State-owned serfs had to pay a tax if they wished to carry on with their own work; the Imperial family had hardly any serfs in Siberia.

Grigori, known affectionately as Grisha, was the youngest of three children. His brother Mikhail, three years older, helped his father on the land, his sister Vara helped in the house: they had at that time one servant, a kind, elderly woman. Grigori's pleasures were rough and simple: he confessed later to his daughter Maria, that he used to play with the children in the village and quarrelled with them. He was sent to the village school, but was not interested in his studies and was unable to read and write. His father, however, insisted on his learning the Scriptures. Grigori had to listen attentively when his father read the Bible so that he would remember what was said. Possessed of an extraordinarily retentive memory, he was able even in his childhood to recite long passages from the Bible. When he reached the age of ten he was put to work in the fields and look after the livestock. He had a deep affection for horses and spent much of his time in the dim, lantern-lit stables, talking to them, fondling them and rejoicing in their smell. His father felt he was lazy and often scolded him for not working as hard as the others.

In many ways he was unlike his brother and sister. Their thoughts were on everyday events and duties, his were devoted to dreams. With his lively imagination he tried to understand and interpret the meaning of various passages of the Scriptures.

Their house had a large vestibule with a door on the right leading to the section where the family lived. In the main room an immense, solidly built brick stove rose right up to the ceiling: it was used not only for cooking but also for baking bread; on an elongated section it was possible on a very cold night to lie down and sleep. At one end there was a large rectangular dining table with ikons hanging on the wall and a light always burning in front of them. The family's normal dormitory was on an upper level, with wooden bunks along the wall to sleep on.

The door on the left of the vestibule led to the section where visitors could be put up for the night—pilgrims, wandering *startsyi* or holy men in long robes leaning wearily on a tall staff, traders on their way to Tobolsk or Tyumen or to Moscow and St Petersburg.

The house, with pot plants on the window-sills, geraniums, cinerarias and roses, had an enormous courtyard with a high fence to screen it from the road. Beyond the large stable were sheds for carts and sledges. At the back of the house, at the far end of the courtyard, was a structure containing a Russian steam bath, a feature of almost every peasant home.

The main road from Russia to Siberia and the Far East ran through the village. Because of this Pokrovskoe was full of animation and life, even in winter. There was a small shop, a village blacksmith, a social centre where one could gather and sing and dance, and of course the church, its white steeple surmounted by an attractive golden cross which glittered in the sunlight; its carillons could be heard for miles.

Grigori's father Efim Andreievich supplied the horses for the mail service and occasionally drove the coach himself, travelling 400 versts* to Irbit in the Urals for the Fur Fair; at other times his elder son took over, or perhaps one of the men who worked for him on the land.

This was before the days of railways in Siberia. A line linking Perm, amid the pines of the Urals, with Ekaterinburg where the exiles were unloaded and made to walk for days still further eastward, was built in 1878, when Grigori was six; six years later the line was extended to Tyumen, the chief centre for navigation on the Siberian rivers. The Trans-Siberian Railway was not begun until 1891, by which time Grigori was nearly twenty.

---

* A verst is two-thirds of a mile.

The Call of Religion

That Grigori was unlike other children became noticeable quite early. One autumn evening the village elders, with high Slav cheek-bones, some young, all of them bearded, arrived at the house in their long high-necked blouses belted at the waist and in knee-length boots, and sat on benches round the stove to gossip while they sipped their China tea and discussed local problems with their headman Efim Andreievich Rasputin. Grigori, aged twelve and suffering from a feverish cold, lay wrapped in blankets in a bed made for him on the stove.

The discussion, carried on in lowered voices because of the child's illness, was chiefly about the theft of a horse belonging to one of the poorer villagers: it was his only horse, and he had no money to buy another. The talk went on for some time. Could it have been stolen by one of the wandering mendicants, or had someone in the village taken it and concealed it somewhere? The possibilities were explored but led to no solution. Suddenly little Grisha threw off his blankets and clambered down from the stove. With an accusing finger he went to the best-dressed, most highly respected man in the village. 'You,' he said, 'you stole the horse.'

The man was furious, the village elders were flabbergasted and Efim Andreievich was very angry. 'Get back to bed,' he hollered. Had the child been well he would certainly have cuffed him about the ears. 'He is sick,' Efim Andreievich explained apologetically to the man who had been so wickedly accused. 'It is just a feverish delirium. Don't take any notice of the child. I'll deal with him later.'

By the time the villagers left the incident was practically forgotten. But not by all. Two of them followed the man who had been accused, keeping at a safe distance in the darkness and feeling that, if guilty, he would betray himself in some way. They noticed that he was uneasy, for he kept looking round to see if he was being followed.

When he neared his home the well-to-do villager glanced once again over his shoulder and, finding that no one was in sight, went into the stables, opened the door carefully so that it would not creak, and brought out the stolen horse. Leading it to the edge of his land he shoo-ed it away. At this the two men rushed up, seized him and with a

5

flow of vile curses beat him severely. Then, leaving him bruised and
bleeding, they rescued the horse and restored it to its delighted owner.

It caused much comment in the village. Early the next morning a
number of women, with shawls drawn over their heads, assembled
outside the thief's house and shouted angry abuse. There was no question of handing him over to the police; he had been dealt with already
and the stolen horse had been restored.

But when the excitement died down, what was talked of then and
for years afterwards, was how did little Grisha, who had been in bed
for some days and so could not have seen the theft of the horse, come
to know who had stolen it? Little Grisha could not answer; he didn't
know, he just saw it happen while he lay ill in bed.

Had it not been for its position at the crossroads and on a busy river
where steamers called and passengers embarked and alighted and with
a staging-post for the Imperial mail, Pokrovskoe would have been no
better than any other Siberian village. It retained, of course, all the
familiar signs of a Siberian village—dogs nosing the rubbish heaps,
children playing games in the streets, women in wide skirts talking in
loud voices and gesticulating at their front doors, carts rumbling by,
horses being taken to the village blacksmith to be shod, and hens flap-
ping their wings and cackling as they tried to avoid the traffic.

In a small shop in the main street one could buy clothes for men,
women and children: the range was limited, the garments were in the
style the peasants had worn for centuries. Food was grown on the
farms: there was a wine shop which sold vodka and madeira and sweet
wine. Alcohol had to be consumed on the premises at the village centre:
some of the older men sat there for hours drinking; they were not
pressed to pay at once, and as a result the debt mounted. Occasionally
their homes as well as their horses and cows had to be sold to pay the
debt.

Grigori, as he grew older, used to drift into the place with his friends,
the closest of whom was Dimitri Petcherkine, intelligent and cheerful
like Grigori, but also, like him, considered rather odd, for they used to
spend hours together discussing the interpretation of certain passages
in the Scriptures. But that interfered in no way with their gaiety; they
joined heartily and noisily in the singing and dancing. The women
usually danced in a circle, waving a handkerchief, with the men in the
centre. After a time the men leapt into the air or danced the *kazachok*,

with bent knees, shooting out alternate legs. Grigori danced well. By
the time he was fifteen admiring eyes followed him round the floor as
he danced the *komorinskaya* with a village girl. The village girls were
drawn to him: they found him irresistible. Tall for his age, thin, with
dark brown hair, the beginnings of a small beard, a large fleshy nose,
his most compelling feature was his steely blue eyes: they could convey
a wide range of emotions—admiration, tenderness, affection, devotion
—and seemed to be able to ferret out the secrets of one's soul. Their
effect was magnetic.

His father, while approving of his intense interest in religion, often
scolded him for being lazy and spending hours singing and dancing.
He did not mind Grigori sitting at the table listening to the wandering
pilgrims, who always had their meals with the family: they talked
about the impressive monasteries they visited, the wonderful ikons on
the walls, the deeply moving chant of the monks and of their long
journeys often walking hundreds of miles barefooted. The boy listened
with sparkling-eyed fascination and longed to follow their example.
One afternoon, without a word to the family, he set out for Verkhoture, the most famous monastery in Siberia, to which thousands came
on a pilgrimage to see the sacred relics of St Simeon the Just. But a
villager, seeing the boy stumbling along the deep snow to the distant
horizon, felt he was much too young to make the journey of 300 versts
alone, and ran to tell Efim Andreievich.

Springing on to a horse, Efim dashed after his son and overtook him
three miles from the village. He brought him back and cuffed him in
the courtyard. 'You'll do anything except work,' he said. Some days
later he put Grigori on to driving one of his carts. It would give him an
outlet: he liked meeting people and talking, he might just as well work
and earn money. In a year or two, he told the boy, you can take
pilgrims to Verkhoture, but not now, you are much too young to
undertake such a long journey.

In recent months a closeness had begun to develop between Grigori
and his brother Mikhail. Until now the age-gap of three years had kept
the elder brother from regarding Grigori as a suitable companion in his
varied activities. But now they went riding together and raced against
each other, swam together in the swift river Tura, or sat on the river
bank fishing: occasionally they went out with the fishermen and helped
to cast their nets and haul in fish for the markets at Tobolsk and
Tyumen.

Mikhail showed hardly any interest in religion and could not be encouraged by his father to follow Grisha's example. The boys went together in the evenings to join the peasant girls in the crowded village centre. They were joyous evenings of singing and dancing, but quite often Grigori did not come. He would be with his friend Dimitri Petcherkine, discussing religion, and they spent hours on their knees saying their prayers. Mikhail could not understand it. Grigori appeared to him to have a dual personality. He had no intention himself of sacrificing pleasure for prayers.

Life with the Monks

One summer afternoon, with the sun blisteringly hot, as it often is in Siberia in the summer, the brothers stripped to the waist and leapt into the roaring river. Both were excellent swimmers. Mikhail, the faster of the two, got well ahead, but soon seemed to be in difficulties. Desperately Grigori strove to reach him, but was unable to fight the river. About twenty yards ahead a villager jumped in, rescued Mikhail, and then dragged Grigori out. Misha, suffering from acute exhaustion, was carried home and put to bed. He was said to be suffering from inflammation of the lungs. The next day he died.

Grisha was desolate. He blamed himself for not being able to rescue his brother. There were moments of acute dejection when the family feared that he might throw himself into the river. For weeks he kept away from people and hardly talked to anyone, even at home. After a time he began to sit with the family again for meals, nibbling the *zakoski (hors d'oeuvres)* or pickled fish and stuffed eggs. What the pilgrims and the *startsyi* said struck much deeper roots now than before. He was resolved to set out like them, barefooted, weighed down with chains, and to experience their religious ecstasy himself, not just sit and receive it at second hand. Since his brother's death he had taken on Mikhail's work on the land; and it did not now seem right, with his parents still grieving over the death of one son, that he should go away for several months, or possibly a year or more, for the pilgrims spoke with pride of the years they spent wandering.

Efim Andreievich noticed the effect of these talks on his son. When the boy reached the age of sixteen, he told him he could take the cart and go to the monastery at Verkhoture. 'It is 300 versts away, too far to walk, you can do that when you are older. The cart can be used on the journey for transporting goods and people, some of whom may also want to go to Verkhoture.'

It was the moment Grigori had longed for: for months it had been noticed that hope and excitement had been bubbling within him. He could now take the road which would lead him to the goal destiny had reserved for him.

Before he had got very far he was hailed by a travel-stained youth wearing a long cotton gown and leaning on a tall staff. The youth asked if he could be given a lift for part of the way to Verkhoture. 'I am going to the monastery to be a novice.' Grigori stretched out his hand and hauled the youth into the seat beside him. 'I am going there myself,' he said.

'As a novice too?'

'No. I shall stay for a while and decide later what I shall do.'

The novice's name was Mileti Saborevski. He was about a year or two older than Grigori. They talked chiefly about religion. Grigori knew much more about the Scriptures and recited long passages, which they analysed together, trying to find their true meaning. Mileti, on the other hand, knew much more about the saints and martyrs: he could read, Grigori could not. Simeon the Just, he explained, had been a very rich man. He gave his wealth to the poor and went to Verkhoture to become a monk.

Grigori listened attentively and nodded. Mileti advised him to stay at the monastery, learn to read and write, and become a monk. Grigori said he did not want to be a monk. To be a member of an order did not appeal to him. He wanted to be free, to make his own personal contact with God. The dialogue should be direct, not channelled through others and given an interpretation by some intermediary.

It took just over a week to get to Verkhoture. High on a hill in that small, busy town on the river Tura stood the early seventeenth-century monastery—a large white building with a tall surrounding stone wall. Beyond the town were farm-lands, which in turn were encircled by a dense wood. On the further side of the wood, some miles from the town, lived an aged hermit, odd and regarded by some as crazy; his shelter was a tiny hut and he never took the heavy chains off his arms and legs. All who came to see the bones of St Simeon the Just, said to have healing powers, never neglected to walk the seven miles to see Father Makari and seek his blessing. His small, round wrinkled face was elongated by an untidy beard, his voice was soft and sometimes barely audible; it was said of him that if the words did not always reach your ears they certainly reached your heart. A large number of hens and chickens kept strutting round his hut. He used to call them and talk to them, and one felt that he had established some sort of understanding with them. Men and women came across Siberia and even from Western Russia to see him. Some had walked barefooted for months, others came in carriages and carts—well-to-do merchants, aristocrats, army officers, soldiers, peasants—they came to ask for his blessing and to seek his advice and guidance. In small towns and remote villages they knew of Makari, even in Moscow and St Petersburg they had begun to talk of him.

Grigori was greatly attracted to Verkhoture and the monastery and often thought of the wealthy St Simeon who had given up all his riches and dedicated his life to the service of God. Grigori had no desire for wealth or luxury. He wanted to serve others. In the fields he joined the monks, tilling, sowing, and went with them into the town to give the poor the food they had grown.

But Grigori had no wish to stay for long in the monastery. After some weeks he discovered that, in a separate building, heretics sent from various parts of Siberia were held for correction. Some of them were said to belong to the *Khlysty* sect, who practised flagellation and indulged in sex orgies. Grigori spoke to some of them; the gentleness and tenderness instilled in him by the Scriptures made him recoil at the very thought of flagellation. He stayed on only because of the hermit Makari, with whom he spent many hours day after day listening eagerly to his simple philosophy. 'When you go back to your home,' Makari said, 'you must learn to read and write. It is essential.' Grigori promised he would.

After four months Grigori left Verkhoture. Mileti Saborevski tried to persuade him to stay and join the community, but Grigori firmly refused. The monks, who had come to like and admire him, made a collection and gave him more than enough money for the journey home.

His father was not pleased at his long absence. The horses could have earned money during those lost months; and Grigori, eager to tell his father all he had seen and heard, did not enjoy being welcomed with a shower of angry abuse. Some days later Efim Andreievich tried to draw him out. His son's answers were short, his attitude indifferent. He showed his independence by seeking employment with a carter-contractor at Tobolsk. A *telega** and two horses were assigned to him, and though he lived at home and was affable enough towards his parents and his sister, the atmosphere had changed.

The biggest change in fact was in Grigori. His stay in the monastery had altered his outlook and his way of life. Religious thoughts absorbed him. He acknowledged the greetings of the village girls with a smile,

---

* A kind of cart.

but no longer spent the evenings with them singing and dancing. He helped occasionally in the fields, but most of the time he was away driving the rough, swaying cart with bottles swinging from hooks in the roof and bundles falling constantly off the crude rack. At home he spent long hours fasting, meditating and praying.

One day, on his return from a long journey, he went to see his employer and reported that one of the two horses of his *telega* had broken loose and had gone to the river for a drink, but unfortunately fell in and was drowned. The contractor refused to accept the story. The police were called. 'This young scoundrel has sold the horse,' he said. Searching him, the police found twenty-one roubles in his pocket. It made them suspicious. How on earth could a youth receiving a small salary have so much money. Instantly they arrested him. Grigori shook himself free. 'What do you think you are doing?' he asked.

'How did you get so much money. You stole the horse and sold it, that's obvious.'

Grigori explained that the money had been given to him by the monks at the monastery. In fact they had given him more; the twenty-one roubles was what was left.

The police refused to believe him. At his trial in court his explanation was rejected. 'It's a lot of money,' the magistrate said. 'Monks have no money. A term in prison will cure you of stealing and lying.'

'Ask the monks,' Grigori said. 'They will tell you how I got the money. And I want to make this clear. I shall take action against the contractor for calling me a liar and a thief.'

The case was dismissed for lack of evidence, and young Grigori Rasputin was free to go home. The contractor apologized and asked him to stay on. Rasputin ignored the request and walked away. But the man ran after him, grabbed him by the arm and persuaded him to stay on as his driver.

A few months later Grigori, his cart laden with goods for delivery in various towns, found to his horror that a large package of furs, intended for a trader in Tyumen, had been stolen. When he reported it to his employer, the police were again called in. Two thefts within such a short space of time was too much for the contractor.

Afraid of losing his job, Grigori told the police that he had been attacked by a gang of bandits. Police inquiries revealed that Grigori, possibly answering a call of nature, had left the cart unattended for a few minutes. When he returned the furs had gone.

The court decided that, though what he had said was near enough to the truth, he should be punished for leaving the cart unattended as well as for not saying exactly what had occurred. The sentence passed at Tobolsk on 14 February 1891 was a flogging and a brief term of imprisonment. It is the *only* known record of his ever having been given a court sentence.

Years later he told his daughter Maria that he had never dared to steal anything because he realized that everybody would know at once that he was a thief. 'If my comrades stole anything *I* knew it at once'— and it seemed to him quite natural that the others would know it too.

On leaving the prison at the end of his brief sentence, he gave up working for the contractor and decided to leave home and wander like the pilgrims who had sat with him at his father's table and talked of their communion with God.

The Barefooted Pilgrim

At about this time a tragic sequence of disasters descended on the Rasputin family. First Grigori's mother, Anna Egorovna, died after a brief illness. She had been the mainstay of their domestic life: she cooked, laundered, worked on the land, kept the house spotlessly clean and brightened all the rooms with flowers.

Her daughter, who had been helping her, took over, but, subject as she was to epileptic fits, could not be relied on to run the house as meticulously, even with the help of their elderly servant. Often Anna Egorovna had washed the family's clothes on the river bank. Now her daughter took on this duty. One afternoon, under a blazing sun and bent over the washing, she had a fit and fell into the swift waters of the Tura. Her body was never recovered.

A third disaster followed shortly afterwards. The house, built entirely of wood like the other houses in the village, caught fire and, despite the efforts of Efim Andreievich, his son Grigori Efimovich and a host of neighbours who fought the flames bravely, almost the entire house was burned down.

Grigori could not leave home now as his father needed him; there were only the two of them left. He helped his father to rebuild the house: they made it much larger, with more rooms and a much bigger parlour; the walls had a double layer of wood and the tall windows were set in attractively carved frames. A garden was laid out in front with an iron railing to protect it. The spacious courtyard was surrounded by a tall, wooden wall with perpendicular white stripes as on the walls of the house.

Village women dropped in from time to time to help with the running of the house. After some weeks, when things seemed to be going a little more smoothly, Grigori decided to go away for a while; he had kept his desire to wander in check for a long time. On leaving he mentioned it to his father, who merely stared at him in wonder. As he walked to Balik he was told there was a religious fête at a monastery at Abalak and made his way there. It was on the river Tobol ten miles to the east of Tobolsk and more than a hundred miles from Pokrovskoe. At the fête he met a tall, slender, attractive girl with bright blue eyes and golden hair who lived in a nearby village. Her name was Proskovia Doubrovina. Grigori was drawn to her and she to him. There was a difference of four years in their age: she was twenty-three and he only nineteen. After a courtship lasting a few weeks he married her and took her home.

Efim Andreievich, now in his late forties, was delighted. They needed a woman in the house and Grigori had very thoughtfully brought one home. She was gentle, understanding, sweet-tempered: it was clear to Grigori that she was not going to nag him and start a quarrel when he set out on his wanderings.

The villagers came in small groups to see Grisha's wife. They welcomed her, for she was like them, a simple peasant, who could not read or write. The new domesticity in the home delighted Grigori and made him settle down: he dismissed all thought of going wandering for the time being. He took his wife, whom he called affectionately Novyk and sometimes Novychok, meaning the New One, to the village centre where they danced together just as they had danced at the fête at Abalak.

Acting on the advice of Makari the hermit, he began now to learn to read and write with the help of his father and the village priest Father Piotr. Knowing the Scriptures by heart, it was not difficult, once he had learned to spell, to recognize the printed text in the Bible.

Early in the following year Novyk gave birth to a son. Grigori was frantic with joy. He danced round the room and kissed his wife again and again in gratitude: the child, named Dimitri, was hardly ever out of his father's arms. With an accompaniment of delighted chatter, Grisha carried little Mitia from room to room, into the fields and proudly through the village street. The change in Grigori Rasputin was the subject of constant comment. 'He will settle down. He won't want to go on pilgrimages any more,' they said.

Six months later Dimitri died. What caused his death is not known, but to Grigori it was a shattering blow. He wept ceaselessly and refused to accept comfort from his father, or his close friend Dimitri, after whom the child had been named, or from the villagers, who had bestowed their warmth and affection on Grigori since his childhood; even his wife's attempt to comfort him had no effect. He refused to see or talk to anyone. For long hours each day he was on his knees and his prayers and lamentations were audible all over the house and in the streets. He ate nothing. Many thought that his mind had become unhinged. After some weeks, during which he never left the house, he suddenly disappeared. They looked for him in the fields and in the village but he could not be found. Some feared that he might have thrown himself into the river in despair and his body had been carried away by the swift waters of the Tura. Then it was noticed that his long white robe and tall staff were missing. His wife and his father breathed a sigh of relief. He had begun his wanderings or possibly had gone to spend some time in a monastery, trying to understand why God had taken his only child from him.

In fact he had set out on foot for the monastery at Verkhoture. It took him the best part of a month to reach it barefooted. The monks gave him a delighted welcome. The novice who had travelled as a passenger in his waggon, Mileti Saborevski, was still there. Grigori had little to say to any of them. He walked into the woods to seek Makari, whose religious faith was quite detached and without any sympathy for the *Khlysty* flagellants. Sitting down on the hard soil in front of his hut, Grigori found Makari at prayer and waited for some time until at last, when he had finished, Makari looked up to see who his visitor was.

Grigori's distress was only too apparent. His chains rattling as he raised his hand to bless Grigori and make the sign of the Cross, Makari listened attentively to all Grisha said and tried to comfort him as he wept over his son's death. 'Everyone,' Makari said, 'is weighed down by his own grief. Only those who know God will understand why he has been so afflicted.'

They prayed together for some hours. Being with Makari was comforting and reassuring; it provided him also with the key to what he had really been seeking in life—a way to God. Words alone were not enough.

'Have you learned to read and write?' Makari asked.

'Yes. I find reading easier than writing. But I shall improve with time.'

'God bless you, my son. He has sent you to me and I hope I have helped you to understand and accept the Lord's decisions.'

'Yes, holy father.'

Makari had helped him to find God. Every evening in Pokrovskoe large numbers of men and women of the village came to attend his prayer meetings, for they realized now that Grigori, being a *staretz*, could help them to attain salvation.

The village priest, Father Piotr, who gave religious instruction in the school and was a friend of the Rasputin family, did not like this at all. The congregation was deserting his church. Very few came to his services even on Sundays. He decided to talk to Grigori and warn him that unless he stopped luring his parishioners away, it would be his duty to report the matter to the Bishop of Tobolsk.

But on the day before he had intended to come and see Grigori a strange thing happened. It was early Spring, the morning was bright. While working in the fields, Grigori saw a dazzling light in the sky. Looking up, he saw the figure of the Virgin Mary in the sky. Her eyes were fixed on him and she kept on gesticulating, as though she was trying to say something. He was excited yet bewildered. Was it a dream or a real vision? He shut his eyes for a moment, but on opening them he saw that the Holy Virgin was still there. But the clothes she was wearing were quite different from her clothes in any ikon he had ever seen. He got down on his knees and prayed, then rushed to the woodshed in the courtyard and returned with a large wooden cross, which he planted where he had been standing when he saw the Holy Virgin.

Nothing was said about this to his wife or his father. As the morning wore on they saw he was no longer in the field, and once again they noticed that his long robe and pilgrim's staff were missing. He had gone possibly to some monastery to solve a fresh religious doubt. In fact he had gone to see his friend Dimitri Petcherkine to tell him about the vision. Dimitri was most excited and they decided to go to Verkhoture together to see the hermit Makari and seek his interpretation of what the Holy Virgin had been trying to say.

Once again the journey was on foot. The two young men stayed in the monastery with the monks, joining in all the religious services. Petcherkine was greatly attracted to the life and told Grisha that he would perhaps one day be a monk. But Grisha merely shook his head. 'I have come here only to see Makari.' He took Petcherkine with him through the forest to the hut and described in detail the lovely vision he had seen.

'Those gestures,' Makari said, 'the sweeping, forward movement of the Holy Virgin's hand clearly meant that you must go—go on a long pilgrimage. God has obviously chosen you for work of great importance. To undertake that work you must develop your spiritual powers. You must go to Mount Athos in Greece and pray there.'

'May I go with him?' Dimitri Petcherkine asked.

C

'Certainly. Though the vision was not vouchsafed to you and you have received no sign yet of the work that lies ahead for you, nevertheless it would be to your advantage to further your own spiritual training. So go with Grigori to Mount Athos.'

On returning home Grigori informed his wife and his father that he was setting out for Mount Athos, the most famous and sacred of all monastic places. Efim Andreievich had a vague idea that it was very far away, perhaps 1,000 miles. In fact it was about 2,300 miles from Pokrovskoe. Efim asked his son if he intended to walk there. Grigori said he could go no other way on a pilgrimage. Dimitri Petcherkine would be going with him. His wife dissolved in tears, but made no attempt to dissuade him, though deeply distressed at the thought of what was to be a long absence.

'How long will you be away?' she asked.

'That God will decide,' he said.

A few days later he and Dimitri set out. Efim did not like being left without his son's help in the fields and with the livestock, but had to accept the situation. All he said was: 'Grigori has become a pilgrim out of laziness—nothing else.'

They had to cross the rugged, in parts 5,000-feet high, Ural mountains, for Greece lay to the south-west of Pokrovskoe. That was all they knew: details of the route would have to be picked up as they went along. Barefooted and wearing chains, they covered each day about eight to ten miles and knocked on the doors of simple country people to ask for a night's shelter in a corner of the floor; when the weather was fine they slept out under the stars. In every village the people came out and invited them in. The family gathered round. Food was brought from the kitchen and endless cups of tea were provided by the *samovar*. Questions were asked about the towns and villages they had come through, about the people they met on the road, and about some of the more knotty points in the Scriptural texts. From time to time while they walked someone would run and grasp Grigori's arm, and with tears in her eyes would kneel and beg him to come and see her poor mother who was dying; or her ailing child perhaps; or her aged father. He would go in and pray by the bedside—there was nothing else he could do. Then he would rise, make the sign of the Cross over the patient and say, quite suddenly, the words coming spontaneously from his lips: 'She will not die—soon she will be well again.' And they would kiss the hem of his garment as he left; and he would tug it away from them gently: 'It is God's doing, not mine,' he would say.

At harvest time Grigori and Dimitri went into the fields to help; they joined the fishermen on the river to haul in the nets; and at times the villagers gathered in the street to hear Rasputin preach in his gentle melodious voice and join him in singing psalms and sacred songs. Always when they saw a monastery, Grigori and Dimitri would go in to attend divine service and celebrate Mass, staying to discuss the Scriptures with the monks.

After crossing the Urals they made for the Volga, the longest, widest and most important river in Russia. They did not follow it all the way down to the Caspian Sea where it discharges its waters through seventy mouths, but skirted Saratov, crossed to Rostov on the river Don, then circled the northern and western coast of the Black Sea, going through Rumania and Bulgaria to Greece.

It took ten months to reach their goal. Mount Athos, rising to a height of 6,000 feet, dominated a picturesque tongue of land jutting out into the Aegean Sea. On and around the peak, revered as the holiest citadel of the Orthodox Church, are strewn more than a score of monasteries of various denominations. Some sponsored by the Russians are richly endowed: almost all have priceless treasures of Byzantine art and vast collections of historic documents. Not all the architecture is attractive: the rectangular, wooden-balconied buildings are pleasing; others have a quaint but delightful beauty. The churches, surmounted by cupolas, towers and onion domes, stand in quadrangles. Wherever one turns the landscape is very lovely: the gardens are rich in colour and perfume, the thickets strewn with pink and white oleanders, the meadows filled with grazing bulls. There are no cows. In 1060 the Emperor Constantine IX passed a law to prevent the entry 'of any women, any female, any eunuch, and any one with smooth visage'. Even now no woman is allowed to set foot in any part of the sacred mountain and female animals are still excluded. As a distinguishing mark, and providing the right of entry, all the men were required to grow beards.

The total population is about 7,000. Less than half are monks, the rest are lay brothers. Apart from their religious devotions, they till the fields, grow corn and vegetables for the table, set out in boats to fish, and are skilled in various handicrafts.

Equipped with the necessary documents, Grigori and Dimitri

Petcherkine were allowed to enter and were welcomed by the monks as their guests. Both Grigori and Dimitri were delighted. From the summit the view was breathtaking. The chants in the churches, the pageantry in the streets, the very air was vibrant with the call of religion.

By the end of the week Petcherkine, enchanted by the life and the setting, informed Grisha that he had decided to become a monk and was going to take the vows of a novitiate. His efforts to induce Grigori to do so too were brusquely brushed aside. 'I do not like this place,' Grigori said. 'There is nothing but dirt and vermin and moral filth here.' Without women, he added, the only natural outlet for their human desires would be through homosexuality.

For some days he had been busy ferreting out what was going on behind the scenes and saw enough to substantiate his fears. His surmise, he found, was proved to be right. 'I have no wish to spend another night here,' he told Petcherkine. 'I am leaving. I find the atmosphere utterly insufferable. May God bless you and guide your steps away from these corrupting pitfalls.' Both got down on their knees and prayed, then they embraced and parted.

CHAPTER FIVE

The Holy Land—
Then Home

Instead of returning home Grisha took the road to the Holy Land. Crossing the sea to Asia Minor, he wandered southward through Turkey and eastward to Aleppo, then took the coast road to Tripoli, Beirut, Damascus, Jerusalem, Bethlehem, Bethsheba, Nazareth and Golgotha.

It took him another 1,000 miles away from Pokrovskoe, but dressed in his long pilgrim's robe and with his tall staff to lean on, he walked on undaunted. Alone now, he relied on the company he met on the road and the hospitality of the peasants, Greek and Turk and Jew, who gave him food and shelter and delighted in asking him about his travels.

What he saw in the Holy Land moved him deeply. Each town was steeped in sacred memories. These were God's pastures. Christ had walked here, suffered here and performed his miracles here. Its echoes filled the years ahead. Constantly he talked of it—talked so vividly that those who listened spellbound felt that they had walked with him in the sacred pastures. It was a verbal record; a written record was made by Grigori Rasputin when he returned to the Holy Land about twenty years later.

There was no means of keeping in touch with his wife and father during his long absence. He could give no address, so he received no letters, no news of what was going on in his home. A few days before he left home his wife thought she was pregnant. Would there be a son again to take the place of Dimitri, his first-born? God may grant him this great joy if he deserved it.

After an absence of two and a half years, during which he had walked nearly 7,000 miles, he returned to Pokrovskoe. He was no longer the young man of twenty. Though almost twenty-three now, he looked at least fifteen years older. His beard was longer and fuller; his dark brown hair hung down to his shoulders, his steely blue eyes had become hypnotic. His wife stared at the stranger at the door, his clothes dusty, a bag hanging at his side. To her he was just another wandering *staretz*. 'Come in, come in,' she said affably. 'I will bring you some tea and food and I will prepare a bed for you for the night if you should care to stay.'

Grigori's laugh was explosive. 'I hope you *will* let me stay here,' he said. His voice and laughter brought recognition. She wept as they embraced, kissed and embraced again.*

'Wait here,' she said.

'Can I not come into the house?' he asked.

'Wait,' she cried as she hurried in. A moment later she returned carrying in her arms the child born to him during his long absence.

He stared at the child, now two years old. 'It's my Dimitri,' he said at last. 'My Mitia has come back. God has given him back to me.'

Efim Andreievich came in from the fields to see what was going on. Who was the strange man at the door and what had caused all that familiarity and laughter?

His eyes widened as he recognized his son. After a long, warm embrace, he held Grisha at arm's length to survey the changes wrought on him by travel and experience. He had reached maturity. In the depths of his steely eyes there was a more penetrating, searching look now, which seemed to probe thoughts and reach deep into the soul. What Efim Andreievich saw was a fervent, unshakeable dedication to God.

The news spread rapidly through the village. Within minutes the people came hurrying to the house to see their Grisha and to ask him a thousand questions about his travels. But first he made them gather round him in the courtyard, get down on their knees and join him in prayer. They prayed and chanted for nearly two hours, then crowded into the parlour, some sitting on the wooden benches against the wall, others standing, while Grisha's wife and father passed round plates with black bread, pickled fish and stuffed eggs, and tea to wash it all down. Grigori had given up eating meat and asked his wife not to serve it to him nor to cook his food in animal fat. Having heard only tit-bits from Grigori about his travels, the villagers came again the next evening and the next. The talks were always preceded by a prayer. A few days later, with their help Grigori began to build a chapel in the courtyard, and when it was finished he held long services there every evening. The prayers were interspersed with sermons, based on his personal experiences and reflections, which gave an edge and reality to what he said. Every evening they came to the chapel. The service and the talks went on for hours, and then they came into the house for refreshments in the *gornitsa* or parlour and still more talks. They began now to call him Father Grigori.

---

* For years the family talked of this and his daughter Maria wrote about it.

The village priest's wrath was roused again. This time he resolved to take action. A lengthy report was sent to Bishop Anthony of Tobolsk, describing the flagellation and promiscuous sexual orgies as practised by the *Khlysty* sect at Verkhoture and now taking place in the courtyard of Rasputin's house. He did not pause to wonder why Grigori, if he found that method of religious devotion pleasing, did not stay in the monastery at Verkhoture.

The Bishop, greatly disturbed, sent a commission to Pokrovskoe with strict orders to ferret out all that was going on.

The members of the commission, all of them priests, called on Father Piotr first, then visited in turn all the villagers, talking to those who attended the prayer meetings as well as those who did not. Numerous questions were asked. After the inquiry was closed, and on the assumption that, if there were *Khlysty* practices, Grigori would resume them now, a policeman was sent from Tobolsk dressed in peasant's clothes to attend one of the services in the chapel. Slipping in unrecognized, he joined in the prayers and was so greatly impressed that he knelt before Grisha and kissed his hand.

The commission refused to reveal to Father Piotr what their findings were: the report, they stated, would be delivered to the Bishop, who, in due course, would give his verdict.

It was not what Father Piotr had expected. Grigori Efimovich's religious services were found not to be remotely heretical. There was nothing that resembled *Khlysty* practices in any way or that could be described as departing from the Orthodox Christian ritual. His preaching was highly commended and tribute was paid to Father Grigori's understanding and interpretation of the Scriptures.

Delighted to be home with his wife and son, Grigori abandoned all thought of going wandering again for the present. He confined his wandering to the rooms of the house with his son in his arms, singing, dancing, elevating him high above his head and then taking him into the fields where the farm hands gathered round and supplied an accompaniment of admiration, laughter and song.

The child was told about Mount Athos and the Holy Land, but merely smiled, for he loved listening to his father's soft, gentle voice with its haunting musical lilt, though it could when necessary reveal a roughness and anger when challenged by Father Piotr and other critics.

He worked in the fields by day, went to the white-spired village church on Sundays and two or three mornings a week to celebrate Mass there, and went with his fishermen friends on the river Tura and occasionally took his wife to the village social centre where they joined in the singing and dancing.

The pilgrims, the *startsyi*, the travellers passing through, the itinerant traders, the mendicants, even the soldiers came to see him, sat at the table and, while the food was passed round, listened with fascination and wonder to his account of the many thousands of miles he had covered, the Tartar towns he had been through, the small scattered villages on the shores of the Black Sea—a vast world most of them had never heard of and would never see. Before they went they knelt and prayed with him, and they left with his blessing.

When he saw that the people had begun to look on him as a saint he angrily brushed it aside. 'There is no holy man on earth; so long as man lives, he sins,' he said—it was his recurrent response. Nevertheless they were able to prove his saintliness, for they had heard of his ability to heal the sick and had in their own village seen those who were dying leave their beds. A 'miracle-worker' they began to call him. 'It is not a miracle,' Grisha said. 'All that is necessary is to ask God's help. Prayer can do anything.'

Visitors passing through Pokrovskoe made his name known in the remote eastern reaches of Siberia as far as Mongolia and Manchuria, westward beyond the Ural mountains to Moscow and St Petersburg, and southward to Kiev and Kazan.

To Kiev and Kazan

After spending ten months at home Grigori again began his wanderings. He did not travel far. His desire was to visit Kiev and Kazan, especially Kazan to see the famous miracle-working ikon of the Holy Virgin to know if it was how She appeared to him in his vision. A few weeks before leaving he learned that his wife was pregnant again: would it be another boy, or perhaps a girl?

His wife wept when he blessed her and said good-bye; she always wept, but never tried to persuade him to stay at home a little longer. He went as the Lord prompted: it would be wrong for her to interfere.

Although Kazan, on the other side of the Ural mountains, was only 650 miles from Pokrovskoe, Grigori went first to Kiev, 800 miles further on.

Kiev, one of the oldest and most beautiful cities in Russia, was important 1,000 years ago for its position on the trade route between Byzantium, capital of the Eastern Roman Empire, and the north. It is picturesquely situated amid wooded heights on the banks of the river Dneiper, here 500 yards wide. As the earliest centre of Christianity in the country, it was looked upon as a Holy City. Pilgrims, numbering a million a year, poured in from all parts of Russia. They slept in barrack-rooms, ate at the common table, visited the sarcophagus containing the remains of St Sergei and kissed the golden cross placed on the red velvet sheet that covered them.

Grigori arrived in time for the great festivals in July and August at the Lavra, the Monastery of the Caves, built in the eleventh century and revered as the most sacred monastic institution in Russia. Down in the catacombs he walked along the narrow passages and saw the small rectangular chambers where the saints are entombed: of the 385 canonized Russian saints, 100 are in these catacombs.

Here there is neither gold nor silver [writes Grigori Rasputin], the very silence seems to breathe, and the saints repose in simplicity without any silver shrines but in plain oak coffins. One realizes one's worthlessness. . . . I have seen such marvellous sanctuaries. These sanctuaries were hewn from bare rock by the hand of God, and here the monks took refuge from the onslaught of the people from foreign lands.

Among the impressive cathedrals he visited was the green-and-white-walled St Sophia with its fifteen gilded domes, four of them spangled with stars, and rich with mosaics and frescoes.

After some weeks at Kiev, praying, preaching and talking to the high priests, he left for Kazan by the mile-wide Volga with its gay boatmen, known as *burlai*, who sing as they move along the water. A city founded by the Tartars in 1438, it has a number of mosques, for the Golden Horde (so called because yellow was the Mongol colour and the word *ordu* meant camp) had by then become Moslems. They were driven out by Ivan the Terrible a hundred years later. About 30,000 Tartars still live in Kazan. The Kremlin, high on a hill, is the most striking feature of the city. Within its walls is a tall 246-foot red-brick tower, a relic of Tartar architecture. Near the Kremlin is the Bogoroditski convent, built in 1579 to house the miracle-working ikon of the Virgin of Kazan which was found buried in the earth. But Grigori did not see it there, for it was moved in 1612 to Moscow, and, a hundred years later, to Peter the Great's new capital, St Petersburg.

Grigori was welcomed by the monks of the magnificent sixteenth-century monastery in the Kremlin: he attended their services, listened to their preaching and joined the student discussion groups. Kazan must have cast its spell on him, as on all who go there; in the markets he lingered at the stalls, heavy with the smell of new leather, examined the oriental slippers with their tips turned up, the saddles, the boots, the belts; the fruit stalls had a gay display of colour—luscious red oranges, plums, greengages, melons, figs, pears and apples. He was to return to it again and again.

On arriving at his home in Pokrovskoe in the following Spring he saw his wife Proskovia Dourovina with another child in her arms—his daughter Matriona. Lovingly he took the two-month-old baby and covered her face with kisses. He was motioned to a chair by Novychok, who knelt before him to fulfil her wifely duty by taking off his tall, heavy, travel-stained boots.

For well over a year he stayed at home. The visitors kept him fully occupied. Apart from the evening services in his courtyard chapel, they used to drift in during the day, bringing an ailing child, a sick mother or, on a stretcher, a feeble old man no longer able to walk.

'Please help us, Father Grigori. The doctor can do nothing more,' they begged.

He would gaze at the patient, touch the forehead with the palm of his large, long-fingered hand, not so rough now as it used to be, then kneel down and pray, sometimes for ten minutes, or it might be for half an hour or more. Then he would say: 'He will get well,' and always the patient seemed to get better, the suffering was eased; occasionally a complete cure was effected.

His gift of healing was talked of not only in the village, but in Tyumen, Tobolsk and even at Ekaterinburg and beyond. People brought their sick across the Ural mountains and from the remote southern and eastern regions of Siberia.

To express their gratitude they brought gifts—a hen perhaps, or a duck, or a bottle of vodka (Grigori never drank vodka, he liked madeira or sweet wine); sometimes they placed some roubles on the table. He ignored the gifts and gave them to the needy. To a poor aged woman he gave all the money that had been given him.

From Tyumen, Tobolsk and further afield they sometimes came in a carriage or perhaps a cart to convey him to the sick-bed of the Governor's wife or of a paralysed father. He always answered the call and would sometimes be away for three or four days.

After eighteen months of healing and prayer he went wandering again. Just before he set out in 1897, his wife gave birth to a second daughter, whom they named Varvara. 'I do not know how long I shall be away,' he said. 'When God wills it, I shall return home.' His wife wept. His young son Dimitri and his daughter Maria held on to his hands affectionately. His father merely nodded, thinking no doubt that Grisha had been of no help at all in the fields during the past eighteen months.

These wanderings were of vital importance in the development of his personality. His close association with others, wanderers like himself seeking the same path to salvation, provided thoughts to exchange, reactions to discuss, some fanatics, others sectarians, many emphatic, assertive and even quarrelsome and after a while penitent. More and more, as he listened to the dogmatic sectarians, he realized how much more reliable the Scriptures were as a guide. The wandering widened his understanding and his sympathy; he encountered the despairing and hopeless and tried to instil new hope in them. One had to help the weak and the needy: that was his only code, it could not be said of him that he looked the other way and quickened his pace, nor was he ever malicious or spiteful: he wanted to give not take.

This time Grigori went eastward further into Siberia, travelling from village to village, a dozen or more miles apart. Everywhere, as they saw his tall, lean figure, long-haired and bearded, leaning on a pilgrim's staff, they came out of their houses, for they realized at once who it was. They asked for his blessing; they told him their problems, sought his advice and guidance, got down on their knees with him and began to pray in the street, then kissed his hands; some, treating him as a saint, kissed the hem of his long, belted kaftan. 'No! No! No!' he would say. 'I am *not* a saint. I am human like you and the rest of you. The Lord has been kind to me and has given me the strength and the ability to help you.'

His preaching held them spellbound. He quoted from the Scriptures, giving counsel. 'Whatsoever thy hand findeth to do, do it with thy might; for there is no work, nor device, nor knowledge, nor wisdom in the grave where thou goest.' Each text he quoted was enlivened by examples drawn from his own experience, acquired during his wanderings. He talked at times for an hour or more and was often so carried away by what he was saying that he would begin to sing and dance, which to him were part of the religious ritual, for did not King David dance before the Ark of the Covenant?

Often they begged him to say what the future held for them. 'I am not a prophet,' he replied; but he had the gift of prophecy, which could not be summoned, but suddenly found utterance. And when it proved to be true, the word was passed round and winged its way from town to town, arousing the curiosity and the hopes of all who heard it.

At the same time Father Piotr, furious that the Bishop of Tobolsk had absolved Grigori from indulging in *Khlysty* practices and sex orgies, began to spread the vilest accusations against this man of deep religious sincerity. While many in the villages he visited came up and fell on their knees before him, a few now began to whisper: 'He is not a holy man really. He is a sex maniac. He rapes little girls and stirs up their desire by flagellation. He has a whip hidden in his long peasant blouse.'

There was no evidence to support any of these stories: what we do know is that his intense interest in religion began when he was fifteen. Nevertheless the malicious gossip spread. Grigori Rasputin was branded a humbug, a fornicator and, with an additional flourish, a drunkard, though there was no evidence up to now that he was ever drunk.

Stories were invented and passed round. It was exciting gossip—waylaying and raping young girls, stealing horses and furs and selling them to get drunk on more and more vodka.

On 2 September 1900 a woman named Lisavera Nikolaievna Bul, hearing some of this gossip, went to the police station at Tobolsk and accused Grigori Rasputin of trying to murder her.

She was offered a chair and the police inspector brought out his ledger, dipped his pen in ink and wrote down her accusation. While walking along the road from Fagast to Kazan, she said, she saw Rasputin in a field having sexual intercourse with two young girls. Shouting at him to leave the children alone, she walked on to the field to take the girls away from him; but he turned on her and would have murdered her had she not run away and hidden until it was dark.

The police asked her what work she did and what caused her to be on that road at that time. She explained that she was a dancer and got jobs with travelling circuses and sometimes with theatrical troupes.

When, she was asked, did she see Rasputin and the young girls in the fields? 'On 31 August,' she said.

'You were near enough to Kazan then, why have you come to Tobolsk, which is more than 600 miles away? And how did you manage to travel 600 miles in three days?'

The police realized that there was no truth in her story. Rasputin was no doubt still in eastern or southern Siberia, nobody knew exactly where. They made inquiries at Fagast and Kazan and learned that no charges had been made about any disorderly behaviour against any young girls.

During these wanderings Grigori was usually away for eight or ten months, then spent some weeks at home with his wife, his three children and his father, who was now in his early fifties and is said to have taken to drinking rather heavily. There were spans of sobriety, we are told, but sometimes he would be noisily drunk for three or four days.

Grigori Efimovich was still in his twenties—twenty-eight when the circus dancer Lisavera Nikolaievna made her allegations about him and the little girls. His son Dimitri, affectionately called Mitia, was seven years old now, Matriona, called Maria, was five, and Varvara, called Vara, was three. Both the girls were flaxen-haired like their mother—

the boy's hair, fair until he was five, was by now a pale brown. All three looked more like their mother than like Grigori.

The religious wanderers originated in Siberia and were strongly influenced by the Buddhist and Hindu wandering mendicants. Buddha himself gave up his aristocratic status and his entire wealth and wandered among the poor to tell them how to attain *nirvana* by practising asceticism and meditation and by helping those who were poor and ailing. His priests, with shaven heads and wearing long saffron robes, preached his doctrines, making converts in China, Mongolia and Manchuria, and walked westward across Siberia and into Russia.

Many Hindus have also adopted religious mendicancy and may still be seen wandering about India, crossing the Himalayas and the Hindu Kush mountains into Tibet and the vast southern expanse of Siberia. Some of the Hindu wanderers are *yogis*, popularly called *jogis*: basically they believe in *yoga* philosophy, practise asceticism and meditate deeply in the hope of attaining superhuman powers—they don't all attain it, many give up their mendicancy and become fortune-tellers and conjurers. The *sanyasis* smeared their bodies with ashes, put on a small tiger skin and a rosary of berries, and allowed their hair to grow long, matted and filthy. People began to say this about Grigori Rasputin. His hair was always worn long, and doubtless during his wanderings it became matted and filthy: but at home, with a steam bath in his courtyard, and considering his mania for going to the public baths in the towns he visited, it is unlikely that he called on friends unwashed or in dirty clothes. All through his life he found baths irresistible.

The Hindu wanderers who resembled the *startsyi* most closely, were the *sadhus*: that word, like the word *startsyi*, means Holy-men. They preached, they helped the poor—it was their duty to take from the rich and give to the needy. Many became hermits like Makari and lived in small tumble-down huts in the mountains, praying, telling their beads, and often being visited by those who sought their guidance and blessing.

Grigori Rasputin would have fitted into the *sadhu* category: in many ways he was like them, but though he sought solitude from time to time to meditate and pray, he was worldly enough to mingle with people, to wander through the villages, talk, help, heal and to set right, if he could, the little bit of the world around him.

He returned to his home some months after Lisavera's accusation about the two young girls. On being told of it, he went to the police and asked them to bring the woman into court as he would like to confront her. A search was made in Kazan and Fagast and in numerous other places in and beyond that area. She could not be found. 'It was a fictitious charge,' the police told Grisha, 'we never thought there was any truth in what she said.'

Some months later he went across the Ural mountains and once again visited Kazan. Greatly attracted to this oriental town, he decided to stay there for a while. He visited the monks, attended their seminars, took a prominent part in the discussion of the Scriptures, was welcomed by the townspeople, who gathered round him in the streets. They tugged at his sleeves, knelt before him and wept as they talked of the sick and dying, the paralysed and the blind in their family. In most cases the patient recovered. We are told that a man who was paralysed got up with some difficulty and walked. This has been known to happen even in western hospitals, when a doctor, feeling that the patient lacks confidence to trust his weight to his legs, tries persuasion and finally gives a sharp command which startles the patient and makes him rise and stagger forward for a few yards. In Rasputin's case legends, often greatly exaggerated, were circulated about his miraculous cures. Some of them certainly seemed miraculous, and these shall be described later, but what is unlikely is that a paralysed man, whose legs had shrivelled, would be able to get up and walk.

During his stay in Kazan, Grigori Rasputin made many friends. He came to know the Katkoff family well, and a few years later, in 1908, brought his daughter Maria to stay with them.

In St Petersburg

On leaving Kazan Rasputin went once again to Kiev. Here, too, during his stay he made many friends. At the house of one of them he met the Grand Duchess Militsa: she had seen him in the courtyard sawing wood, asked who he was and when told was most excited at the prospect of meeting him and talking to him.

Militsa and her sister Anastasia were the daughters of King Nikita I of Montenegro, a country since absorbed into Yugoslavia. Blest with an oriental attractiveness, they married two Russian grand-duke brothers closely related to the Tsar: Anastasia married the elder, Nikolai Nikolaievich, appointed Commander-in-Chief of the Russian forces on the outbreak of the First World War; Militsa married the younger brother, Peter Nikolaievich.

On being invited to come in and meet the Grand Duchess, Rasputin merely glanced up from the courtyard and went on sawing wood. 'He will come in when he has finished,' Militsa was told. 'He feels that any task that has been begun has to be completed.'

She laughed. 'I'll wait.' She could not take her eyes off the tall man (being slender, he looked taller than he was), his stained cotton blouse with a leather belt at the waist, his faded black trousers and coarse muddy boots.

When he came in she rose from her chair, but said nothing, for his blue eyes held her magnetically. 'I have been told wonderful things about you,' she said at last. 'A man of your mystic—your *supernatural* powers is needed in St Petersburg. Will you come as my husband's guest and mine?'

He was off-hand in his dismissal of the suggestion. 'There is nothing *wonderful* about me. I am no different from others. I have no powers. When God thinks fit he guides me.' He nodded and was about to leave the room, but Militsa turned to her host and hostess. 'Can't we together persuade him to stay for a while and talk to us?'

The two Montenegrin princesses were deeply interested in spiritualism, table-rapping and the supernatural, and had picked up many so-called prophets and miracle-workers later found to be charlatans, introducing each in turn to the Russian nobility and even to the

Tsaritsa. There was Dr Philippe, whose real name was Philippe Nizier Vachot. Militsa had found him in France. He was the son of a butcher who worked in a village not far from Lyons. Fully trained in the practice of hypnosis, Philippe had built up a considerable following in Paris and was pressingly invited by rich hostesses to their salons.

Militsa, while in France with the Tsar and Tsaritsa, introduced Philippe to them. He was brought to St Petersburg and, to give him some status at the Imperial court, the Tsar made him a military doctor and State Councillor. The Tsaritsa received him often at the palace. Her longing, she told him, was to provide an heir to the throne: so far she had had only girls. He assured her that it was in his power to guarantee that her next child would be a boy. So strong was his assurance and his hypnotic influence that before long the Empress became pregnant. There was great joy in the Palace: the Tsar wanted an heir and Dr Philippe had guaranteed it. As the months passed and the pregnancy became more and more noticeable under her maternity gowns, the doctors got busy estimating the date of the child's delivery, examined her Imperial majesty and found she was not pregnant at all. All Russia had heard of the expectation of an heir: it would be embarrassing now if it got about that her so-called pregnancy was nothing more than the prompting of hysteria. Dr Philippe would have to be disposed of. Heaping gifts upon him, so that it should not be thought that the Empress was the dupe of a French charlatan, he was packed off back to France.

Philippe was replaced by a succession of bogus prophets of God: Daria Ossipova, who muttered incoherently, was later found to be mentally defective; next Militsa and her sister Anastasia found Mitia Koliaba, a cripple with amputated arms and a faulty palate. Every epileptic fit he suffered was said to be the voice of God. A sexton named Egorov went everywhere with him and acted as interpreter. The Tsaritsa asked Mitia if he could tell her whether she would provide an heir. Piercing screams were his answer. It was impossible to stop him, and the Tsaritsa, shaken by the horrifying ordeal, had hysterics. The interpreter explained to her Imperial Majesty that Mitia was merely saying that it was much too early to foretell the birth of an heir to the throne. Even after this hysterical ordeal, the Tsaritsa continued to see him.

Now, looking at Rasputin as they stood facing one another in the drawing-room at Kiev, Militsa asked him to sit down. He did not sit

D

down. She then asked how long he would be staying in Kiev. He said he would go when God told him to go, and walked out of the room.

A few weeks later he left Kiev and returned to Pokrovskoe. He had been away for the best part of a year and was happy to be with his children again. Dimitri, Maria and Varvara were old enough now to join in various games with him, listen to him talk about his wanderings, go for walks with him along the river bank and on to the quay to see the boats come in and go out, and sometimes he would harness a *troika* to a farm cart and take the three children tearing madly along the roads towards the dark cluster of forests.

His daughter Maria has described their happiness when their father was at home.

[In] the *gornitsa*, the state room, the blue flame of the lamp was always kept burning in front of the ikons. Below was the spacious *isba* with its wooden benches running all round the walls, where we usually sat round the Russian stove. In this room my father would often take us on his knees, my brother Mitia, my sister Varvara, and myself. He would tell us wonderful stories with that tenderness he always showed and that absent look in which seemed to be mirrored the countries he had visited and the strange adventures he had met with on the road. He spoke to us of the great Russian nation stretching from the Baltic to the Caspian Sea, of its thousand cupolas of gold and silver stretching towards the sky. He told of the great rivers down which he had travelled, the enormous boats laden with travellers, gipsies, sheep, fruit vendors, *moujiks*. He described the Tartar towns with their bright sunshine and narrow streets, their bazaars sparkling with untold riches, and their markets overflowing with great juicy fruits ablaze with every colour of the rainbow.

At other times, again, he would speak of the deep silence of the Siberian forest and the wild beauty of the steppes. He praised the piety of the *straniki*, those wandering pilgrims whose lot he had shared. He told us about Makari the hermit who had made him realize his vocation for this wandering life. His voice would suddenly become graver and slightly hoarse. We looked at him in surprise. And suddenly, almost in a whisper, as one says a prayer, he would call up one of those visions that had come to him in the solitude of the forest or the fields—a woman of splendid beauty, always with the features of the Holy Virgin, speaking softly to him—and while, trembling, our eyes raised towards his, we drank in his words, he would suddenly pause and make over our heads the sign of the Cross.

They enjoyed listening to the Russian fables he told them about the dragonfly and the ant, the peasant and the snake, the rich man and the cobbler, the poet and the millionaire. In the autumn he took them to the village fête, and at harvest time, even though revered as a *staretz*, he helped in the fields and presided at the servants' and harvesters' meals and pronounced the blessing.

In the evenings there were services in his chapel in the courtyard: the chapel was by now full of ikons and figures of saints. The children had to attend and found it tedious and boring, Maria tells us. And of course he spent a lot of time talking to pilgrims and mendicants and healing the sick.

The months passed quickly and pleasantly and suddenly the year ended and a new year came. Before long it would be the Spring, the snow would melt, the trees would put out young green leaves, and the children knew that Papa would sniff the air, pack his bundle, take his staff and not be seen again until possibly the end of the year.

Grigori Efimovich Rasputin set out in that Spring of 1903 westward: he crossed the Ural mountains, spent a few weeks with his friends in Kazan, then walked 200 miles to Nijni-Novgorod,* where the Volga and the Oka rivers meet: a large city with most attractive old buildings. He arrived in July in time for the opening of the great fair at which furs from all over Russia are sold.

Hearing that the Tsar was going to canonize a monk named Seraphim at Sarov, a small town not far from Nijni-Novgorod, Grigori went there to attend the religious ceremony. The story of this remarkable man, a legend in his lifetime, was taught in every school. Drawn early to a religious life, he became a hermit and, like Makari, spent many years in a forest. Most of the food brought to him he gave away to the birds and the bears who became his friends. In 1825 the Tsar Alexander I went to see him. Seraphim died in 1833, and seventy years later people still talked reverently of his miracles.

---

* Now called Gorki.

Grigori, standing with his face towards the silver shrine containing Seraphim's relics, prayed long and fervently, then seemed to go into a trance. Suddenly, raising his voice, he announced to the congregation that a miracle was soon to be seen in Russia. Within a year a son would be born to the Tsaritsa. The prophecy was fulfilled within the time mentioned. The heir to the throne was born in August of the following year, 1904.

From there Grigori went on to Moscow, for centuries the capital of Russia until Peter the Great built St Petersburg and transferred the capital there. Rasputin had not been in Moscow before. There was much to see and much to do: he went to the Kremlin, where, in the fifteenth-century Cathedral of the Assumption, under whose five golden domes the Tsars were crowned, he gazed with wonder at the numerous ikons studded with costly precious stones (the weight of their gold alone is six tons) and at the enormous chandelier of solid silver hanging from the basilica; then he visited the quaint St Basil Cathedral in Red Square, with its eight domes, each a different shape and decorated in various colours. After a relatively brief stay of three weeks, he continued to the famous Trinity and St Sergiev Monastery at Zagorsk, about sixty versts out of Moscow. The white-stone Trinity Cathedral, its walls inclining inward, was built in 1422, and the Whit Monday church fifty years later. The monastery was heavily fortified in the following century to resist attacks from the Tartars, who descended on Moscow in 1571, set fire to the city and slaughtered more than 100,000 people. Grigori, welcomed by the young monks wearing bright mauve brimless velvet hats, stayed with them for ten days. He found the gentle, soft-voiced chants in the Assumption Cathedral, built by Ivan the Terrible, deeply moving: 'Their prayers came from the depths of their souls,' he said. In the cathedral he saw the vault which contains Boris Godounov's tomb.

From there he began his 300-mile walk to St Petersburg. Though he had heard and read and seen pictures of the capital, his first sight of it must have been breathtaking. For one who was always conscious of beauty, as his later impressions of the Holy Land show, the vast loveliness of the city spread across miles of water, islands and tongues of land—strewn with spires and cupolas and crossed by impressive wide avenues penetrating inland from the shores of the Baltic and cut at intervals by canals which mirrored the pale green sky and the huge stone buildings—would have made an immediate impact. We can picture him pausing on the inviting embankments, leaning against the parapets and looking at the islands sprinkled on the water and the handsome bridges that linked them together. But Grigori had not come for that. What he most wanted to see was Kazan Cathedral, built to house the famous ikon of the Holy Virgin of Kazan, an attractive, arresting structure at the most fashionable end of the Nevsky Prospekt, with two impressive semicircular colonnades in front, echoing the architecture of St Peter's in Rome.

Rasputin stood misty-eyed before the ikon, its golden frame, weighing 360 lb., inlaid with hundreds of gems. As he gazed at it he saw that the Holy Virgin was dressed exactly as he had seen her in the sky at Pokrovskoe—in a purple-brown veil and a dress of the same colour, with the Infant Jesus beside Her, with His head almost level with Hers. Grigori stood there a long time, thinking of the ikon's many miracles: first the capture of Kazan from the Tartars by Ivan the Terrible, then the victory of the Cossacks over the Poles in 1648, and eventually the shattering defeat of Napoleon at Moscow in 1812. In the crowd around the ikon was a man who kept looking at the strange *staretz*, and when Grigori left, he followed him, threading his way through the cluster of spectators admiring the French flags and banners and eagles captured during Napoleon's retreat from Moscow. He followed him into the Nevsky Prospekt, the finest and most impressive street in all Russia, and watched his reactions. The building of this strange city had been begun in 1703 when Peter the Great laid the foundation stone of the St Peter and St Paul fortress. Scores of thousands of peasants were brought from all parts of the Empire to fill in the swamps, hew down the forests, erect the buildings, many of them on stilts, and make the roads: many thousands of the workers perished. In 1712 it was made the new capital of Russia. Nevsky Prospekt, about 120 feet wide and three miles long, was the only street not cobbled but paved with wood-blocks. Some of the houses were of stone, others of stucco painted pink or pale blue or orange or yellow. He paused to look at an enormous bazaar, the Gostiny Dvor, built on two floors, with 200 shops selling ikons, beautiful hanging lamps, coins, snuff-boxes, old furniture and pictures. Swarms of customers bargained wildly, as they would in any oriental bazaar, a practice acquired doubtless from the Tartars.

Attracted by the clatter of horses' hoofs, Grigori turned to look at a group of cavalry officers dressed in blue and crimson uniforms with gold and silver braid galloping along the street; then a *troika* went by, then another with the driver standing on the shaft with a whip in his hand, like a Roman charioteer. Occasionally a motor car went past. There were tram cars here, as elsewhere in the city, some still horse-drawn, others with electric overhead wires. At the street corners there were policemen in black uniforms with green facings.

As Grigori moved away the stranger, a round-faced man of medium height with a neatly trimmed beard, introduced himself. His name, he said, was Georgei Petrovich Sazonoff, and he was a journalist with a St Petersburg newspaper. Inviting Grigori to take tea with him, he led him into a small restaurant in a side-street. From answers to his probing questions he learned that Rasputin had only just arrived in St Petersburg and was looking for a monastery in which to stay for a few days.

'I have a comfortable flat for my wife and family,' Sazonoff said. 'Why not stay with us?'

When they finished their tea Sazonoff rose from the table and, handing Rasputin his tall staff, escorted him to his apartment not far from the Nevsky Prospekt.

Rasputin had not come to St Petersburg for sightseeing. Here, as in Kiev, Kazan and elsewhere, his interest was in religion, and within a day or two of his arrival he made his way to the Alexander Nevsky Monastery. It lies on the south-eastern edge of St Petersburg and covers a vast area, for it contains a cathedral, twelve churches and a large number of chapels, all enclosed by walls and moats. It was tremendously impressive. In the Cathedral of the Trinity he saw a reliquary containing the bones of St Alexander Nevsky, the hero-saint who won a great victory over the Swedish Knights of the Teutonic Order in 1241. Peter the Great brought the bones here himself. In the various churchyards are the graves of Dostoevsky, the composers Glinka, Tchaikovsky and Anton Rubinstein, the historian Karamazin, the poet Zhukovsky and others. It is the seat of the Metropolitan of St Petersburg, and connected with it is the Imperial Theological Academy where Grigori made his way to listen to the discussions and take part in them.

It was there apparently that he met Father John Sergeiev of Kronstadt, who had been confessor to the previous Tsar Alexander III and was now the spiritual adviser of the Tsaritsa. Seventy-four years old, he had been for nearly fifty years a priest at Kronstadt, Russia's principal naval base, not many miles from St Petersburg. His outlook was old-fashioned, many called it medieval: he believed that the Tsar must rule as an autocrat, making no concessions to democracy. Revered by the nobility, he was said to have effected some miraculous cures of the sick and dying.

Grigori Rasputin met him again the next day when Father John was celebrating mass in a St Petersburg church. So as not to keep the congregation waiting, Father John had adopted the practice of getting his entire congregation to confess at the same time in loud voices: if the priest did not hear them God did: the confessions were deeply moving, for many beat their breasts and sobbed.

When at the end of the service he held up the sacraments and said: 'Approach in faith and in fear of God,' he surprised the congregation by suddenly crying 'Stop!' Spotting Grigori in the church he beckoned to him. Every head in the congregation turned to look at the tall, bearded pilgrim, and everyone kept their eyes on him as he walked up to the altar.

Father John of Kronstadt blessed Rasputin and then asked for his blessing. The congregation was bewildered. Who was this young *moujik*, and why had he been singled out by the priest and accorded so much deference?

It was through Father John, it is thought, that Rasputin met the Archimandrite Theophan, head of the Alexander Nevsky Monastery. A frail old man with dreamy blue eyes, unworldly and as reactionary as Father John, he was very much liked by the Tsaritsa. But others think that they met when Rasputin was at the Theological Academy listening to a student discussion into which he was drawn. His answers had a note of originality and depth and greatly impressed not only the students, but the Archimandrite Theophan, who in his turn arranged that Rasputin should meet Bishop Hermogen of Saratov, the largest town on the Volga about 1,000 miles from St Petersburg. The Bishop, who was often in the capital, was one of the most popular religious figures in Russia.

All three, weary of the table-rapping and the succession of charlatans at the Imperial court, had decided to create a new saint in order to direct the thoughts of the Tsaritsa in a different direction. It was they who suggested that the early nineteenth-century monk Seraphim, who had made some pleasing prophecies to the Romanovs, should be canonized. Despite intense opposition from other leaders of the church, they had got their way, and, as we have seen, Grigori while at Sarov prophesied the birth of the heir. To them he represented a tremendous asset. As leading members of the reactionary political organization known as the Union of True Russians, which stood against democracy, against the freedom enjoyed in the western countries of Europe, against Judaism, and which firmly supported the sternest possible action to suppress demands from the people for reform, it was their resolve to make Grigori a member. Unlike the spiritualists and fortune-tellers, the bearded *moujik* was young, a peasant from the steppes, without guile and with an impressive sincerity while unquestionably being a man of deep religious faith. Should the nobility be drawn to him, it would bring about a cleansing of St Petersburg, which was hourly becoming more and more decadent, for the aristocracy practised little restraint in its drinking or sexual indulgence, displayed hardly any social responsi- bility and devoted its time to gambling in night-clubs until carried out at dawn by flunkeys and taken to carriages or sleighs.

They succeeded in persuading Rasputin to join the organization. The full scope of the Union of True Russians was possibly not made clear to him, but in any event it is unlikely that Rasputin would have thought for a moment why he should not join a movement of which three of the most honoured elders of the Russian Orthodox Church were members.

One of the senior students at the Theological Academy was Sergei Trufanov, possibly, like Rasputin's mother, of Samoyed origin, with very marked Mongol features, high cheek-bones and tight lips. Shortly afterwards he became a monk and was sent as a priest to Tsaritsyn,★ more than 200 miles south of Bishop Hermogen's see at Saratov. Like Rasputin a peasant by origin, he adopted the name of Illiodor and won an enormous following with his outspoken, rousing sermons. He de- nounced the aristocracy, their corrupt morals and their dabbling in spiritualism; at the same time he shared the reactionary views of the two bishops and supported the autocracy of the Tsar. Inconsistently, however, he would launch out suddenly in his sermons on the need to improve the condition of the poor.

From their first meeting in the Academy, when Grigori Rasputin had taken part in the student discussions, Illiodor became his devoted admirer and some years later invited him to Tsaritsyn, where he spoke of his plan to build a new monastery on a hill. It would have a lofty tower and would be called Mount Tabor. The large congregation who came to hear his sermons, which were based on his visits to brothels and

---

★ Later Stalingrad, now Volgograd.

gambling halls for the purpose of denouncing them, responded generously to his appeal for money and brought bricks and mortar for the building of the tower; some even took an active part in its building: the tower was begun, but was never completed.

At the end of the year, after spending six months in the capital, Grigori Rasputin left St Petersburg without having made any effort to see the Grand Duchess Militsa and walked all the way back to his family in Pokrovskoe.

First Meeting with the Tsaritsa

In the summer of 1905 Grigori Rasputin returned to the capital and again stayed with his journalist friend Sazonoff.

'Shortly after you left St Petersburg in December 1903,' said Sazonoff, 'I met the Grand Duchess Militsa at a reception. She had read what I had written about you and asked if you were still here. I told her she had missed you by two or three days. She exacted a promise from me that I would let her know when you returned.'

Rasputin spread out his hands and turned away with a look of indifference. During the following week the grand duchess sent a carriage to Sazonoff's house for him.

Grigori found when he arrived at the large palace on the English Quay on the Neva that it was just a family gathering—Militsa's husband the Grand Duke Peter Nikolaievich, her sister Anastasia and her sister's husband Nikolai Nikolaievich. The two brothers were gigantically tall and handsome. The atmosphere was not remotely formal: there was a warmth in their manner as they talked to Rasputin, and at the same time a respectful deference to his saintliness. Only fleetingly did their talk touch on religion: the grand duchesses wanted to delve more deeply into the supernatural and tried to direct his thoughts towards it. They asked about his miracles: 'The miracles are not mine,' he said. They asked about his prophecies: 'Only God can tell me what to say.' But when they asked about spiritualism, he became very angry: 'That is of the Devil,' he said. 'It has nothing to do with God. Leave it alone.'

They fell silent, for all four had been steeped in table-rapping and the other variations of spiritualism. The Grand Duke Nikolai patted the head of his small frail dog, possibly to cover his embarrassment. Rasputin looked at him and patted the dog too.

'He has not been very well for some time,' said the Grand Duke Nikolai. 'We brought him with us just to give him some fresh air.'

'Poor pet,' added Anastasia. 'Nobody knows what is the matter with him. The vets say he cannot live more than two months or so.'

With his hand still on the dog's head, Rasputin got down on his knees and began to pray. His prayers went on for half an hour. One heard just the faint murmur of his voice and the heavy breathing of the dog. The others watched in silence.

After a while the dog's breathing became less audible. The Grand Duchess Anastasia looked at her sister anxiously. The Grand Duke Nikolai took a step towards the dog, but Rasputin, though his eyes were shut, waved him away.

The prayer over, Rasputin rose, and so did the dog: it licked Rasputin's hand, then went to render a like tribute to the Grand Duke Nikolai and his wife Anastasia.

'He seems better,' said Nikolai Nikolaievich. 'Will he live?'

'He will get better as the days pass and he will live for some years.'

The prophecy proved to be accurate. Nikolai Nikolaievich as an expression of his gratitude tried to press Rasputin to accept if not money, which had been firmly refused, then perhaps some gift—but Rasputin would accept nothing. Some years later, when Rasputin's wife was ill and a serious internal operation was necessary, Nikolai Nikolaievich insisted on her coming to St Petersburg, engaged a room for her in a nursing home and secured the best surgeon to attend her.

The Tsar Nikolai II and the Tsaritsa Alexandra Federovna were close friends of the Grand Duchess Militsa, whose husband Peter Nikolaievich was first cousin of the Tsar's father Alexander III; at Peterhof, on the shore of the Gulf of Finland, where the Tsar and Tsaritsa spent part of the summer, Militsa lived in Znamenka Palace, barely ten minutes away from the Imperial Palace. Their friendship was indeed so close that when the Tsar and Tsaritsa went to Paris in 1900, Militsa went with them. That was when she had met M. Philippe and taken him to Compiègne, just outside Paris, where the Tsar and Tsaritsa were staying.

Now it was to be Rasputin. When Dr Philippe was sent away from Russia laden with gifts, it was revealed that he had been advising the Tsaritsa on the political and military appointments that should be made by the Tsar. As a parting present Philippe gave her a bell and told her to ring it when she wanted to keep all political and other advisers who did not agree with *her* views away from the Tsar. Then he kissed her hand, bowed low and said: 'Your Majesty will some day have another friend like me who will speak to you of God.' Militsa, having heard recently that Philippe was dead, was convinced that the new friend in Philippe's prophecy was Rasputin.

Much had happened to the Tsar and to Russia since Rasputin left St Petersburg at the end of December 1903. Barely six weeks later, on 6 February 1904, war had broken out with Japan. Some years earlier, when he was heir to the throne, the Tsar had visited the Far East and been greatly impressed by what he saw, for Siberia had already acquired vast territories in the east, and there was so much more that could be added. While in Japan he had been saved by Prince George of Greece from a fanatic's attempt at assassination.

Bit by bit his dream was being fulfilled: more and more land was being taken from China; soon Russia had control of all Manchuria. The Japanese, equally greedy, had their eye on Korea. The Tsar regarded this not as a challenge but as an impertinence. When Hiroboumi Ito, Japan's astute statesman and architect of his country's impressive development, arrived in St Petersburg to discuss a compromise settlement, he was treated with discourtesy and finally left the country in disgust.

The Tsar approved of war with Japan, which anyway now seemed inevitable, and was supported with wild enthusiasm by those who felt that imperial conquest was an effective way of stopping the people agitating for reforms. But the war proved to be a disaster. After the destruction of almost the entire Russian fleet at Tsuchima on 27 May 1905, it became clear that the war could no longer continue. Japan, with complete command of the sea, had annexed a large part of Manchuria and also taken possession of all Korea. Throughout the brief months of the war every blow delivered by the Japanese roused the people of Russia to still greater fury and brought revolution ever nearer. On 19 January 1905, soon after the fall of Port Arthur, the Russian Far Eastern base, a gun was fired from the fortress of St Peter and St Paul towards the Winter Palace: the Tsar was so shaken by this that he left St Petersburg and never lived there again. The atmosphere in the capital became jittery. Three days later, when peaceful groups of unarmed workers accompanied by their wives and children and carrying ikons and portraits of the Tsar marched to the Winter Palace to ask the Tsar to improve the condition of the factory workers, singing patriotic and religious songs as they went, the palace troops opened fire while mounted Cossacks charged with drawn sabres and cut down men, women and children; then a cannon was fired along the Nevsky Prospekt, killing many who were trying to escape death: one of them, named Nijinsky, was aged fifteen and on his way to a dancing lesson when he was struck on the head, and he lay unconscious in the street as the crowd tore past him; luckily he survived to become one of the world's most famous ballet dancers. The Tsar, essentially a gentle, kindly man, but haunted by assassinations and revolutionary outbreaks —his grandfather Alexander II had been assassinated just as he had completed a plan for granting representative government to the people, which, of course, the assassin did not know—now asked what the casualties were that morning outside the Winter Palace. He was told that 150 people had been killed and 200 wounded. 'Are you sure,' he said, 'that you've killed enough people? Only by killing enough of them could you keep the murderers and assassins off the streets.' But these men, women and children had come unarmed, singing gaily and carrying portraits of the Tsar. The day was known as 'Bloody Sunday' and the Tsar was often referred to as 'The Murderer', though he was not in the Winter Palace at the time; but as the sole autocratic ruler of the country he was held responsible for the horrifying slaughter by his troops.

Half-way through the Russo-Japanese War, the heir to the throne, prophesied by Rasputin at Sarov, was born and named Alexei Nikolaievich. When the child was fourteen months old the Tsar and Tsaritsa met Rasputin for the first time. It was at the house of the Grand Duchess Militsa and the Tsar made a note in his diary on that day, 1 November 1905: 'We have got to know a Man of God—Grigori—from the Tobolsk province.' It was a meeting of vital importance, for it contributed to the easing of the heir's suffering from haemophilia, for which medical science had no cure.

Not long after that meeting Grigori left St Petersburg for Pokrovskoe. His time during the five or six months in the capital had been very crowded: people kept coming to the house of Sazonoff, the journalist— priests, monks, women with children, beggars, down-and-outs and charlatans who sought his support to sell worthless shares to gullible people with the blessing of this man of God; others came out of curiosity because they had heard that he was a miracle-worker who could pick up a fistful of earth and magically turn it into a rose and that he could foretell their future more accurately than any fortune-teller.

He stayed in Pokrovskoe with his family for six months: it was joy to be with them again. The children were growing fast. He taught his son Mitia, now nearly thirteen, to drive the cart, and one day, when

Grigori happened to be out with four fishermen on the river, the boy was leading the horses to the cart when his grandfather Efim Andreievich came running from the fields and ordered him angrily to take the horses back to the stables.

Mitia was frightened he would tell his father when he came home in the evening, but Efim didn't. It was not until some months later, after Grigori had set out on one of his wanderings and grandfather happened to be out, that Mitia, accompanied by his sister Maria, went to the stables and brought out the horses.

Mother was busy cleaning the stove, which was drawing badly [says Maria], and our grandfather Efim Andreyevich had gone to see the *starost* about a tax they were demanding from him. We softly opened the stable door and put the horses in the sledge. I grazed the skin off my hands with the harness. Dimitri, who was thirteen and passionately fond of horses, astonished me by his knowledge. Soon we were perched on the *troika* behind our three wildest horses and set off at a gallop over the snow. Dimitri drove as well as a *yemstchik*, and at first all went splendidly. He cracked his whip; the horses pricked up their ears, their manes blew in the wind, and we shot forward like an arrow. The bells jangled as we passed, drawing people to the windows, and in a twinkling the village had vanished behind us. Then suddenly the horses doubled their speed. Dimitri tugged at the reins with all his might, but the pace did not slacken. . . . Suddenly a violent shock threw us both forward—the horses had run into a mound. The sledge overturned. Peasants dashed up on their little horses. I was found unconscious in the snow, and a little further on was Dimitri who, luckily, was only bleeding from the nose.

When they got home their grandfather poured out his anger in curses. Nothing was told to their father when he came home some months later. He had been to Kiev where he attended many religious gatherings and presided over some of them. During his stay he made many friends, one of whom was Nikolai Soloviev, whose son Boris later married Grigori Rasputin's daughter, Maria.

From Kiev he went on to St Petersburg.

CHAPTER NINE

The Iron-gloved
Tsaritsa

Militsa kept telephoning Sazonoff during Rasputin's absence from the capital, for he had been away again visiting remote monasteries and it was not until the Spring of 1907 that he was back in St Petersburg. It was then, at Militsa's, that he met Anna Alexandrovna, the daughter of Alexander Taneyev, Director of the Tsar's Private Chancellery, a post held by his family under five Tsars. A composer, and uncle of an even better composer, Sergei Taneyev, he attracted the friendship of the Tsaritsa, who was fond of music. His daughter Anna was appointed a lady-in-waiting, and became in time her majesty's closest friend: she was twenty-three, red-haired, plump, attractive rather than pretty, simple-minded, good-natured, kind and deeply religious.

A husband, the Tsaritsa decided, must be found for 'dear Anya' without delay. But Anna, as it happened, was deeply in love with General Orlov, who was in command of the Lancers and was a close friend of the Empress. The Tsaritsa knew of their love, but felt that the general was too old for Anna. She selected a young naval officer Lieutenant Boris Vyroubov for her: he had been serving at Tsuchima when the Japanese sank almost the entire Russian fleet, and had ever since suffered from shell shock—it was still discernible in his manner.

Anna was greatly disturbed by the Tsaritsa's plan to marry her to this man. In her distress she sought the advice of Militsa and was invited to her home to meet Rasputin. His appearance and manner startled her. He had apparently walked from Pokrovskoe to St Petersburg and was still barefooted and wearing the clothes of penance. That he was an uneducated man was only too obvious; he looked rough, his gaze was penetrating, but clearly he was a man with a mission. His eyes pierced through her as he looked at her round, pink-and-white baby face, her small turned-up nose and blue eyes with long lashes.

'Your marriage will be unsuccessful. It will not last long. It will fail,' he said.

Though she had her own fears of it being an unhappy union, what Rasputin was saying shook her. How did he know? He had never met her or the naval lieutenant. Yet there was an unmistakable tone of prophecy in his voice.

Anna told the Empress what Rasputin had said and begged her not to force her to go on with the marriage. The Empress brushed all that aside. The date has been fixed, she said, nothing can be done about it now.

From the outset things began to go wrong. The warm friendship between Anna and the Tsaritsa disturbed her husband Boris Vyroubov. Why should she spend so much time with the Tsaritsa? He wanted more of his wife's company.

The atmosphere soon became almost intolerable and the Tsaritsa, observing it and realizing that she had made a sad mistake, decided to work out a solution for Anna's happiness. She arranged for the transfer of the young naval lieutenant to a ship about to start on a world cruise. Vyroubov said good-bye to his wife and left for Kronstadt, where the ship was at its moorings.

On arriving he was informed that there was engine trouble and the ship's departure would be delayed for some days. For a moment he hesitated, wondering if he should stay in the ship or go home. He decided to go back to his wife as their separation would inevitably be a very long one.

At their villa at Peterhof, where the Tsar and Tsaritsa resided in the summer, he found his approach barred by a large number of troops. He explained that it was his residence, but was told that he could not be allowed to enter while the Tsaritsa was there. Not allowed to go in even after the Tsaritsa had left, he forced his way into the villa. Angry voices were heard, mainly his. The quarrel went on for some time, then Anna rushed out screaming. Her face was bruised: her husband had beaten her unmercifully.

Sobbing uncontrollably, she made her way to the Imperial Palace to seek the Tsaritsa's protection. The Tsaritsa, furious at his vile and brutal behaviour, tried to comfort Anna, who kept saying: 'I will *not* go back to him.' She was going to live with her parents, she said.

'I will arrange your divorce,' the Tsaritsa told her. 'We shall get it done as speedily as possible.'

The wheels were set in motion and Rasputin's prophecy was fulfilled within a very few months.

A few weeks later Anna Vyroubova was instrumental in bringing Rasputin into closer association with the Tsaritsa and other members of the Imperial family because of the illness of the infant Tsarevich. The birth of the heir to the throne, as we have seen, had been awaited with longing and disappointment for ten years; each arrival had been a daughter, and by now they totalled four. In her desperation the Tsaritsa had turned to priests, bishops, archimandrites, doctors, quacks, charlatans, spiritualists, table-rappers and fortune-tellers: each gave her comfort and assurance, but no heir arrived. Grigori Rasputin, speaking not to her but in a crowded church at Sarov, made a prophecy which was fulfilled within a twelve-month. It may have been just chance, as may also be true of his prophecy over Anna Vyroubova's marriage, but it so happened that both prophecies were fulfilled.

The young Tsarevich, the pride of his father and mother and the delight of all Russia, was found before long to be suffering from haemophilia: it is not hard to realize how bitter the blow must have been to his parents when told by the doctors. Haemophilia is inherited only by a male child through his mother: girls never get it, and fortunately not all the boys in a family are afflicted.

In the case of the Tsar's heir, Alexei, it had been passed down through Queen Victoria, one of whose sons, Leopold, had had it. The Tsaritsa, her granddaughter, passed it on to her son. Another granddaughter Irene, who married Prince Henry of Prussia, transmitted it to two of her sons; one lived for only four years, the other was fortunate enough to survive until forty-five. There were other female carriers among Queen Victoria's many descendants: one was her daughter Beatrice, who married Henry of Battenburg: two of their sons had the disease. Beatrice's daughter Queen Victoria-Eugenie, who married King Alfonso XIII, the last King of Spain, transmitted it to two of her three sons.

The Tsar, heir to the throne at the time, fell in love with Alix (her mother was Queen Victoria's daughter Alice) when she came to St Petersburg for the marriage of her elder sister Elizabeth to the Grand Duke Sergei, an uncle of the future Tsar Nikolai II. Alix was only fourteen then. Writing in his diary on 2 January 1892, three years after that meeting, Nikolai said: 'My dream is some day to marry Alix H.* I have loved her a long while, and still deeper and stronger since 1889 when she spent six weeks in St Petersburg. For a long time I resisted my feeling, trying to deceive myself by the impossibility that my dearest

---

* Her father was Louis IV, Grand Duke of Hesse.

E

dream will come true.' She was certainly very pretty, with well-chiselled features and lovely red-gold hair, but Nikolai's family saw many disadvantages in having her as the wife of a Tsar: she was very shy, blushed constantly, dressed badly, danced badly, was inclined to be neurotic, but worst of all she was assertive and arrogant. Her future mother-in-law, the Empress Marie, did not like her at all and was totally opposed to the marriage, but was comforted by the fact that her husband Tsar Alexander III, who did not like the girl either and did not want his son to marry a German, would never permit it. They tried to find other brides for Nikolai, but he would not consider any of them and threatened that if he could not marry Alix he would rather become a monk. It might have been the salvation of Russia if he had, for Alix shed none of her failings as the years passed; in fact they became worse.

Two years after this entry in his diary, Nikolai left for the Far East. In the following winter Tsar Alexander III, a tall, broadly built, powerful man, always in robust health, became ill and his vitality began to fade. For thirteen years, haunted by the assassination of his father, he had surrounded himself by police and dealt ruthlessly with every sign of revolt. His son, now twenty-six, was, he knew, lacking in experience and quite unqualified to rule. That Nikolai had as mistress the tiny, vivacious nineteen-year-old ballerina Mathilde Kschesinskaya he also knew: it might not be serious, he felt, but Nikolai did go to see her dance at Krasvoe Selo every day. Later he began to take her out riding in the evenings, and stayed with her all night—it was not over yet; they were still seeing a lot of each other. What his son needed, he felt, was a stabilizing force: marriage with someone suitable would provide it; but since Nikolai would marry no one but Alix, he was left with no alternative. So, most reluctantly, his father agreed to the marriage.

At the time of her christening, with Tsar Alexander III and King Edward VII as her godfathers, Alix was described as 'a sweet, merry little person, always laughing' and was called 'Sunny' by her mother. Having won his battle against his formidable father, Nikolai too began to call her Sunny. But the family knew that, despite the pet name bestowed on her by her mother, Alix was obstinate and bad-tempered: this aspect of her emerged after her mother's death when Alix was only six. Her grandmother Queen Victoria now took her under her wing: her influence was powerful; it made Alix narrow-minded and left her without any appreciation of taste and fashion. But what she did get from her grandmother, apart from her unyielding obstinacy, was her love for politics: she hoped to be, like Queen Victoria, the most power-ful ruler in Europe.

Nikolai and Alix became engaged in the presence of Queen Victoria, who came to Darmstadt for the marriage of Alix's elder brother Ernest, the reigning Grand Duke of Hesse. Nikolai, after a brief visit home (when he broke the news to Kschesinskaya, she wept), went to England where he and his fiancée stayed in a cottage at Walton-on-Thames as guests of Alix's eldest sister Victoria, who was married to Prince Louis of Battenburg and became the mother of Lord Mountbatten of Burma and grandmother of Prince Philip, Duke of Edinburgh.

On returning to Russia, Nikolai found that his father's condition had deteriorated. He was moved to the Imperial Palace at Livadia in the Crimea, and there Alix joined them. When she arrived Alexander rose from his sick bed and put on full-dress uniform: it was, he said, how the Tsar of Russia should receive the future Tsaritsa.

Her conversion to the Orthodox religion of Russia was arranged, and, deeply devoted though she was to the Protestantism in which she had been brought up, she accepted the new faith and in time became even more dedicated to it than she had been to the old.

The focus of attention by doctors, ministers and others in the bed-room of the dying Tsar was of course on Alexander. But Alix resented it. Her fiancé, who was to be Tsar at any moment, should, she felt, be given much more deference and attention. Her feelings about this were so strong that she picked up Nikolai's diary and wrote in it:

> Be firm and make the doctors come to you and tell you how they find him . . . so that you are always the first to know. Don't let others be put first and you left out. . . . Show your own mind and don't let others forget who you are.

For the rest of her life she treated him in exactly that way—as a weak, limp, spineless man who had great power but needed a firm assertive wife to tell him how that power should be used.

The Emperor Alexander died in November 1894, aged forty-nine. To Russia it was a shock; to the new Tsar Nikolai II it brought panic. Weeping in the arms of the Grand Duke Alexander Mikhailovich, who was married to Nikolai's sister Xenia, he said: 'Sandro, what am I to do? What is going to happen to me . . . to Alix, to mother, to all Russia? I am not prepared to be a Tsar. I never wanted to be one. I know nothing of the business of ruling. I have no idea of even how to talk to the ministers.'

A week after the impressive funeral in St Petersburg, attended by Queen Victoria's eldest son, later King Edward VII, and her grandson, the future King George V, and sixty other royal mourners, the marriage of Nikolai and Alix (henceforth to be known as Alexandra) took place in the chapel of the Winter Palace, both bride and bridegroom holding lighted candles. The new Tsaritsa, writing to her sister about it, said: 'Our marriage seemed to be a mere continuation of the Masses for the dead with this difference that now I wore a white dress instead of a black one.'

Because the court was in mourning there was no reception afterwards and no honeymoon; the young couple went to live with the Tsar's mother, the Dowager Empress Marie, at the Anichkov Palace in the Nevsky Prospekt. All the accommodation they had there was six rooms: the new bride, always quick to take offence, resented having to spend the entire winter with her mother-in-law. Neither liked the other; what Alexandra resented most was the amount of time her husband spent with his mother: night after night when dinner was over, he stayed on to talk to his mother. The newly wed couple saw little of each other, as most of the day was spent by the Tsar with his ministers. Alexandra hated being left alone and she was far too shy to make friends. Occasionally, by way of providing some diversion for her that winter, Nikolai took her wrapped in furs for sleigh rides across the lovely white landscape. But she wanted much more than that: she wanted his constant attention and his entire devotion.

In the Spring the Tsaritsa found she was pregnant. The Alexander Palace at Tsarskoe Selo, fifteen miles south of St Petersburg, was selected as their home. They hoped the child would be a son; but it was a girl, weighing nine pounds. She was named Olga.

In May of the following year the Coronation took place in the Cathedral of the Assumption in Moscow where the Tsars were always crowned. From every corner of Russia people swarmed into the city— peasant women from Siberia wearing embroidered blouses with brightly coloured shawls over their heads, Moslems from the Tartar cities in red fezes, Caucasians in long red coats—Russia's entire conglomeration of races was represented. At the end of the service cannon were fired in salute and all the church bells in the Kremlin were set ringing.

The festivities lasted for three days. But for the superstitious there were two frightening omens. In the cathdral, as the new Tsar walked towards the altar, the chain of the Order of St Andrei fell off his shoulders. Few noticed it, but those few were sworn to absolute secrecy.

Far worse was the second omen. It was customary on the day following the Coronation for the ordinary working people of the city to be invited to an *al fresco* feast, the counterpart of the banquet given in the Palace for 7,000 guests, which was attended by foreign royalty, grand dukes, ambassadors and others, with just a sprinkling of the proletariat, invited because their forebears in preceding centuries had saved the life of one or other of the Tsars: they were placed in a separate room by themselves.

For the *al fresco* party, which was to be held in Khodynka Meadow, which the Moscow garrison used for their training, thousands began to arrive the evening before. The night was passed without any sleep and by the first light of dawn there were half a million there. Soon waggons laden with beer for the evening's festivities and souvenir enamelled cups bearing the Imperial crest, which were to be distributed as gifts, began to arrive.

An unfortunate rumour that there would not be enough beer for all if the crowd kept growing, caused a panic rush to the front of the meadow, in attempts to be certain of getting served first. The rush caused an appalling and unforgettable tragedy. For the training of the troops the meadow had been cut up into shallow ditches and trenches. In the rush, men, women and children fell into the ditches, and those who came behind them trampled inevitably on their bodies and faces. Hundreds were killed and many thousands gravely injured. By midday the beds of Moscow's hospitals were full.

The news spread rapidly. For that night a ball had been arranged by the French ambassador in the Tsar's honour, but Nikolai, stunned by the awful tragedy, said he could not attend but would retire to a monastery and pray for the victims and their families. Unfortunately he was persuaded by his uncles and other members of the family not to stay away, as it would give great offence to France, Russia's only European ally. So he and the Tsaritsa went: she was in a state of great distress, and her eyes were reddened by tears, the British ambassador stated in a letter to Queen Victoria. 'We expected that the party would be called off,' said Sergei Witte, the Tsar's finance minister. 'It took place as if nothing had happened and the ball was opened by Their Majesties as if nothing had happened.' The people never forgave them for it, although the Tsar and Tsaritsa spent the next day visiting the injured in the hospitals.

As his wife realized from the beginning of their life together, the Tsar lacked his father's strength of character; and yet it was on his father that he was trying to model himself. His four uncles, only too aware of what was lacking in the new Tsar, took upon themselves the task of training him to be like their brother Tsar Alexander III.

The first ten years of his reign Nikolai II spent [says his cousin the Grand Duke Alexander] sitting behind a massive desk in the Palace and listening with near awe to the well-rehearsed bellowing of his towering uncles. He dreaded to be left alone with them. . . . Down on the table would go with a bang the weighty fist of Uncle Alexei— 250 lb. packed in the resplendent uniform of the Grand Fleet. Uncle Sergei and Uncle Vladimir developed equally efficient methods of intimidation.

Paul, the youngest of the four, only eight years older than Nikolai, 'was less blustering and assertive'.

On his accession the progressive, liberal-minded people hoped that the young Tsar would bring Russia out of its medieval backwater. The *Zemstvo* (County Council) of Tver, in their address to His Imperial Majesty, appealed for 'the voice of the people and the expression of their desires to be listened to'. But on the advice of his uncles, his mother and his tutor Pobedonostev, who was Procurator of the Holy Synod, Nikolai not only rejected their demands *in toto*, but rebuked them for their 'senseless dreams of the participation by the representatives of the *Zemstva* in the affairs of the internal administration of the country'; and then added: 'I shall maintain the principle of autocracy just as firmly and unflinchingly as it was preserved by my unforgettable dead father.'

Despair descended, and the revolutionaries decided that reform could be achieved only by bomb and bullet; in the succeeding years their ranks were swelled by thousands and eventually by millions.

It was not until the end of 1903 that the Tsar began to rule without persistent interference from his uncles. By now he was thirty-five, and his children numbered four grand duchesses—Olga, Tatiana, Marie and Anastasia; his son Alexei arrived in the summer of the following year. As an autocrat he appointed his own ministers; they were not answerable to a democracy but to him alone. Often he dismissed them quite arbitrarily without the vaguest hint as to why the minister was dismissed. To avoid unpleasantness, Nikolai would receive the minister in a most friendly manner, agree with what the man said and make him feel that all was well. The minister would go home delighted, only to receive a note of dismissal the next morning.

The Tsaritsa meanwhile took on her own role as Empress. Her grandmother, Queen Victoria, aware of her embarrassing shyness, had been acutely uneasy about Alix's swift transition from a German princess in the small duchy of Hesse to Empress of the largest country in the world. At her receptions and balls, the guests, as they filed past the tall, beautiful Empress, noticed her coldness, her aloofness, her indifference, for she hardly ever smiled or said a word, and eventually they attributed it to her utter boredom with the entire palace ritual. It did not take long for every invitation to be regarded by the guests as a passport to agony in a magnificent imperial setting. They disliked going there and disliked the Empress. They preferred to invite and entertain one another and spend the entire evening pouring out their contempt for the Tsaritsa.

Soon they had even more reason to criticize and dislike her. The behaviour of the nobility and the well-to-do in St Petersburg was severely condemned by her as being grossly immoral: irregular love affairs were being proudly flaunted. She disapproved strongly of all-night parties. The normal and quite natural feelings of young girls received this denunciation: 'The heads of the young ladies of St Petersburg are filled with nothing but thoughts of young officers.' Decolleté gowns shocked her. During a court ball at the Winter Palace she sent a lady-in-waiting to tell a woman who was dancing happily with a high-ranking officer: 'Her Majesty, madame, wants me to tell you that in Darmstadt we don't wear dresses like this.' To which the lady replied: 'Please tell Her Majesty that we wear our dresses like this in Russia,' and promptly pulled the front of her dress down even lower.

From a bad beginning it never got better but grew steadily worse. During the first ten years, when the Tsar was dominated by his uncles, the Empress suffered a series of bitter disappointments as each pregnancy, welcomed with fresh hopes and prayers, brought yet another girl. She felt she had failed her husband and had failed Russia in not providing an heir. Her spiritualist sessions were joined by the Tsar, who sought by table-rapping the advice of his father on how the country should be ruled. His mother disapproved of it strongly. The idea of constantly calling on the spirit of her dead husband infuriated her. She had never liked her daughter-in-law, and now she blamed the situation on her, for it was she who got Militsa to arrange these spiritualist seances. The Dowager Empress Marie became increasingly aware that the Tsaritsa's strong influence over the Tsar had weakened her relationship with her son.

When at last an heir arrived, the feeling of failure left the Tsaritsa. She had achieved something of the utmost importance for her husband and the nation. No longer was there any need for her to give a thought to the members of the Imperial family, who put on such airs of superiority. They would have no further say. Her husband was Tsar and she would at last be able to guide him.

CHAPTER
TEN

Healing the Heir to the Throne

The heir was only six weeks old when the first signs of haemophilia were discovered.

> Alix and I have been very worried [the Tsar noted in his diary]. A haemorrhage began this morning without the slightest cause from the navel of our small Alexei. It lasted with but a few interruptions until evening. We had to call the surgeon Federov, who at seven o'clock applied a bandage. The child was remarkably quiet and even merry but it was a dreadful thing to have to live through such anxiety.

It recurred the next day.

> This morning [the Tsar wrote] there again was some blood on the bandage but the bleeding stopped at noon. The child spent a quiet day and his healthy appearance somewhat quietened our anxiety.

There were no further signs of bleeding for some weeks. But as the child began to grow and crawl and walk, inevitably he stumbled and fell, his legs and arms were bruised, and it was noticed with horror that dark blue swellings began to appear. Haemophilia prevents the blood from clotting quickly, as it does normally, and it continues flowing for some hours. Eventually a clot is formed, but the pain is excruciating. The doctors do what they can to help; tight bandaging, for example, helps, but certain parts, like the inside of the nose, cannot be bandaged.

The parents realized now that it was something they and the infant Tsarevich would have to live with for the rest of their lives. But they decided to keep it secret, for they did not want anyone—the grand dukes, the other members of the nobility, the artisans or the peasants—to know. But for how long could it be kept secret?

Tsarskoe Selo was near enough to St Petersburg to be regarded as a Russian Windsor. It was selected as a country retreat by Catherine I, the wife of Peter the Great. Two palaces were constructed there: the Catherine Palace, a vast, impressive structure, planned to surpass the magnificence of Versailles; and a modest two-storeyed building, the Alexander Palace, which Nikolai and Alexandra chose as their home. The tall pillared central section contained the state apartments, reception rooms and ballrooms. The Tsar and his family lived in one of the two wings, the other was occupied by the court officials and ladies- and gentlemen-in-waiting.

Before moving in the Empress had the royal residential wing re- decorated and refurnished. Her favourite colour was mauve. It appeared in almost all the rooms she used: her boudoir was mauve throughout: carpets, curtains, furniture, even the flowers—lilacs, violets and mauve orchids. The bedroom in which she and the Tsar slept together in a double bed had a vast mauve carpet. Off this bedroom was a small private chapel with hanging lamps and an ikon. Off the other side was the Empress's bathroom: her prudishness required that not only the toilet but the bath tub also should be covered completely when not in use. None of her six personal maids saw her undressed or in her bath: they came in after she was dressed. The nurseries, planned soon after their marriage, were on the upper floor: bright English chintzes were used there; all the massive old furniture had been cleared out even from the main reception rooms; the traditional Romanov hard camp-beds were covered for her daughters with richly coloured English cretonne. One could have mistaken the whole of this wing as part of an English country house, save for the four enormous Negroes in red trousers, gold-embroidered jackets and white turbans who stood on guard: their duties were in fact confined to opening and shutting doors.

Here the heir arrived nine and a half years after the family had moved in; here he lay in his small cot, his head a shock of golden curls, his eyes a very bright blue, trying to take in everything and everyone.

His falls while toddling brought bruises and swellings, but did not cause any alarm. When he was three and a half he fell in the garden. His face began to swell rapidly and soon his eyes were completely closed. Anxiety was caused by the fear that the blood would seep into the muscle or tissue, or, worse still, into a joint where it could destroy bone, cartilage or tissue. When the bone foundation is affected the limbs move into a bent position and become rigid, and the patient must be confined to his bed for some weeks.

The Tsaritsa phoned her sister-in-law the Grand Duchess Olga and begged her to come. By the time she arrived the child was in great pain, and his limbs were growing distorted. The doctors, says Olga, were unable to do anything to help. In her despair the Tsaritsa sent a messenger to find Rasputin and ask him to come. Apparently he was with a group of friends at one of the all-night gipsy entertainments on the outskirts of St Petersburg, attended largely by the nobility. Some say he was drunk, but the moment he was told of the illness of the heir, he went down on his knees and prayed; then he rose, mounted a horse and hurried to Tsarskoe Selo. On entering the nursery he got down on his knees again and prayed, then went up to the child's bed and made the sign of the Cross. Alexei opened his eyes slowly. 'Don't be afraid,' said Grigori, 'everything will be all right. Your pains will go.'

The next morning the Empress took her sister-in-law to Alexei's room. 'I just could not believe my eyes,' says Olga. 'He was sitting up in bed.' Three weeks later, the Tsar, writing to his mother in London, said: 'Thank God, the bumps and bruises have left no trace. He is well and cheerful.'

As a precaution to prevent his falling again, two sailors, Derevenko and Nagorny, were appointed as Alexei's bodyguards. In Spain, the two royal haemophilic boys were protected by heavily padded clothes, and even the trees in the part of the park where they played were padded.

The Tsarevich Alexei was high-spirited. He enjoyed running noisily down corridors, getting under the dining table, pulling off the women's shoes and taking them to present to his father, for which of course he had to be scolded.

As he grew older he had to be told why he had to avoid falling down and hurting himself. He listened, but hated not being able to do what other children did. 'Why can't I have a bicycle?' he asked. 'Why can't I play tennis like the others?' And sometimes he would cry; or defiantly he would do what he was told not to do. The Tsar, while inspecting some troops on the parade ground, was horrified when he saw Alexei coming towards them on a bicycle. He stopped the parade and sent men to surround the boy and close in on him as gently as possible. Another time at a children's party at the Palace he was seen leaping from table to table. The sailor Derevenko had to stop him and calm him down.

The Tsar and Tsaritsa, to divert his thoughts to other things, bought the most elaborate and costly electric toys, which needed only the pressing of buttons for ships to sail, warships to attack, church bells to ring, clockwork passengers to get into railway trains and get out at different destinations and battalions of tin soldiers for him to manœuvre. Alexei was also given a Cossack uniform, which he proudly wore in the winter with a fur cap and long boots; in the summer a sailor's uniform was worn with the badges of the Russian navy.

His sisters were deeply attached to him. Olga, the eldest, and Marie, the third daughter, were very Russian and strikingly Romanov, says Anna Vyroubova. Olga was the cleverest, had a strong will and a hot temper; Marie was blonde-brown haired, sweetly disposed and inclined to be stout. The prettiest of the four was Tatiana—tall, slender with rich brown hair and very like her mother in appearance. Anastasia, the youngest, and only three years older than Alexei, was a tomboy, says Anna, clever and full of practical jokes. They joined their brother in the same indoor and outdoor games. Music appealed to them all: the girls played the piano while Alexei strummed the *balalaika*, which he played well. All of them adored pets: his was a spaniel called Joy, and a playful circus donkey, named Vanka, who was full of tricks.

From 1906, when Alexei was two years old, a Swiss tutor, Pierre Gilliard, was engaged to teach French to his sisters. He rarely saw Alexei; occasionally he caught glimpses of him tearing down the corridor or driving out in a sledge on the snow, and sometimes the boy would burst into the classroom and interrupt the studies of his sisters.

> At times his visits would suddenly cease [says Gilliard], and he would be seen no more for a long time. Every time he disappeared the Palace was smitten with the greatest depression. My pupils' mood was melancholy which they tried in vain to conceal. When I asked them the cause they replied evasively: 'Alexei Nikolaievich is not well.' I knew he was prey to a disease . . . the nature of which no one told me.

Some years later Gilliard was asked by the Tsaritsa to teach him French. Alexei, he says, was rather tall for his age.

> He had a long, finely chiselled face, delicate features, auburn hair with a coppery glint in it, and large blue-grey eyes like his mother's. . . . He had a very quick wit and a keen penetrating mind. He sometimes surprised me with questions beyond his years which bore witness to a delicate and intuitive spirit.

The tutor's problem was to teach him discipline, which had never been imposed on the ailing child. But bit by bit discipline was imposed by explanation and gentle persuasion. Gilliard felt that the constant protective presence of the two sailors was damaging to the development of the boy's self-control:

> What the child gained possibly in safety, he lost in real discipline. I thought it would be better to give him more freedom and accustom him to resist the impulses of his own motion. Besides, accidents continued to happen. It was impossible to guard against everything.

Although the doctors disagreed, the Tsar and the Tsaritsa decided to give it a trial.

> Everything went well at first [writes Gilliard], and I was beginning to be easy in my mind when the accident I had so much feared happened without warning.

Alexei was standing on a chair in the classroom when he slipped and fell. His right knee struck a piece of furniture and the next day he could not walk. 'The swelling,' says Gilliard, 'which formed below the knee rapidly spread down the leg.' The pain grew worse every hour; he moaned and cried. 'Every now and then the door opened and one of the grand duchesses came in on tiptoe and kissed her little brother. . . . For a moment the boy would open his large eyes, around which the malady had already painted black circles.' Dr Derevenko (he happened to have the same name as the sailor) was anxious. But the Tsaritsa prayed and held vigil by the child's bed. Had it been critical she would have sent for Rasputin.

It was always Anya, as the Tsaritsa called Anna Vyroubova, who in such an emergency had to find Rasputin and tell him that there was nothing more the doctors could do for the child. At other times she could say that the Tsar and Tsaritsa would be delighted if he would come to Tsarskoe Selo for a cup of tea and a talk. Sometimes Anna was present when he came, but mostly he saw just the Tsar and Tsaritsa, staying an hour perhaps or a little longer if the Tsarevich came down in his long blue bath robe to say goodnight to his parents and ask Rasputin endless questions about Siberia and the Holy Land and about his sleeping in fields under the stars during his wanderings. Occasionally the girls joined them for tea and made it a small family party.

The Tsar, as we know, made a note in his diary when he first met Rasputin at Militsa's. In the following October their second meeting was recorded. 'This evening we were in the Sergeievskaya (the cathedral of St Sergei) and saw Grigori.' After a further interval of some months, Grigori was invited to the Palace at Tsarskoe Selo: 'Grigori arrived at a quarter to seven; he brought a picture of St Simeon of Verkhoture, greeted the children, and talked with us until a quarter to eight.' After he had left the two Montenegrin Princesses dined with the Tsar and Tsaritsa, for the entry in the diary adds: 'Militsa and Stana [Anastasia] dined with us; we talked of Grigori the whole evening.'

That was the beginning. Anna met Grigori in the following year, 1907, when she went to Militsa's just before her marriage. She described the meeting to the Tsaritsa and both women were most deeply impressed when, a few months later, his prophecy that the marriage would fail proved to be true.

Later that same year Grigori was called to the Palace because the doctors could do no more for the suffering heir. Grigori knelt by the bedside and prayed, then made the sign of the Cross over the child and said that Alexei would be well. The improvement began a few hours later.

In the years that followed he visited the Emperor and Empress about once a month when he happened to be in St Petersburg. The Tsar said to General Dediulyn, Commandant of the Imperial Palace and A.D.C. to the Tsar: 'Whenever I am oppressed by care, doubt or worry it is enough to talk for five minutes with Grigori. I feel at once strong and calm again. He always says exactly what I need to hear, and the effect of his good words lasts for weeks.'

In his manner Grigori was natural, frank and when necessary blunt. There were no polite, adulatory phrases. He called the Tsar '*Batiushka*' (Little Father) and the Tsaritsa '*Matushka*' (Little Mother). If he did not agree with what they said he never failed to contradict. The Tsar, who was deeply interested in spiritualism and table-rapping talked to Rasputin about it. Grigori looked at him with a disgusted scowl. 'I have nothing to do with it, and thou shouldn't. It is the work of the Devil.'

The Tsar then asked him how he was able to foresee the future.

'I know nothing of clairvoyance,' Grigori replied.

Often Grigori was away from the capital and spent some months with his family in Pokrovskoe, wandering at intervals through villages, visiting monasteries, praying, preaching and healing the sick.

A great deal of his time while in the capital was sought by John of Kronstadt, Bishops Theophan and Hermogen, the young preacher Illiodor and other heads of the Russian Orthodox Church, largely because they admired him and respected his knowledge and interpretation of the Scriptures. But they saw more in him than that: here was a new Messiah from a remote region of the Russian Empire—a prophet, a healer, with a simple saintliness. They saw that to the Church his cooperation would be of the utmost value; wandering as he did he could spread the political tenets of the Union of True Russians, of which they had made him a member, and thus convert the agitators and bring peace to the nation.

Grigori Rasputin had always been a loyal supporter of the Little Father and looked on the Tsar as anointed by God to rule the people. To that extent he was at one with John of Kronstadt, Theophan, Hermogen and the others. But his sympathies were always with the poor and the underdog—the peasants, the workers in the factories, the afflicted and the minority groups such as Finns, Poles, Armenians, Jews and others. He was not prepared to give his support to any activity that went against these ingrained moral and spiritual convictions. Though he sought to bring about reforms, he refused to support the left-wing revolutionaries because they were materialists and preached atheism. In time those who sought his help in the church as well as the extremist reformers were to discover this and to turn bitterly against him.

The Lion of Society

Militsa and her sister Anastasia had opened for Rasputin the doors to the dazzling splendour of the palaces of the aristocracy. Invitations were showered on him. He had a childlike joy in diversions, particularly if they included singing and dancing and the gay laughter of men and women of all ages. Bowed to by liveried flunkeys, many of them wearing eighteenth-century wigs, he walked through vast chandeliered rooms with tapestried walls and richly painted ceilings; a lively orchestra perhaps played the *Blue Danube*, while beautiful girls in low-cut, half-naked gowns, and tiaraed big-bosomed women, heavily jewelled in breath-taking, costly dresses, whirled round with handsome young officers in the uniforms of their regiment and with generals heavily laden with gold braid. In some houses there were two or even three ballrooms, as well as rooms where restless men and women sat at green-baized tables to play bridge or *chemin-de-fer*; and there were gorgeously furnished and curtained drawing-rooms where men and women gossiped, running down some of their most intimate friends who were at the party but who happened not to be in the room. In corners couples were locked in voluptuous embraces. Nobody took any notice; each hoped it would be his or her turn next.

As Grigori went through these rooms all eyes were turned on him. His very presence was arresting, doubtless because he looked different: his clothes stained and torn, his hair and beard possibly blown by the wind; but combed they would have been, for he always carried a comb, and he would not have been dirty and smelly, for he rejoiced in taking a bath. There were many public baths in St Petersburg—luxurious steam baths with private rooms and male masseurs to pummel one's body, and baths for the masses who were charged five kopeks* per person, with a communal room for the men and another for the women; and, as we know, in Pokrovskoe, he had a steam bath in his courtyard, and on the blazing hot days of the Siberian summer he often bathed twice a day.

---

* 100 kopeks=1 rouble=2s. 1¼d. in the early years of the present century.

His rich hostesses and others who were not so rich soon began to give him long silk blouses, sky-blue, cream or scarlet, often very beautifully embroidered; later the Tsaritsa and her two elder daughters, Olga and Tatiana, also made and embroidered blouses for him. To wear with the blouses he was given velvet trousers—black velvet or burgundy; and soft kid boots to replace his rough shabby leather ones.

Some of the most memorable receptions were given by the Grand Duke Nikolai Nikolaievich and his wife Anastasia, and by his brother the Grand Duke Peter Nikolaievich and his wife Militsa. Princesses and countesses fought to get Rasputin to their parties. Not because he was an oddity or a nine-day wonder or a man of God, but chiefly because women seemed to find him irresistible and his bluntness fetching, while above all his eyes were welcoming, penetrating and mesmeric. They took his hand and kissed it; some kissed the hem of his garment. Militsa told Anna Vyroubova before her first meeting with Rasputin: 'Do not be astonished if I greet him peasant fashion, which is with three kisses on the cheek'; and she did so greet him. The Princess Golitzin, the Countess Ignatiev, Princess Tatiana Chakovkaia, Madame Golovina, the widow of a state councillor, and her pretty fair-haired daughter Mounia, who had been in love with a handsome young nobleman, invited him to their parties, at one of which he met Prince Felix Yussupov, a friend of Golovina's. Anna Vyroubova, living alone in a small house near the Tsar's Palace in Tsarskoe Selo, did not give big parties, but entertained just a few friends, including the Tsar and Tsaritsa: generally the Tsaritsa arrived with footmen behind her bringing cakes and sandwiches and fruit. Anna was generally at most of the big parties Rasputin attended.

He loved opera and ballet and was taken to the Marie Theatre to hear Chaliapin singing in Mussorgsky's *Boris Godounov*, and Rimsky-Korsakov's *The Snow Maiden* and *Tsar Sultan*. At the ballet he never tired of seeing Kschessinskaya, one of Russia's greatest dancers: she was a *prima ballerina assoluta* at the Maryinsky when only twenty-three—a title bestowed only twice in the theatre's history—and the first Russian dancer to perform the 32 *fouettés*. The Tsar's mistress before his marriage, she wept when he left her and, after marrying his cousin the Grand Duke Andrei, was known as the Princess Romanovsky-Krasinsky: born in 1872, she died in Paris in her hundredth year.

Others took Grigori to spend an evening with the gipsies—he never tired of these professional entertainers who came to St Petersburg in

F

the winter and lived in tents in the Novaia Deresvnia, a district known as 'The Islands'. The men were dressed as Russians in bright blouses, baggy trousers, long-sleeved black kaftans, top boots and wide black hats; the women, bronze-complexioned, their hair jet black, their eyes sparkling, wore long full skirts, shawls, head scarves tied at the back of the neck, and made an abundant display of big barbaric brooches, silver bracelets and necklaces of large coins. Some of the women were very pretty, but they allowed no liberties: marriage possibly, but no one would be granted a clandestine love affair.

The entertainment was given in a vast room with divans along the walls; in the middle of the room there were small tables and numerous chairs. Bright lights suspended from the ceiling and tall lighted candles on the tables helped the visitors to enjoy the wild abandon of the gipsy singers and dancers. An explosion of voices in the distance heralds their coming and their exhilarating display begins. Spontaneity prompts their feelings and guides their dancing and singing: neither is fettered by pattern or tempo. Suddenly a singer steps forward. The solo starts slowly and moodily, the voice metallic, barbaric . . . then surprisingly the rhythm changes, becomes more animated, rises to a very fast beat and descends to a whisper. At one moment it is rousing . . . at another it is sad and deeply moving. Most of the audience stay till the dawn. In their joyful abandon they throw gold coins to the gipsy women, which are added to those already dangling on their foreheads and cheeks.

Grigori, so long as the music, the singing and the dancing lasted, found it impossible to leave. Often his hosts got drunk and no doubt Grigori at times also had more to drink than normally. He was talkative, joined noisily in the singing, and often, because he could not keep still, joined in the dancing to the delight of the audience and the gipsies.

The high priests and the aristocratic hostesses were not his only contacts. He used to be waylaid in the streets by people he did not know; he was, of course, used to this in Pokrovskoe and during his wanderings. But some of those who stopped to talk to him were well dressed and had an air of affluence. They touched his arm and suggested that they might slip into a restaurant for some tea: it would be more comfortable to sit down and talk. As the friend of all who sought his help, he went in, wondering whether the man—or occasionally woman—wanted religious guidance or advice on a personal problem. It was neither. They wanted Grigori, who knew so many influential and wealthy people, to do them a personal favour. Then the scheme would be unfolded. They had a proposition—a money-making proposition; or possibly an invention that, if backed by a man of wealth, would make a fortune. 'You know people who are rich,' he was told. 'With your blessing. . . .' Grigori shook his head. 'I can't bless something I don't understand.' He finished his tea and rose from his chair. Occasionally, when the man was very persuasive and Grigori's heart was touched, foolishly he would give a note of introduction, saying, 'Go and see this man and tell him about it yourself. He may understand what you are saying, I don't.'

Some of these casual contacts in the street or elsewhere led to the formation of a close relationship. Aaron Simanovich was a jeweller he met in Kiev. Of middle-age, short, his head small, his cheeks and jowl wide, he was pale-complexioned with brown hair and a full moustache. His eyes were intelligent but cunning. He had two sons, one of whom suffered from St Vitus's dance.

Simanovich had sold jewels to the Tsaritsa long before he ever met Grigori. The Empress used to bargain about the price, and when at last the figure was agreed, the sum was paid in instalments, spread sometimes over years. But jewels were not the only thing he was interested in: he owned night-clubs, recruited cabaret artistes and ran gambling dens. Some regarded him as unreliable.

My second son Joann Aaronovich, who was in his teens [says Simanovich], was seriously and incurably ill. His right hand trembled continuously and the whole of his right side was paralysed. Rasputin asked me to bring my son to him early one morning, put him in the room adjoining his bedroom, then knock on his door and go. I did that. Shortly after I left, Rasputin came into the room, my son told me, and sat in a chair facing Joann. He then placed his hands on my son's shoulders and gazed fixedly into his eyes. After a while Rasputin was seized with a severe trembling which persisted for some time, then slowly Grigori Rasputin became his normal self again.

Quite suddenly he sprang from the chair and shouted: 'Go away, you silly boy! Go home before I give you a thrashing!' My son jumped up and ran home as fit as a fiddle. The illness never recurred.

Swamped by a feeling of intense gratitude, Simanovich saw Rasputin often. How much he relied on Grigori's influence for his further advancement, Simanovich does not say. A friendship was established, and no doubt Grigori, understanding nothing in his simplicity as to what was afoot, made comments that were regarded as prophecy.

> Most people [says Simanovich] believed my success was directly attributable to my friendship with Rasputin. This was by no means entirely the case, although, of course, the friendship was of great value to me. As it was, my popularity with the Tsar's household and with the Court came into being long before Rasputin set foot in St Petersburg.

He often called himself Rasputin's secretary. His son Joann, who now has a restaurant and night-club of his own in Monrovia, Liberia, called the 'Rasputin', decorated in the Russian style and serving Russian food, with African waiters dressed as Russian peasants in high-necked blouses with ropes round their waists, writes:

> My father's duties as Rasputin's secretary were rather unlimited: he used to read to him letters of all kinds asking for help and assistance; and also expressed his point of view on various matters. Very often my father acted as intermediary for Rasputin and talked to various high officials and their wives, all of whom wanted Rasputin to help them with various propositions; and at times it was not possible for callers to meet Rasputin without first explaining to my father what they wanted to see Rasputin about.*

Another hanger-on was Manasevich Manuilov, the son of a Jewish merchant. As a boy he attracted the homosexual Prince Meshchersky, who had been a close friend of Dostoevsky. The prince had the boy's clothes made by the best tailors and took him as his protégé to the best salons in St Petersburg. When he grew up he joined first the secret police, then went to Paris to ferret out anti-Tsarist revolutionaries. Short in stature, he dressed with an exaggerated elegance and had impeccable manners. His outstanding achievement was the deciphering of the Japanese secret code during the Russo-Japanese War, and he was rewarded with the Order of Vladimir by the Tsar. There was, however, an unsavoury side to his activities. His main interest was money; he was

---

* In a letter to the author.

paid enormous sums by many who were eager to escape military service. The promises he made were never kept. His attitude towards Rasputin had for a time been contemptuously hostile; but later he realized that Rasputin would, in his ignorance of worldly affairs, have not the remotest inkling as to how he was being used.

We shall come across him again, for Manuilov maintained the link for many years; and we shall also meet others who hitched themselves on to Grigori and became his self-appointed secretaries. At least four of them claimed to hold that office. Grigori always scribbled his own brief letters and notes of introduction: that was the only writing he did. He kept no diary, though on his second visit to the Holy Land he did keep a badly scrawled but interesting record, some of it excellently phrased, of what he saw and what his feelings were.

Oddly enough, although they knew he was ignorant of business transactions, buying and selling on the stock market and of investments, businessmen, some of them affluent, would come to seek his advice. 'Do you think these shares are worth buying?' they would ask. Possibly they were expecting a prophetic pronouncement from the *staretz*. Slowly his simple mind would get to work and make a commonsense analysis; and he would say the shares were good and would go up in price, or that they should be left alone. How far his analyses were right we do not know. But the investors, sometimes women, kept coming to him again and again, hoping for a prophetic pronouncement to make them rich—or richer.

What Grigori Rasputin much preferred was wandering through the streets, often in the poorest quarters on the eastern fringes of St Petersburg. There he met people like himself from a working-class background. However unselective and widespread his sympathy, he realized that they were far more in need than most of those who waylaid him and begged his favours: to heal the sick one made no choice, but, to help in other ways, preference had to be extended to those who lacked such necessities as food and shelter. The Union of True Russians, in which he had been enrolled by the high clergy, did not take this into consideration: he therefore refused to remain a member. Persuasion was tried, but was unavailing, and eventually they became his enemies.

Walking through the streets of the capital, he paused to look at the fortress of St Peter and St Paul on one of the central islands: in its dank dungeons, he had been told, a great many political prisoners, Dostoevsky among them, had been incarcerated for months awaiting trial and deportation to Siberia. It had been to Chelyabinsk, known as the Gate to Siberia and barely 200 versts from Pokrovskoe, that these prisoners had been taken, thousands upon thousands of them, and sent to remote eastern camps, too remote for escape. In the St Peter and St Paul Cathedral in the fortress he saw the white marble mausoleum of the Romanovs with a gilded bronze double-headed eagle at the corners: in the centre lay Peter the Great.

There was so much that was strange and so much that was beautiful in St Petersburg—an endless succession of palaces wherever one looked, along the embankments, overlooking the Neva and the canals, such riches, such immense wealth: it was said that Prince Felix Yussupov's family was the richest in the country. Anna Vyroubova told Grigori that Felix was a charming, warm-hearted and friendly young man; she and Felix used to go to dancing classes together when they were children, she said. His palace was splendidly situated, in the most fashionable part of the capital overlooking the Moika Canal.

CHAPTER TWELVE

The Unyielding Autocrat

There was no doubt in Grigori Rasputin's mind that, as God's anointed ruler, the Tsar could fulfil his obligations to the vast Empire of Russia only as an autocrat. In this he was wholly at one with the archimandrites and the bishops. Further than that he would not go with them: his sympathies were with the varied sections of a population which consisted of no less than 120 different nationalities, 119 of them classed as *inorodtsy* or aliens: these included Poles, Finns, Jews, twenty million Moslems and numerous heathen nomad tribes.

In the early years the stern exercise of autocracy had been essential for national defence—the people had suffered under the Tartar yoke for two and a half centuries between 1240 and 1480—and also to deal with the annual invasions that reduced the peasants to slavery.

Tsar Alexander I, in 1811, the year before Napoleon was driven back from Moscow, was given advice by Speransky, the greatest of his statesmen: advice which his successors would have been wise to have adopted. 'An autocrat decides everything,' said Speransky, 'but only on the basis of official information and advice served up to him by those qualified to give it and who have themselves been appointed by the Tsar for that very purpose.' The Council of State was created in that year: as its members served for life, we might regard them as life peers.

Nikolai II, no matter what advice his ministers gave, often acted on his own impulses. Of the five Tsars who immediately preceded him three were assassinated. His father Alexander III, who died in his bed, was his own Prime Minister. Nikolai had no Prime Minister, nor did he take on the role himself. The result was chaos. The ministers quarrelled and conspired against one another. The Russo-Japanese War provides an example. Sergei Witte, who had served Alexander III, was Nikolai's ablest minister. He was totally opposed to Russia going to war with Japan. Plehve, the tough, stern Minister of the Interior, was for it. The country, Plehve said in 1903, was on the brink of revolution, and 'a small victorious war would be just the thing to stop it'. Being in charge of the police force, Plehve, a reactionary of the extreme kind, embarked on widespread repression—an enormous number of peasants were flogged in Ekaterinoslav; *pogroms* were launched against the Jews; and he was opposed to the reforms planned by the *Zemstva*, the democratically elected county councils set up by Alexander II, grandfather of Nikolai II. Witte warned Plehve that such actions would lead to his assassination. The Tsar promptly dismissed Witte, the Russo-Japanese War broke out in February 1904 and Plehve was assassinated by a terrorist a few months later on 28 July. The 'small war' proved to be disastrous for Russia, and Witte was sent to do the best he could in arranging a peace treaty. All through the war, news of defeats and loss of territory to the Japanese led to disorders, riots, strikes and assassinations, which included the Tsar's uncle the Grand Duke Sergei, who had married the Tsaritsa's sister Elizabeth. On the Black Sea the crew of the battleship *Potemkin* mutinied, killed the officers and opened fire on Odessa.

The workers began to form unions; the first of these were unions of factory workers and railwaymen; then came the peasants' union, which demanded that all their land should be returned to them. Soon almost the entire working population was absorbed in unions of various kinds. There followed next the first of the Soviets, or councils of elected delegates, and eventually all these organizations were gathered together in the Union of Unions. Many feared that the expected revolution had already begun.

To replace Plehve the Tsar appointed General Dimitri Trepov as Governor-General of St Petersburg with absolute power over the entire police force of the Russian Empire. Trepov's order 'Don't spare the cartridges' was enthusiastically commended by the Tsar. The peaceful march of unarmed workers on 'Bloody Sunday', 22 January 1905, to the Winter Palace was met, as we have seen, with bullets, a charge by the Cossacks with drawn sabres and finally cannon fire, which swept along the Nevsky Prospekt and killed many trying to escape. Grigori Rasputin was not in the capital at the time; he had left in December 1903 for Pokrovskoe and did not return until the summer of 1905.

Witte, heavily built, robust, with a lofty bare forehead and a droopy moustache, made a count for his brilliant handling of the Peace Treaty with Japan, went with Count Kokovtsev, Minister of Finance, to see the Tsar and stated that a national assembly should be set up on the English parliamentary pattern, with elected members. The Tsar, after much hesitation, agreed to receive a deputation and discuss it further.

Grigori Efimovich Rasputin (*René Fülöp-Miller*)

Rasputin's house in Pokrovskoe, Siberia (*René Fülöp-Miller*)

Rasputin with his three children, Maria, Varvara and Dimitri, in the courtyard of his house in Pokrovskoe (*René Fülöp-Miller*)

Queen Victoria and some of her descendants. Seated on
her right, her grandson Kaiser Wilhelm II and on her
left her daughter, the Kaiser's mother; standing behind
him, Tsar Nikolai II with his wife the Tsaritsa Alexandra, grand-daughter of Queen Victoria; standing
behind the Tsar is Queen Victoria's eldest son, the future
King Edward VII (*Mansell Collection*)

Tsar Nikolai's nineteen-year-old mistress, the famous ballerina Mathilde Kschesinskaya

Tsar Nikolai's wife the Tsaritsa Alexandra shortly after her marriage (*Mansell Collection*)

Alexander Palace, Tsarskoe Selo. In the colonnaded section were the State rooms, which were hardly ever used. The Tsar and Tsaritsa lived on the ground floor of the wing on the right; the floor above had the children's nurseries; the Palace officials lived in the other wing (*Larry Burrows/Time-Life*)

The Tsar and Tsaritsa with their four daughters—Olga
was the eldest, then came Tatiana, then Marie and
finally Anastasia. Their son Alexei was born in 1904,
a few months before this picture was taken (*Radio Times
Hulton Picture Library*)

Rasputin during his first few months
in St Petersburg in 1903

Rasputin with Bishop Hermogen and
the monk-priest Illiodor (*René Fülöp-
Miller*)

The Winter Palace, St Petersburg (*Radio Times Hulton Picture Library*)

Kazan Cathedral, St Petersburg (*Radio Times Hulton Picture Library*)

Anna Vyroubova's house in Tsarskoe Selo (*René Fülöp-Miller*)

Rasputin in his apartment in St Petersburg with some of his friends who had been to Mass with him. Anna Vyroubova is the third woman standing on the left; Maria Golovina (wearing a hat), and her daughter Mounia are seated on Rasputin's right (*Radio Times Hulton Picture Library*)

Witte (*Mansell Collection*)   Stolypin

Rodzianko   Guchkov

The four most important ministers of the Tsar

At its head was Prince Sergei Trubetskoy, who warned the Tsar that if the people were not granted representation they would rise against 'all who are called their masters. Do not linger, Sir. Great is your responsibility before God and Russia.'

A plan for the formation of a Parliament, to be called the Duma, was drawn up on 17 October 1905. It was to be a consultative not a legislative body; and it was required to co-operate with the various departments and the ministers chosen by the Tsar. The Tsar did not wish the Duma to be democratically elected. Large sections of the population, including almost all the professional classes, were to be denied the vote. Liberals, reformers, members of the *Zemstva* and the town councillors —the last two already democratically elected—were disgusted with the restrictions imposed on the election to the Duma and the limitation of their influence: they could speak, but they were not allowed to do anything other than co-operate with the Tsar's ministers in such activities as the Tsar indicated. The workers' reaction grew steadily worse. There were disorders, a railway strike that paralysed the country, and then a general strike.

Witte, widely respected by the people since the Japanese war, pointed out to the Tsar that he had a choice of only two alternatives—either appoint a military dictator or grant a constitution and make the Duma a legislative body with the assurance that no laws would be passed without its assent. The Tsar discussed this with his cousin the Grand Duke Nikolai Nikolaievich, the obvious choice for a military dictator. The Grand Duke said he would shoot himself if the Tsar insisted on his taking on the task. So the second alternative was adopted, and the Tsaritsa never forgave the Grand Duke Nikolai. The Tsar would not, however, agree to the concessions Witte desired. The Duma was not to be made a legislative body as such, though he agreed to form the ministers he appointed into a Cabinet and to nominate a Prime Minister. That office was given to Witte, who thus became the first Prime Minister in the history of Russia; it was a change the Tsar always regretted having made.

The franchise was widened a little by Witte to give illiterate peasants the opportunity to elect literate representatives, who in turn elected others. The elections took place during a series of savage risings in the Baltic provinces, in Moscow, and most violently at Saratov. The First Duma's 524 delegates were received by the Tsar in May 1906 in the brownish-ochre Winter Palace, with its enormously tall pink granite column in the square in front, erected by Alexander I to commemorate the victory over Napoleon in 1812. The reception was in the magnificent chandelier-lit throne-room. After the Tsar's speech the new Prime Minister Goremykin,* weak, aged, his abundant white moustache descending to his lapels, told the members quite bluntly that such demands as land for the peasants were inadmissible. A vote of censure was immediately proposed by one of the Duma members and was followed by a recital of the widespread high-handedness of the existing government. They thus infuriated the Tsar, who was not prepared to discuss, let alone grant, any reforms. Ten weeks later the Duma was dissolved.

Grigori Rasputin, not in St Petersburg since December 1905, knew little about politics. Certain things seemed wrong to him, such as the persecution of the *inorodtsy*, the aliens, and especially the *pogroms* that brought misery and death to thousands of Jews merely because they were Jews; and there was also the flogging of the peasants—*they* had their rights too, and so did the workers in the factories and on the railways. All that seemed terribly, terribly wrong to him—a cruel, unfeeling mockery of the word of God. He felt that the bishops and the archimandrites, concerned about the Union of True Russians, should give some thought to the creatures of God who were being victimized.

After his return to the capital early in 1907, when he met Anna Vyroubova for the first time, Grigori spent most of the year in St Petersburg, for he was still in great demand, not only by the wealthy hostesses, but by the large number of disciples, women as well as men, who had attached themselves to him. Some of them were young members of noble families, others were students, others just working people: they sought his religious guidance and often a visit by him to an ailing relative or friend: it took up a great deal of his time, but it was the work to which he had dedicated himself.

He visited the Tsar and Tsaritsa at Tsarskoe Selo at their invitation three or four times that year, once when the Tsarevich was critically ill. Much time was spent also with Bishop Theophan, so meek and gentle, and the sturdy, vigorous Bishop Hermogen. Their concern was over the Tsaritsa, whose interest in mysticism, the supernatural and the occult had disturbed them for many years. They told Grigori about the charlatan Dr Philippe; on his departure from St Petersburg a man named Papus, a bogus French gynaecologist claiming to be a disciple of

---

* Witte had been dismissed a day or two earlier.

Philippe's, was received by the Tsaritsa, who saw him quite often. Fortunately, now it was Father Grigori, not a foreigner or a charlatan, but a true Russian, a man of the soil, a simple man, dedicated to God, well versed in the Scriptures, which he could quote so appropriately. While so many religious scholars groped for an interpretation of the obscure, Grigori saw it with clarity, satisfying to the uneducated and indeed often also to the learned. The high priests were intensely interested to hear about his pilgrimages. Not many of them had undertaken such arduous 1,000-mile walks barefooted and laden with chains of penance. His influence with the Tsar and especially the Tsaritsa would, they felt, undo the harm that for more than a dozen years had been caused by spiritualists, table-rappers and dabblers in the supernatural. Grigori had denied that he was a clairvoyant: occasionally he voiced a prophecy which proved in time to be true. He denied too that he had taken any lessons in hypnotism: his eyes were certainly mesmeric, a power that was latent in them, apparently from birth. The bishops and other high priests admired his frankness, his sincerity and his independent attitude. It was a blessing from God that he had been sent all the way from a remote village in Siberia to help the church to cleanse the wickedness and sin in the capital. The monk Illiodor all but worshipped him. They came from the same humble background, but whereas Illiodor was ambitious, Grigori Rasputin was not.

When Grigori returned to Pokrovskoe in the autumn of 1907 he told the family that Bishop Theophan had talked to him about the education of his children. His daughter Maria states: 'My brother Dimitri was sent to Samara, where, however, he only remained for one year, and I, for my part, was taken by my father to Kazan, where I was to attend the Gymnasium.' She stayed with the Katkoff family whom Grigori had met during an earlier visit to Kazan; they lived in one of the 'houses with tall façades painted in vivid colours and near the teeming harbour'.

Leaving home for the first time she wondered: 'Shall I ever see again our wooden house at Pokrovskoe, its impressive palisade, the white tower of the church near-by, the red Easter eggs on the great table, and the joyous bustle of the fête mornings with the accordions passing under our windows and the *telegas* bringing from the neighbouring villages their loads of laughing girls.'

Early in 1908 Grigori, after a short stay at Pokrovskoe, took his wife with him to St Petersburg to be operated on for a tumour in the stomach. The Grand Duke Nikolai Nikolaievich and his wife Anastasia did everything for her care and comfort, engaged the most skilled surgeon, obtained a room for her in one of the best nursing homes and went frequently to see how she was progressing. After leaving the nursing home she stayed for a few weeks in St Petersburg to convalesce, sharing the rooms the Sazonoffs had set aside for Grigori. Grigori looked after her with the utmost tenderness and, to show her something of the capital, hired a *droshky* and took her along the Nevsky Prospekt to see the Winter Palace and across the River Neva to the St Peter and St Paul fortress and asked the driver to take them next to the Kazan Cathedral. Proskovia Dourbovina, or Novychok as Grigori still called her, found it all very tiring. Everything was too big. 'I don't want to live here,' she said, and some days later he took her home by train to Tyumen, then by boat to Pokrovskoe, where he stayed with her and his father until early in 1909.

Grigori tried to persuade his father to visit St Petersburg. 'Come with me,' he said; but Efim Andreievich shook his head violently. He had heard enough from his daughter-in-law not to want to go there. So Grigori went back alone. Some months later, to his surprise, Efim Andreievich arrived. 'He only once visited St Petersburg,' says his granddaughter. 'Exhausted and terrified by the complications of the journey, the poor man's first gesture on arriving in the capital and seeing the swarming traffic, was to make the Sign of the Cross. A few days later, unable to acclimatize himself, he went back to his native village.'

A year or so afterwards Maria came to St Petersburg.

My father [she says] was still living with his friend Georgei Petrovich Sazonoff. To begin with he sent me as a boarder to a girls' school, the *Pension Seimann*. Dreadfully homesick, I found this anything but pleasant and a few months later my father took me to live with him. Then we both lived at the Sazonoffs, whose daughter Marie became my bosom friend. Later I went to the Steoline Kamersky Gymnasium in the Liteini Prospekt, where I was joined by my younger sister Varvara; we attended this school for nearly five years.

For the first two years or so they lived at the Sazonoffs'. It was not until 1912 that Grigori moved to a small apartment of his own: it had five rooms on the third floor of a house in Gorokhovaya, a straight, long street, near the Nevsky Prospekt at its starting-point in Alexander

Garden, but extending at a slant, like the spoke of a wheel, and deteriorating as it went.

Having his daughters with him did not tie Grigori to the capital. He went to Pokrovskoe every year and stayed there for some months; his daughters returned home for their school holidays.

The girls soon came to know Anna Vyroubova, and it was at her house that they were presented to the Tsaritsa and eventually got to know her four daughters.

In the Crimea in the early autumn of 1909, Anna, who was staying with the Imperial family, describes the recurrence of the Tsarevich's bleeding and the parents' and doctors' fear that it might suddenly become serious.

The sufferings of the child were so acute that everyone in the Palace was rendered perfectly miserable. Nothing much could be done to assuage the poor boy's agony, and nothing except the constant love and devotion of the Empress gave him the slightest relief. We who could do nothing else for him took refuge in prayer and supplication in the little church near the Palace. . . . The Empress, the two older girls Olga and Tatiana, two of the Tsar's aides and myself assisted in the singing.

The feared crisis did not develop, or Grigori would certainly have been sent for.

| # Life at Tsarskoe Selo

Goremykin, Witte's successor as Prime Minister, resigned soon afterwards and was succeeded by Piotr Arkadyevich Stolypin in July 1906, the third Prime Minister in three months. An extremely able man with a wide forehead, a dark moustache with curled ends, a beard confined to his chin, and immense courage, Stolypin had handled the outbreaks in the turbulent province of Saratov by defying a shower of bullets and walking unarmed to the rioters to warn them not to force him to use the power he possessed. He was for reform: he wanted to show the country that he intended 'to get away for ever from the old police order of things'. He realized he would need the support of the Duma, and called for the election of another, but the Tsar narrowed the franchise still further, thus excluding enormous numbers of voters.

The Prime Minister, the Minister of the Interior, the Ministers of Finance, Education, and so forth, it must be remembered, were not appointed by the Duma, were not even members of the Duma, but were nominees of the Tsar. Stolypin, who wanted to work with the Duma, had his house in the country blown up by a bomb. His daughter was crippled for life, his son injured and about forty guests and servants killed or wounded, but Stolypin, writing at his desk, escaped with only ink splashes on his clothes and face. The Tsaritsa offered to send Grigori Rasputin to see him, but Stolypin declined the offer.

The horrifying and crippling consequences of the bomb did not deter him from carrying out the reform he planned, which was to give every peasant the right to claim his share of the village holding as his personal property which he could pass on to his heirs. It was an essential adjustment to the Emancipation granted by Alexander II in 1861; the peasants had waited for it for nearly half a century.

Stolypin was responsible for the election of the Second Duma, but the others around the Tsar were totally opposed to it and told Nikolai that, without a Duma, he could recover his full authority as an autocrat. From the moment of its election the Tsar waited impatiently for its dissolution. An Imperial manifesto was issued before long, accusing the Duma of having plotted against the Tsar, and it was dissolved early in the morning of 16 August 1907; like its predecessor, it had had a short life—in this case of just over three months.

The franchise was now narrowed still further—most of the towns were merged into the provinces for electoral purposes: where indirect election was necessary a complete predominance was given to the country gentry. The whole of the Central Asian part of Siberia was disenfranchised; in other parts of Russia, the franchise was manipulated to give a substantial majority to the Cossacks. Thirty-one Social Democratic members of the earlier Duma were sent as prisoners to Siberia.

On this narrower basis the Third Duma was elected and met in November 1907. It contained fifty reactionaries, including Vladimir Purishkevich, who had been in the Second Duma and nine years later was to join forces with Prince Felix Yussupov to murder Grigori Efimovich Rasputin. Less diehard were the Octobrists, who took their name from the 'League of 17 October', bearing the date of the Tsar's manifesto of October 1905 which set up the Duma: they were Conservative reformers, and 153 of them were elected under the leadership of Alexander Guchkov, the grandson of a serf: an attractive young man of gentleness and charm, whose party proved to be an effective force throughout the life of the Third Duma, which stayed the full five-year course to June of 1912.

Guchkov's speeches were brilliantly pointed. He criticized the army and navy estimates, referred to the humiliation the country had suffered in the Japanese war and put the blame not on the forces but on the government. The effect on the public was electric: it proved that the Duma had begun to work and the people were now ready to give it their support. Even so, only the Tsar and the ministers he appointed could make decisions: the elected members of the Duma were allowed merely to talk: some years later two of its members, one of them Guchkov, waited on the Tsar in his railway carriage and received his abdication.

Away from St Petersburg for almost the whole of 1906, Grigori knew little about the first two Dumas; but he was there for the Third Duma elections and learned much from what was said about the aims and ambitions of the outstanding political personalities who were striving to guide the country without having any power.

One evening in the autumn of 1907 the Tsar's youngest sister Olga was taken after dinner to the children's nurseries on the upper floor. The Tsarevich and his four sisters, all dressed in white pyjamas, were about to go to bed. In the middle of the room Olga saw Rasputin standing and talking to the children. Olga says:

> I felt that gentleness and warmth radiated from him. All the children seemed to like him. I still remember their laughter as little Alexei, deciding he was a rabbit, jumped up and down the room. And then quite suddenly Rasputin caught the child's hand and led him to his bedroom and we three followed. There was something like a hush as though we found ourselves in church. In Alexei's bedroom no lamps were lit; the only light came from candles burning in front of some beautiful ikons. The child stood very still by the side of that giant, whose head was bowed. I knew he was praying. It was all most impressive. I also knew that my little nephew had joined him in prayer. I really cannot describe it—but I was then conscious of the man's sincerity.

After the children had been put to bed, the Tsar, Tsaritsa and Olga went down to the mauve boudoir and Rasputin was asked to join them. 'I realize,' says Olga, 'that both Nicky and Alicky were hoping that I would come to like Rasputin. I was certainly impressed by the scene in the nursery and I allowed the man his sincerity. But, unfortunately, I could never bring myself to like him.' She was impressed by his eyes, she said, but 'I never felt I was hypnotized by Rasputin. . . . It was almost impossible to keep up a conversation with him. That evening I noticed that he leapt from one subject to another and he did use so many biblical quotations.' She said quite firmly that, apart from having tea occasionally at the Palace, he usually came to see Alexei or to discuss religion with the Tsaritsa. He never had a meal there. The girls were always glad to see him because they saw what he was able to do for their brother when he was suffering.

Lili Dehn, wife of Captain Charles Dehn, an officer on the Tsar's yacht *Standart*, met the Tsaritsa for the first time in 1907 and became her close friend. They used to play Halma* together. 'We had two or three games,' she writes, 'she was greatly addicted to Halma, but she

---

* A recently invented game played on a chequer-board of 256 squares with nineteen men on each side if played by two people and 13 each if played by four; also known as Hoppity, because one could leap over any adjoining counter if there was a vacant space beyond.

had one little lovable weakness in connection with it. She never liked to lose!' The Tsar meanwhile played dominoes in the next room and smoked cigarette after cigarette.

Lili tells us that, while at Tsarskoe Selo, she and the Tsar's daughters

used to ride on the wooden switchback which was set up in one part of the Palace. It was tremendous fun and we slid and played together for hours, but I quite forgot that I was a married woman and that I had hopes of becoming a mother in some months' time. However the Empress had some idea of my condition, and one day, after she and Anna had been watching our performance on the switchback, Anna drew me aside. 'Lili,' she said. 'I've a message for you from the Empress. She wants you to be very careful just now.' She held up a playful finger. 'So no more switchback.'

In due course Lili came to know Grigori Rasputin. Her child Titi was seriously ill.

It was thought that diphtheric conditions would set in and the poor little boy lay tossing from side to side in a delirium. Anna, who made constant inquiries, at last phoned. 'Lili,' she said, 'my advice is—ask Grigori to come and pray.' I hesitated—I knew my husband's distaste for anything touching the supernatural. But when I saw how ill Titi was I hesitated no longer. At any rate no one could possibly condemn the prayers offered for a sick child. Rasputin promised to come at once, and he arrived in the company of an old woman dressed as a nun. This quaint creature refused to enter the boy's bedroom, and sat on the stairs praying.

'Don't wake Titi,' I whispered as we entered the nursery, for I was afraid that the sudden appearance of this strange peasant might frighten the child. Rasputin made no reply but sat down by the bedside and looked long and intently at the sleeper. He then knelt and prayed. When he rose from his knees he bent over Titi. 'Don't wake him,' I repeated.

'Silence—I *must*.' He placed a finger on either side of Titi's nose. The child instantly awoke, looked at the stranger unafraid and addressed him with the playful name which Russian children give to old people. Rasputin talked to him and Titi told him that his head ached 'ever so badly'.

G

'Never mind,' said Rasputin, his steel eyes full of strange lights. Then addressing me: 'Tomorrow thy child will be well. Let me know if this is not so.' And bidding us farewell, he departed with his odd escort. Directly Rasputin had gone the child fell asleep and the next morning the threatened symptoms had disappeared and his temperature was normal. In a few days, greatly to the doctor's amazement, he was quite well. After this I could hardly dispute Rasputin's peculiar powers. I always saw him whenever he came to the Palace—this on an average once a month. It is only fair to Rasputin to say that he derived no material benefits from these visits, in fact he once complained to me that he was never even given his cab-fares.

The Empress, Lili adds, was perfectly frank in her belief in Rasputin's powers of healing.

She was convinced that certain individuals possess this gift and that Rasputin was one. When it was urged that the services of the most skilled physicians were at her disposal, she gave the invariable answer: 'I believe in Rasputin.' As for the stories that Rasputin and Anna Vyroubova gave the Tsarevich poisons and antidotes, I dismiss these with contempt—they belong solely to sensational fiction. Anna Vyroubova would have been too frightened to give a kitten a dose of medicine, much less would she have tampered with the medicines given to the Tsarevich.

Sir Bernard Pares, who knew Russia and its leading figures well, writing about Rasputin and the Tsar and Tsaritsa, says:

What was the nature of Rasputin's influence in the family circle? The foundation of it all was that he could undoubtedly bring relief to the boy, and of this there was no question whatsoever. As his [the Tsarevich's] last nurse Teglova put it to Sokolov [a legal investigator]: 'Call it what you will, he could really promise the Empress her boy's life while he lives.' Mosolov [head of the Emperor's Civil Chancery] speaks of his 'incontestable success in healing'.

A new hanger-on now attached himself to Grigori Rasputin—Piotr Alexandrovich Badmayev, an elderly doctor who was born in the eastern section of Siberia beyond Lake Baikal, went to school at Irkutsk and then to St Petersburg University, where he was converted to Orthodox Christianity and changed his name of Shamzaran to Piotr: the Emperor Alexander III was his godfather, and this gave him an entry to the Imperial court for life. There are letters in existence between Dr Badmayev and Alexander III going back to the year 1893, so his link with Nikolai II and the Tsaritsa was in no way connected with Rasputin, who did not meet the Tsar until 1905.

On leaving the university Badmayev joined the civil service and was appointed to the Ministry of Foreign Affairs. As he had travelled in Mongolia and China and had studied Chinese, he was entrusted with important missions in the Far East: an entry in Nikolai II's diary states: 'After breakfast I discussed Mongolian affairs with Badmayev.' During the Japanese war he persuaded the Mongolian chiefs to join the Russians and used the 200,000 roubles given him by the Tsar to bribe them.

Badmayev claimed that his ancestors had an extensive knowledge of Tibetan medicine, much of which was secret. His brother Zaltin had kept up the family tradition and used herbs to bring about miraculous cures. Eventually Badmayev took over his practice, which soon began to flourish. But he was not able to help the young Tsarevich: on haemophilia his herbs had not the slightest effect. Nevertheless the Tsar kept in touch with him and often sought his advice on the appointment of ministers and high officials. As soon as it was known that he was a friend of Grigori's it began to be said that he was being used by Rasputin to give small doses of poison to the Tsarevich so that Rasputin could come along and cure the child. Many believed that was the basis of Rasputin's miracles. They seemed to be unaware that the doctors at the bedside of the sick child would have discovered the plot, analysed the poison and eliminated it themselves; nor is it explained why poison should have caused the bleeding, which began after the child had fallen and hurt his leg, his arm or his nose.

The Tsar's sister the Grand Duchess Olga says:

> There were thousands upon thousands of common folk who firmly believed in Rasputin's gift of prayer and healing. . . . There is no doubt about that. I saw those miraculous effects with my own eyes more than once. I also know that the most prominent doctors of the day had to admit it. Professor Federov, who stood at the very peak of the profession and whose patient Alexei was, told me so on more than one occasion; but all the doctors disliked Rasputin intensely.

'Not Worth Fighting
For'

Uninvolved in any way in politics, Grigori found himself advising the
Tsar at a moment of crisis. It was in October 1908, when suddenly and
quite unexpectedly Austria annexed the Slav states, Bosnia and Herze-
govina.* Thirty years before, unknown to Nikolai II, his grandfather
Alexander II had agreed to allow Austria to annex those two adjoining
countries provided Austria supported Russia in the war against Turkey.
In fact Austria had not assisted Russia at all.

Nikolai was furious, and so was Stolypin. The Serbian Government
appealed urgently for Russia's help; and France and England were ready
to give Russia loyal support. At the same time Germany rallied to the
support of Austria. This could have brought on the First World War
six years earlier. Rasputin told the Tsar: 'Fear war! *Fear* it!' Angry
though Nikolai was at the humiliation he would have to face if he
didn't fight, he paused and reflected. He realized it was little more than
three years since Russia's defeat by the Japanese. As he wrote and told
his mother the Dowager Empress, 'There was nothing for it but to
swallow one's pride, give in and agree.'

But it wasn't the last he heard from Austria. A fresh crisis arose four
years later, and once again Rasputin advised the Tsar not to go to war.
'He always said,' the Tsaritsa reminded her husband, 'that the Balkans
were not worth fighting for.'

Grigori spoke not as a politician, but as a man of acute awareness,
who saw not merely triumph and failure, as a general would or a politician or a Tsar, but as one filled with a surge of sympathy for the
millions of men and women and children, on both sides of the battle-
lines. What would *their* gain be? The death of their loved ones, the loss
of their homes, the inescapable shortage of food. . . . He had seen during
his many wanderings how one thing was dependent on another: the
land had to be tilled, carts had to convey food to the railway trains so
that it should reach those who are hungry. That was what religion
meant to him—to help his fellow men.

To the bishops and the archimandrites dogma and ceremonial were

* Now part of Yugoslavia.

the essence of religion. Not many had risen to their eminence by wearing chains of penance and walking barefooted, praying, begging, serving those who needed their help. In the chandelier-lit ballrooms of the nobility, to the women who gushed as they took his arm, he said: 'Thou art much too pampered, my dears. Follow me to Pokrovskoe, to the vast freedom of Siberia. We will work in the fields and catch fish, and only then thou wilt learn to know God.' The women repeated it with delight to their friends, and Anna Vyroubova quoted it in her book.

He knew he possessed two great gifts conferred on him by the blessing of God—the sudden spontaneous utterance of a prophecy, perhaps giving good tidings and joy or possibly sorrow and grief, over neither of which he had any control; and also the gift of healing of which he was only an instrument, for it required but a prayer to God and it was God who did the healing not he. 'Through faith we understand,' he said quoting from the Scriptures, 'that the worlds were framed by the word of God. Lift up the hands which hang down, and the feeble knees; and make straight paths for your feet lest that which is lame be turned out of the way; but let it rather be healed. Let brotherly love continue. Be not forgetful to entertain strangers: for thereby some have entertained angels unawares.'

Of the priests who sought his company and discussed with him the mysteries of the Scriptures, the one with whom Grigori had most in common was Illiodor, the tall, moustached, narrow-eyed peasant with faith and courage. They met often when they were in St Petersburg and spent many hours together.

In the autumn of 1909 Illiodor invited Grigori to stay with him in Tsaritsyn, for he was proud of the monastery he had built, of his vast congregation, their excitement when he preached, their eager echoing of his virulent denunciation of the follies of mankind and especially of the haughty, wealthy and unfeeling.

Grigori was impressed by his eloquence. There was depth to his spiritual fervour. Aware that Illiodor was an extreme reactionary, Grigori was puzzled on hearing his incessant onslaught on the nobility in language that was violent and often obscene. He was obviously trying to be another Savonarola. There was much more condemnation than sympathy in what Illiodor said. He attacked right and left incessantly—the Russian government, the advancement of civilization so evident in Western Europe, dancing, gambling, brothels, spiritualism.

For some of this Grigori shared the same contempt: taken to a brothel by a rich nobleman, Grigori walked out in anger. 'I will have nothing to do with all that.' But condemnation was not enough. There had to be a balance. If you say, 'Do not take that path, for it is full of pitfalls,' you must indicate at the same time which roads lead to God. A man cannot stand for ever facing the barred path: he needs guidance.

During his stay in Tsaritsyn, Grigori noticed traits in Illiodor that he had not noticed before: he was intensely ambitious, intent on personal advancement and fame, hence his plan to build the lofty Mount Tabor, with an enormous tower on top from which he would speak to the multitude. Grigori felt it was an attempt to emulate Christ and deliver his own Sermon from the Mount. Christ did not build a tall tower to get the people round him. He went among the poor, seeking nothing but the opportunity to help others. Though Illiodor's attitude towards Grigori was that of a disciple, full of admiration and humility, to others, as Rasputin could not help noticing, he was vain, arrogant and assertive. Illiodor was young—younger than Grigori: there was much he would have to shed.

They talked about it. Illiodor did not appear to resent Grigori's critical comments. 'I need your guidance and help,' he said. 'I talk of sin because I have seen its magnetic pull: once you are caught in it you will be sucked into the cesspool.'

Grigori asked if he had experienced it. Illiodor explained that he had visited dance halls, gambling halls, brothels and dens of iniquity and had seen what went on. Asked if he had ever sinned, Illiodor replied that he had not. He then put the same question to Grigori, who replied that he had. One avoided all one could avoid, and did penance when one had failed.

'I have *not* sinned,' Illiodor repeated.

'There must be something lacking in thee,' said Grigori. 'No human being can say with honesty and truth that he has not sinned. Daily in our prayers we ask God to forgive us our sins. Dost thou omit that from thy prayers?'

Illiodor was silent. His eyes looked troubled. Grigori made the sign of the Cross and rose from his chair.

Illiodor took Grigori Rasputin with him when he visited his disciples. On one occasion, just as they were about to enter a house, a young carter rushed up, seized Illiodor's arm and begged him to come and help his wife. 'She is possessed by the devil. She keeps rolling on the floor, screams and says awful obscenities.' Groping in his huge pocket, Illiodor produced a bottle of holy water and sprinkled it over the woman as she tossed about the floor, saying at the same time a prayer to drive out the devil. But it had no effect.

Grigori then volunteered to help. He would have to be left alone with the patient, he said: he had to be left alone, the concentration was too intense—it was so when he treated Simanovich's son Joann. The others left the room and after a time Grigori emerged saying, 'I have driven out the devil.' Going in they found the woman was quite normal. Some days later a young girl, the niece of Madame Lebedev, a prominent citizen of Tsaritsyn, was suffering in the same way. They found the girl unconscious. Illiodor tried, but was unable to help. Grigori struggled for many hours and was trembling as he came out of the room. He had succeeded yet again. Illiodor's heart was flushed with pride when he heard the villagers praise Grigori's divine gift of healing, but a slight twinge of envy crept into his feelings, though it in no way appeared to affect his deep regard and admiration.

In the following year, 1910, Illiodor was invited to visit Pokrovskoe and the two friends set out together, travelling by train to Tyumen, then in a rickety farm cart to Pokrovskoe. Throughout the long journey people kept coming up to pay their respects to Grigori, some kissing his hand, others kneeling in the roadway. Grigori, in his warm, affectionate manner, patted the hand of a man, placed his arm round the shoulder of a woman. Recalling their talk about sin, Illiodor wondered how much Grigori had sinned with women—young, beautiful, ravishing women.

'Have you no regrets?' he asked Grigori.

'It is thou, my friend, who is taunted by regrets,' said Grigori. 'I bear a much heavier load—the cost of penance is formidable.'

They touched briefly on celibacy, which monks and bishops have to observe, but Russian priests do not; they did not discuss sin and human desires again. Illiodor met Grigori's wife and their son Dimitri, now aged eighteen—tall, a pale brown head of hair, broad-shouldered, with very light blue eyes, like his mother's; Grigori's daughters were at home, Maria aged fourteen, Varvara twelve; and Illiodor met Efim, Grigori's father, now in his late fifties, but still immensely strong and energetic.

The villagers kept flocking in—they always did when Grigori was at home. It surprised Illiodor to see how much they revered him. To them he was the messenger of God: when Illiodor said this to him, Grigori laughed. 'They get things into their head. Sometimes when God needs a messenger'—he shrugged—'it may be me or somebody else. I was surprised to hear the Little Father tell me "You are a true Christ." Me!' Grigori laughed out loud.

'By the Little Father do you mean the Tsar?'

Grigori nodded, his eyes twinkling with laughter.

The chapel in the courtyard was used every evening and on three mornings of the week they went to celebrate Mass in the village church. Father Piotr, still the village priest, said to Illiodor: 'Do you also belong to the *Khlysty* sect?'

'I don't belong to any sect,' Illiodor replied angrily.

'He does,' said Father Piotr, pointing to Grigori with his large wide thumb.

'I know Father Grigori well,' said Illiodor. 'He is not a monk and like me he belongs to no sect.'

'Ask him,' said Father Piotr.

Grigori gave a loud guffawing laugh. 'It is not true! I despise flagellation and sexual orgies. It is a form of corruption, a desecration of human values and rights. *He* started this,' said Grigori tilting his head towards Father Piotr. 'He made this charge against me some years ago. The Bishop of Tobolsk sent a commission of inquiry. I was completely freed of this contemptible taint. But the village priest still insists that I am a member of the *Khlysty* sect. He should ask God. God would give him the right answer.'

CHAPTER FIFTEEN

The Hostility of the Church

When Illiodor returned to St Petersburg later that year he was surprised to find that Bishops Hermogen and Theophan had become critical of Father Grigori. Why? Grigori Efimovich Rasputin, he was told, was no longer a True Russian. 'Has he resigned from the Union of True Russians?' Illiodor inquired.

'He was made a member to serve our cause for the greater glory of God, the Tsar and the people of Russia,' said the frail, elderly Archimandrite Theophan. 'It was I who brought him to the notice of the Tsar and Tsaritsa.'

'Was it not the Grand Duchess Militsa?'

'It was through her that the Emperor and Empress first met him, but it was I and, of course, Father John of Kronstadt and our beloved Bishop Hermogen who recommended him to them as a guide and adviser: it was our hope—and we told this to Grigori Efimovich quite clearly—that he should use his influence with the Tsar and Tsaritsa and draw them away from spiritualism—and table-rapping—and supernatural magic. This he has *not* done. He is serving his own interest, not the interest of the True Russians.'

Illiodor defended him. For some months, he said, we have been together—at Tsarytsin and then at his home in Siberia. 'We shared our thoughts with frankness.'

'He will have to fall into line with us,' said Hermogen. 'If he fails, the Holy Synod will have to expel him.' Had John of Kronstadt not died in 1908, it is possible he would have supported the two bishops.

But Grigori Rasputin refused to fall into line. His daughter Maria states:

The Union of True Russians had pushed my father towards the Court in the hopes of being able to make a docile instrument of him. But the Siberian peasant revealed an intelligence too great, a personality too strong, to be merely a dummy in the hands of the party. And yet, seeing faithful followers of the Tsar and sincere patriots among the members of the Union of True Russians, my father remained their ally, thus classing himself among the Ultras, who were at that time his enthusiastic partisans. What spoiled everything was the frankness with which he expressed his thoughts. . . . 'The blame for rebellions and political resistance lies,' he said, 'with those who keep the people in ignorance and darkness. What misery! No hospitals, no schools, nothing but bars . . . ! Instead of organizing *pogroms* and accusing Jews of all evils, we would do better to criticize ourselves!' Those words and that attitude alienated from him the Ultras, who undertook a campaign of underhand calumnies against him in the Press.

'Hermogen,' says Lili Dehn, 'was a firm believer in Rasputin's spiritual powers, and he was also much interested in his arduous pilgrimages.' But the change in his attitude, she adds, started with 'endless intrigues'. Hermogen and the others 'were afraid that Rasputin would become more important than themselves'. The Orthodox Church is the most medieval of religions, she says; modernity, ever a fatal element in religion, is especially fatal to the Orthodox Church.

Though Illiodor remained loyal to Rasputin, he had no wish to fall out with Theophan and Hermogen, whose influence in the Synod was most powerful. But, he realized, to stand by Grigori Rasputin now would be to lose their support. His ambitious hopes made it obvious to him that they could do much more for him than Rasputin. Moreover, the Bishop of St Petersburg, Monsignor Anthony, had been roped in by Theophan and Hermogen to strengthen their ranks.

Their intrigues were soon directed towards having Rasputin banished from St Petersburg by the Tsar. Theophan and Hermogen knew that almost all the nobles would be on their side because of their intense hatred of the Tsaritsa. By driving out Rasputin it would not only shake but shatter her foundations, for when Rasputin spoke to her the Empress heard only the voice of God. It might take time, but they were confident they would achieve it. The Tsar was weak and he was completely under his wife's immovable thumb. Only by painting Grigori in the most horrible, nauseating hues could they make the Tsar see that Grigori Rasputin could not possibly be received in the Palace by His Imperial Majesty. The colours were lurid. It was impossible for them to prove that Rasputin was a liar, a thief, cruel, malicious or spiteful— no evidence could be obtained to support any of this; all the available evidence showed he was kind, gentle and considerate.

The uncouth peasant [says Lili Dehn], who came into the presence of Their Majesties barefooted, wearing the clumsy irons of penance, was in no wise impressed by his surroundings. He spoke freely to the Emperor, who was struck by his sincerity. . . . The Empress always believed in prayer. Rasputin strengthened her in this belief, and I am sure her perplexed soul was soothed by his ministrations. When various people reproached the Empress for being on terms of friendship with a common peasant, and for believing that he was endowed with the attributes of holiness, she replied that Our Lord did not choose well-born members of the Jewish society for His followers. All his disciples except St Luke were of humble origin. She was perfectly frank in her belief in Rasputin's powers of healing. She was convinced that certain individuals possess this gift, and Rasputin was one.

Aldous Huxley, having read the vile avalanche of attacks on Rasputin, sums him up in these words:

At the beginning of his career he seems to have sinned in a not unpleasingly Panic and Arcadian manner. But later, when he had exchanged the country for the town and had become the most influential man in Russia, the primitive candour evaporated and from innocent his sinning became civilizedly sophisticated and, if we can believe the stories told of him, sordid and rather dirty. A great many of these stories are obviously such lies as always crystallize round the name of any extraordinary man after it has remained long enough soaking in the malodorous imagination of the respectable bourgeoisie. . . . The *staretz* turns out to have been, on the whole, a sympathetic character. At any rate, one cannot fail to like and admire him a million times more than any aristocratic rogues, fools, weaklings and neurasthenics, in the midst of whom he accomplished his extraordinary destiny. At least Rasputin was a man. A power moreover. A man with a daemon in his belly—and daemons are always admirable. Anyhow, whatever may be your disapproval of Grigori the man, Grigori the moral philosopher is a personage who must be taken seriously.

For good measure the gossips added that Grigori was not only a member of the *Khlysty* sect, which, as we know, was found to be untrue, but also sexually insatiable, raping young girls, their mothers, exalted titled women and even nuns: it could not be proved and it was extremely difficult to disprove. His daughters, who lived with him in his restricted apartment in St Petersburg, denied that anything like that went on there, though Maria thinks he may have had some mistresses. Madame Golovina and her beautiful young daughter Mounia who saw him constantly, state emphatically that he made no advances of any kind towards them or their friends. Lili Dehn is similarly emphatic.

I know for a fact that many women of my world who had 'affairs' and many demi-mondaines were not dragged further into the mire by Rasputin, for—incredible as it may appear—his influence in such cases was often for the best. I remember that I once met Rasputin when I was walking on the Morskaya with a brother-officer of Captain Dehn's. He eyed me severely, and when I returned home I found a message telling me to come and see him. Out of curiosity I obeyed, and when I saw Rasputin, he demanded an explanation. 'Of what?' I asked.

'Oh . . . thou knowest well enough. Art *thou* going to follow the example of those frivolous society women? Why art thou not walking with thy husband?'

He repeatedly said to women who sought his advice: 'If you mean to do wrong, first come to me and tell me.'

I can do no more than speak of Rasputin as I found him. If I had been a Rasputiniere, or the victim of abnormal passion, I should not be living happily with my husband, and Captain Dehn would never have countenanced my association with Rasputin if he had known of his immoralities. His duty as a husband would have been greater than his devotion to the Imperial family.

Another charge was drunkenness: it was said that he drank vodka in vast quantities. His daughter Maria and others who knew Rasputin were quite emphatic that he never drank vodka. He liked Madeira, which apparently he could get in his Siberian village, and sweet white wine. His daughter says he did not drink heavily until the last two and a half years of his life when the mounting hatred against him became intolerable. He certainly was never drunk in the presence of the Tsar and Tsaritsa.

In the summer of 1910, when Grigori was in St Petersburg, he saw the Church and the nobility draw together for his destruction. The

Press hinted at it, and eventually came out into the open with vicious attacks. The politicians then took it up, and anonymous letters about him kept arriving at Tsarskoe Selo for the Tsar and the Tsaritsa. Sickened by the campaign of vilification, Grigori, who had for some years been contemplating making another visit to the Holy Land, decided to leave St Petersburg and set out on the journey.

Stolypin, the Tsar's Prime Minister and Minister of the Interior, was now approached by Grigori's assailants, urging him to take stern action against Rasputin. It would be better, Stolypin felt, if the Tsar dealt with him. He went to the Palace for an interview and recited the familiar accusations that were being made verbally and in print, and begged the Tsar to expel him. The Tsar displayed no reaction whatsoever, but asked him to prepare a report which would be shown to the Tsaritsa. When it was delivered, the Tsar glanced at it casually, put it in a drawer and asked Stolypin to see Rasputin and judge him at first hand.

Having declined to meet Rasputin in 1906 when a bomb destroyed his home, crippled his daughter for life and killed or wounded about forty guests and servants, it was unlikely that he would receive with an unbiased mind a man he disliked so intensely. Describing the meeting to Rodzianko, President of the Duma, Stolypin said: 'He ran his pale eyes over me, mumbled mysterious and inarticulate words from the Scriptures, made strange movements with his hands, and I began to feel an indescribable loathing for this vermin sitting opposite me. Still, I did realize that the man possessed great hypnotic power, which was beginning to produce a fairly strong moral impression on me, though certainly one of repulsion. I pulled myself together and, addressing him roughly, told him that on the strength of the evidence in my possession I could annihilate him by prosecuting him as a sectarian. I then ordered him to leave St Petersburg immediately of his own free will for his native village and never show his face here again.' Rodzianko, who also disliked Rasputin, adds this: 'It is worthy of comment that by his hypnotic power Rasputin had been capable of producing an impression even on a man of such iron will as Stolypin.' That Rasputin was not a conscious hypnotist has been established: he had taken no training; doubtless it operated unconsciously.

It is obvious that Stolypin had not been authorized by the Tsar to drive him out of the capital: hence, possibly, his use of the words 'of his own free will'. It is not certain that Rasputin mentioned this to the

Tsar or Tsaritsa. Doubtless he said farewell before leaving for the Holy Land, and certainly, despite Stolypin's warning that he must never show his face again in St Petersburg, Rasputin was back in the capital a few months later.

CHAPTER
SIXTEEN

Return to the Holy Land

On his way to the Holy Land Grigori spent a few days at Kiev and visited the Pechersky caves monastery again. It was a place to come to from St Petersburg, he said, because the light in the capital drives one's thoughts towards vain and worldly things, whereas in the monastery the light of silence shines.

From there he went south to Odessa and took a ship across the Black Sea. In the record he kept of this journey he states:

How shall I tell of that great calm? As soon as I left Odessa, on the Black Sea, there was calmness on the sea and my soul became one with the sea and slept in quietness. One could see the little ripples that glittered like drops of gold, and that was all that the eye could behold. And is that not a divine example? How precious is the soul of man; surely it is like unto a jewel. And even as that sea, so is the boundless power of the soul. When you arise in the morning the waves speak, and splash, and rejoice. And the sun shines on the sea as it rises gently, oh, so gently, and the soul of man forgets the world's iniquity and gazes at the glittering sun. And a great joy arises within him, and his soul ponders on the book of life, life's wisdom, indescribably beautiful. The sea arouses you from a sleep of worldliness.

He left the ship at Constantinople and went to see the cathedral of St Sofia, now 'in the hands of the ungodly Turks', who 'even smoke within the temple'. But he saw in the temple 'objects which have remained unsullied. These represent the Saviour (on the altar) and the Mother of God (on the way out of the temple).' He travelled thence to the island of Mitylene, where Paul the Apostle preached; then to Smyrna on the coast of Asia Minor, with the ruins of Ephesus, where John the Divine dwelt for many years, 'and here completed his Gospel, the depth of all wisdom; and for that reason the very sea around this coast is awakened to life from its slumbers. . . . Around Ephesus,' he adds, 'many caves and sanctuaries still remain. You have to go into these caves on all fours.' Then to Patmos: 'Here John the Divine was imprisoned, and it was here he wrote the greater part of his Gospel of the Apocalypse.'

Rasputin was on the Mediterranean for some days and kept thinking of the many apostles who were burnt on these coasts; and he jotted down this reflection.

Nowadays, just as in olden times, all bishops are educated men and very devout, but alas! they are not meek in spirit. And the people will only follow meekness of spirit. They will flock to follow a leader who is meek in spirit, because while devoutness is a great thing, meekness is even greater. A bishop who is without meekness will weep if he is not given a silver cross, whereas if he has meekness, even a tattered cassock will be pleasing to him and it is the tattered cassock that the crowd will follow.

After visiting Rhodes, Cyprus, Tripoli and Beirut (where St George killed the dragon) he arrived at last in the Holy Land. The first place he visited was Jaffa, where Elijah the prophet once dwelt.

The valley of Jaffa is a paradise of indescribable beauty. There is no more beautiful place in the world. Whatever one has heard in church of the bounteous fruits of the earth is to be found there.

Then Jerusalem.

I cannot describe the feeling of joy which overtook me. Pen and ink are powerless to tell of it and it is impossible to relate. There were tears in the eyes of every one of us worshippers, tears of joy. On one side someone sings joyously 'The Lord is risen!' On the other side, someone reminds us of our Lord's agony. The Lord suffered here. Oh, can't you see the Mother of God at the foot of the Cross! You can imagine the whole scene before your eyes, how He suffered here for us.

O Lord, walking these streets and reflecting, a great sorrow seizes the heart, as one sees the people walking about just as they did in those distant days, in the same mantles, the same strange garments that are mentioned in the Gospels. All is just as it used to be. . . . How many thousands will rise up with Him at the Resurrection, and what

sort of people? All simple people of contrite heart, even like ourselves. For God has endowed us with humility while we were on the
sea. We all fast. We eat nothing but rusks, and we meditate upon
salvation. . . .

There are many hangers-on, doing trade in holy things. They run
about crying 'Here's a holy father' and they write your name down
for relics of all sorts. They sell wine, too, a litre for a few coppers,
and people drink it because it is so cheap. It is the monks of Athos
who offend most, and therefore they ought not to be allowed here.
Most of them live just outside Jerusalem. It is difficult to explain, but
those who have been there will know.

He had also been to Athos; he knew.

Going on to Golgotha, he wrote:

How impressive is Golgotha! There is the Temple of the Resurrection where stood the Queen of Heaven, a round hollow has been
made and this marks the place where the Mother of God gazed upon
the hill of Golgotha and wept as they nailed Our Lord to the cross.
. . . O God, what a deed was wrought! And they took down His
body and laid it on the ground. Oh, what sadness and weeping at the
place where His body was laid. O God, O God, why did it all
happen? O God, we will sin no more, we are saved by Thy own
suffering. . . .

We were brought to the Place of the Assumption where the tomb
of the Queen of Heaven is. We walked along the road, led by guides
with torches and the crowd was filled with awe and there were many
lepers, just as it was in the days of Our Lord and the lepers all cried,
'Give us a copper.'

We saw the house of Judas and of Pilate. They are not far from
each other in the same street. And though nobody knows anything
about Pilate, Judas is an example of all kinds of iniquity. With the
crowd we reached the Cave of the Mother of God and all sang
'Despite the Nativity she kept Her virginity; in the Assumption She
did not leave the World', which is a *troparion* in honour of the Mother
of God, and everyone eagerly thronged around Her tomb and all
sang and rejoiced in Her gladness that the Lord had taken Her body
unto Himself.

In the same cave the body of Joseph had been buried, as we are

H

told in history. Here reposes the venerable old man. O most mighty of old men, pray for us now!

We were conducted to the Red Gates where Jesus was tried for the last time. Oh, sad are the thoughts of that trial! How He suffered and all men denied Him and He was condemned to die, the Sinless One who never transgressed. . . .

We came to Gethsemane where Our Lord talked with His disciples before His last great agony, when He prayed about the cup of death. We unworthy ones prostrated ourselves in this place where we were mourned for by His blood-stained tears and were washed in His blood. To think that we stood in the very place where He prayed! All of us were deeply moved. There were tears in everyone's eyes. In the wall there is a stone still stained by the Saviour's blood. One is impelled to pray in such a place where the Saviour stood, and knows that in the Garden of Gethsemane the tears of God flowed in rivers, one is afraid to tread upon this holy ground for every little pebble is sacred—O, it is beyond description. God save us and forgive us in Thy heart.

In the same place, higher up, we saw where the disciples slept amongst the stones and Our Lord came several times to wake them, and we remember that it is not always thus. We are sunk in slumber and fall into evil ways. Lord, awaken us!

Next he went to Jordan and the Dead Sea.

I visited Jordan, and the *troparion* 'Baptising in Jordan' was sung, and everyone immersed themselves in the waters of Jordan. We beheld the wilderness of Jordan whence many fled into Egypt. In the place where Thou, O Lord, wert baptising, all immerse themselves in the water and meditate on the remission of sins. The people of many nations come unto Jordan with great reverence in their hearts, in order to free themselves from their sins. Many thousands from all corners of the earth bring their bodies and souls to be washed. O God, purify us in the water of Thy Jordan.

We saw also the Dead Sea. God's punishment is upon it. We were filled with horror and awe. The Lord waxed wroth because of the iniquity of men, so that here there is to be seen nothing but the oily waves; not a living creature; not an insect may live there, not a fish even, so that you gaze upon it and weep. Woe unto us! God in His anger spares no cities. Lord forgive us, and spare us upon the Day of Judgement. . . .

In Bethlehem there is a huge temple in which are many altars, and facilities are provided for every nation, yet for the Russian pilgrim there is nothing but inconvenience. But when we beheld the cradle of Our Saviour Himself, we forgot our weariness and all the monkish intrigues. We bent over His cradle and our joy was so great we could hardly believe Our Lord had really shown His mercy unto us. There where Christ was born we bowed down and touched the place where He had lain and there was great joy in the faces of us all. Here it was, too, that Herod slew the children. What jealousy and evil made him slay the children in this city? How was it that he did not fear the anger of his own people, and how could he not have pity on the little ones? Insidious as a serpent is jealousy. Here is the cave of all the slain children. There were many thousands of them. The Russian pilgrims pondered with horror on the evil deeds of Herod. Evil and jealousy is with us yet, the great are jealous of those greater still, and crowned heads are filled with intrigue, while truth and goodness, like a blade of grass in an autumn night, awaits the rising of the sun. And when the sun rises, truth will be revealed.

After spending three months in the Holy Land, Grigori left.

When we were on our ship on the way back, we again passed by the place where the whale cast forth the prophet Jonah, and here we sang the Easter Hymn 'Like unto Jonah from the belly of the whale, so Thou hast risen from the grave'. All of us gazed at the place where this miracle occurred. There is a small stone pillar there, with an oblong cavity! The steamer stopped twelve hours at the place.

From Odessa he went once again to Kiev, and from there he made for Pokrovskoe, where he spent some months with his father, his wife and three children.

Anna Vyroubova in Pokrovskoe

In the course of his travels in the Holy Land Grigori sent three or four letters to the Tsaritsa, describing some of the places he visited and how they affected him. He also wrote to her four daughters, Olga, Tatiana, Marie and Anastasia, and sent a card to Alexei, who was now six and a half years old.

The Tsaritsa was deeply moved by his notes. How could Stolypin and the others say such dreadful things about a man whose dedication to God was only too apparent? It was a conspiracy, she felt, by some of the priests and nobles to take their friend away from them. He was hated because they loved him. What would they do if Alexei needed help? He would die if they had not Grigori to come and pray for him. Again and again when the doctors had given up hope because there was nothing more they could do, it was Grigori who had kept the child alive.

The Tsar made no attempt to dispute it. He knew how much he and the Tsaritsa relied on Grigori, and how much comfort he gave them when he sat and talked to them over a cup of tea.

'Do you believe that he has another side to his personality,' the Tsar said, 'as unsavoury as they say it is?'

'No,' the Tsaritsa replied. 'A man of God would not live a double life.' After a moment she added: 'I'll send Anya Vyroubova to stay with him in Pokrovskoe. She will be able to see how he lives and how he behaves when he is away from us.'

The Tsar nodded. 'What a splendid idea! Anna would be able to see exactly what goes on.'

I will say this for the Empress [Anna writes], that although she had the fullest confidence in Rasputin's integrity, she thought it worth-while to make some inquiries into his private life in Siberia, where most of his time was spent. On two occasions she sent me with others to his distant village of Pokrovskoe to visit him. . . . With Mme Orlov, mother of General Orlov, and with two other women and our maids, I made the journey to Siberia, leaving the railroad at the little town of Tyumen. Here Rasputin met us with a clumsy peasant cart drawn by two farm horses. In this springless vehicle we drove eighty versts across the steppes to the village where Rasputin dwelt with his old wife, his three children and two aged spinsters who helped in the housework and in the care of the fields and the cattle.

The household [Anna continues] was almost biblical in its bare simplicity, all the guests sleeping in an upper chamber on straw mattresses laid on the rough board floor. Except for the beds the rooms were practically without furniture, although on the walls were ikons before which faint tapers burned. We ate our plain meals in the common room downstairs, and in the evening there usually came four peasant men, devoted friends of Rasputin, who were called 'the brothers'. Sitting round the table they sang prayers and psalms with rustic faith and fervour. Almost every day we went down to the river to watch Rasputin and the brothers, fishermen all, draw in their nets, and often we ate our dinner by the river, cooking the fish over little camp fires on the shore, sharing in common our raisins, bread, nuts, and perhaps a little pastry. The season being Lent we had no meat, no milk, no butter.

On her return she told the Tsaritsa about his simple pastoral life in Pokrovskoe, adding that the clergy in the village seemed to dislike him while the majority of the villagers, who had known him all their lives, took him for granted. She went with him to the famous monastery of Verkhoture, saw the deeply venerated relics of St Simeon and also went into the forest to talk to Father Makari. 'This aged and pious monk,' she said, 'held Rasputin in higher respect than did the village clergy.'

Anna Vyroubova went to Pokrovskoe a second time, a few months before Rasputin's death. This will be described in the words of Lili Dehn, a former lady-in-waiting to the Tsaritsa, who accompanied Anna to Pokrovskoe on that occasion.

At the end of Anna's first visit Rasputin left Pokrovskoe with her. They travelled together to Kiev. The Imperial family was to be there and were going on to the Crimea. After attending army manœuvres in Kiev, the Tsar and his family went to the opera to see *Tsar Sultan* by Rimsky-Korsakov. Rasputin, waiting in the street with Anna, saw the Imperial carriage arrive, followed by Stolypin's carriage. At this, pointing to Stolypin, Rasputin began to shout: 'Death is after him! Death is driving behind him!' It was yet another example of his second-sight, for an hour or so later, in the theatre, Stolypin was shot by an assassin.

The next morning, in a letter to his mother, the Tsar, who had been seated in a well-guarded State box, said:

> During the second interval we heard two sounds, as if something had been dropped. I thought an opera glass might have been dropped on somebody's head. . . . Directly in front of me in the stalls, Stolypin was standing; he slowly turned his face towards us and made the sign of the Cross. . . . Only then did I notice that his right hand and uniform were blood-stained. He slowly sank in his chair and began to unbutton his tunic.

Falling forward, he said 'I am done for!' While on his way to the opera, seeing the Tsar surrounded by police, Stolypin had said to his Minister of Finance, Kokovtsev, 'We are superfluous!'

Prince Paul Vassili writing during the Tsar's lifetime, states in his book *Behind the Veil in the Russian Court* (1913):

> The whole of Russia was aghast at the assassination of Stolypin; even his enemies were dumb with the horror of it. Expressions of sympathy came from every side; the person who appeared the most unmoved was the Emperor. It was only on the third day after the attack that he visited the dying statesman. He expressed no sympathy to the dying man beyond some conventional inquiries and official words of regret. . . . The Emperor came to his bedside just before the end, and was received by Madame Stolypin, who used the opportunity to address a few tactless words to the Sovereign, which he resented afterwards. Nikolai II remained only a few minutes with the dying man and after some formal expressions of grief he retired. . . . Nikolai did not consider it to be his duty to attend the funeral of his murdered servant. He was to leave Kiev for the Crimea on the very day upon which it took place, and it would have been easy enough to put off his departure for a few hours.

Anna travelled to the Crimea with the Imperial family and Grigori followed by train to join them. The Tsaritsa had been ecstatically thrilled by his letters from the Holy Land; and on his return he had received letters from her, from the two older girls Olga and Tatiana and also one from Alexei.

He had been in the Crimea only a few months earlier while on his way to the Holy Land. A small peninsula, barely 200 miles wide, it juts into the Black Sea and is washed by the Sea of Azov on the east. Its beautiful setting is the pride of Russia. In the south the hills rise to a height of nearly 5,000 feet and are dark with pines. Anna Vyroubova describes it as 'an earthly Paradise'. There is a profusion of flowering trees, shrubs and vines which provide the best wines in Russia. The champagne, she says, is superb. And there are peaches, cherries, almonds, tall cypress trees, trailing roses. The people are mostly Tartars: the men are tall and strong, the women almost invariably pretty, and though Mohammedan by upbringing, they have discarded their veils. The Palace of the Tsar had been a large wooden building, but a new one built of white marble had replaced it—'a gem of Italian Renaissance', Anna calls it, with many small buildings round it which make it almost a town.

But when his train reached Odessa and Rasputin began to make plans for going on to the Imperial Palace at Livadia, he was told by the police that no one was allowed to go to the residence; they were on holiday there and received nobody. Grigori accepted the situation philosophically and made his way to St Petersburg.

The Tsar would have been glad to see him, for he was especially anxious that Grigori should go to Nijni-Novgorod and see the Governor Alexei Hvostov. Stolypin had held two offices in the Tsar's Cabinet: Kokovtsev was appointed to succeed him as Prime Minister, and the Tsar wondered if Alexei Hvostov would be a suitable successor as Minister of the Interior. Anna followed Grigori to St Petersburg and told him that the Tsar wanted him to say whether Hvostov would be worthy of that high office.

Nijni-Novgorod, a large busy town about 250 miles east of Moscow, bristled with *ambars* (covered markets) and Tartars. When Grigori arrived at the Governor's residence, Hvostov had no idea who he was; even the name Rasputin conveyed nothing to him. The Governor refused to see him, but Grigori, having a duty to fulfil for the Tsar, forced his way in. Hvostov was furious on finding the untidy, travel-stained peasant tramping with large dusty boots in his elegant drawing-room. Angrily he ordered Rasputin to leave, and finally rang for his man-servant to remove the intruder. As he turned to go, Grigori told Hvostov: 'The Tsar will receive an unfavourable report.'

Hvostov thought that he was merely boasting. How could an ill-bred, uncouth peasant, unaware of how to behave in the presence of his superiors, come in any contact with the Emperor? But the more he thought of it, the more uneasy he became. If the intruder was acting under the Tsar's orders, it was possible that his report would be sent by telegram. Hvostov phoned the telegraph office and asked if a rough peasant had been there to send a telegram. He was told he had. Whom was it addressed to, he inquired.

'To Tsarskoe Selo.'

'You mean to the Emperor?'

'No,' said the telegraphist, 'to Anna Vyroubova.'

'Will you please read it to me?' the Governor said.

'Tell Mama,' the message stated, 'that the grace of God is in Hvostov, but there is still something lacking in him.'

Hvostov was horrified. The Tsar apparently had him in mind for some high office and stupidly he had ruined his chances. He began to pack his things; he had to go to St Petersburg. A word with the Tsar might put everything right.

The Tsar was puzzled: what was the urgency he wondered? Hvostov explained that he had come to discuss the sewage problem in Nijni-Novgorod. The Tsar frowned. 'It's not urgent or even important business,' he said, then rose from his chair and said good-bye to the Governor. Hvostov did not get the job. The new Prime Minister, Kokovtsev, who wanted his own candidate Makarov to be Minister of the Interior, told the Tsar that 'no one respected Hvostov'.

Shortly after Grigori's arrival in St Petersburg from Nijni-Novgorod, he found that the bishops had worked themselves into a frenzy and were bent on getting the Holy Synod to denounce him. Illiodor, who had been reluctant to abandon his close friendship with Rasputin, had decided by now to give Hermogen and Theophan his full support. He had evidence, he said, of the utmost value: a nun named Xenia, he said, had in the course of her confession stated that Rasputin had raped her. Nothing better could have been hoped for. Whether the nun was brought in to give evidence to the Holy Synod or to the two bishops was not stated: it is possible that they were entirely satisfied with Illiodor's unsupported statement.

But Grigori already knew that Illiodor had tried to rape Madame

Olga Vladimirovna Lokhtina, the young, attractive and frivolous wife of General Lokhtin, who was a State Councillor. She had known Grigori for some years, and it was his influence that had made her turn to religion. She used to go into retreat at the monastery at Tsaritsyn, and on one of these occasions had Illiodor as her confessor. His cell was at the far end of the monastery, and he took advantage of it. Father Grigori's daughter Maria states:

He threw himself upon her and attempted to do violence to her. The poor woman, terrified, cried aloud for help. The monks came running to answer her screams, but Illiodor, feeling the danger he was in, reversed the roles and declared that the young woman, having for a long time pursued him with her attentions, had thrown herself upon him. The monks, scandalized, decided to exorcise the devil of the flesh that possessed the unfortunate woman and found no better means of doing it than a method that belonged to the Middle Ages. They tied the poor woman, with her hands bound, to the tail of a horse. The animal, urged on by whip and voice, went off at a gallop, dragging her almost naked body over the stone flags of the courtyard. When some peasants, taking pity on her, released her, the poor creature had lost her reason. Her family cared for her tenderly, keeping her in quietness and solitude in order to calm her crises of madness. Later she more or less recovered her faculties, but her husband and her parents denounced the abominable conduct of Illiodor and made a complaint to the Holy Synod.

She turned to Grigori Rasputin for solace and used to go down on her knees whenever she saw him and proclaim that he was her Saviour. Maria says her father refused to take any part in this. He had no wish to give evidence against a man who had been his friend.

Receiving an invitation to lunch from Bishop Hermogen, Grigori no doubt felt that it was to thank him for being so considerate, as an exposure of Illiodor would have reflected most seriously on the Orthodox clergy and on the Holy Synod. But, to his surprise, Grigori found a number of other guests there, including Mitia Koliaba, the cripple with stumps for arms whose unintelligible ravings were interpreted by his companion Egorov as inspired prophecies. Militsa had introduced him to the Tsaritsa, who continued to see him until Grigori came into her life. Ever since then Koliaba, and especially his so-called interpreter,

Egorov, had loathed Rasputin. Among the others invited were Illiodor, his brother and a journalist.

Hermogen begged Grigori to ask the Tsar not to punish Illiodor. But he refused to intervene: with his habitual frankness, his daughter says, he told Hermogen 'what he thought of Illiodor and of the Union of True Russians and of the base political intrigue that certain of its members indulged in in order to satisfy their ambitions and their personal grudges'.

This so incensed the others that they all fell upon Grigori. The Bishop seized a heavy crucifix, Illiodor drew an axe which he had hidden under the table, his brother brought out a fencing foil from behind a chest; while Koliaba rolled about the floor screaming, his guardian assaulted Grigori with his fists and the others charged with their weapons. Grigori, unarmed but blessed with prodigious strength, defended himself vigorously; but they drove him with numerous bruises and scratches inch by inch against the closed door. Providentially there was just then a knock on the door. His four assailants took fright, and the battle ended.

CHAPTER EIGHTEEN

Illiodor Steals the Tsaritsa's Letters

Details of the extraordinary luncheon party which ended in a united assault on Grigori soon became known. Various versions, each contradicting the others, were circulated. The Tsar thereupon sent for Rasputin and asked him to state what had really happened. Grigori described it in vivid detail. Furious that a well-known bishop and a monk should have been parties to a crude, unseemly, vulgar brawl, the Tsar asked the Holy Synod to consider carefully the behaviour of these two churchmen and decide what should be done.

Both Hermogen and Illiodor were found guilty by the Holy Synod —Bishop Hermogen was banished to the remote monastery at Girovitz and Illiodor to Florishcheva Pustyn. The bishop meekly accepted the sentence. But Illiodor, avoiding arrest, set out on a tour of Russia, popping up in unexpected places to denounce Grigori Rasputin in wild, fiery speeches and adding that the Tsaritsa was his mistress. While at Pokrovskoe he had stolen from a locked drawer the letters the Tsaritsa and her daughters had written to Grigori. He had them all copied and began now to circulate them to the Press and the public. Here is one of the letters from the Tsaritsa:

My beloved, unforgettable teacher, redeemer and mentor! How tiresome it is without you. My soul is quiet and I relax only when you, my teacher, are sitting beside me. I kiss your hands and lean my head on your blessed shoulders. Oh how light, how light do I feel then! I only wish one thing: to fall asleep, to fall asleep, for ever on your shoulders and in your arms. What happiness to feel your presence near me. Where are you? Where have you gone? Oh, I am so sad and my heart is longing. . . . Will you soon be again close to me? Come quickly, I am waiting for you and I am tormenting myself for you. I am asking for your blessing and I am kissing your blessed hands. I love you for ever—Yours M.*

The Tsaritsa was deeply embarrassed. The Tsar was furious: he instructed Makarov, the Minister of the Interior, to get back the originals

---

* For *Matushka*, meaning 'Little Mother', which was what Grigori always called her.

of all the letters. He succeeded in doing so. Illiodor was arrested, unfrocked and imprisoned in the monastery at Florishcheva, but after dressing up as a woman, he managed to escape through Finland to Norway. There he began to write his memoirs, full of invention and scurrility, and offered to sell the manuscript to the Tsaritsa if she was prepared to pay him 60,000 roubles. She did not even bother to acknowledge the letter. Two years later, after the outbreak of war, he sold the section of the book referring to Rasputin to an American magazine and included the Tsaritsa's letters. Illiodor acknowledged later that he had not adhered strictly to the facts, but had elaborated them for effect; Bernard Pares and others believe that the Tsaritsa's letters had also been doctored: the Tsaritsa, in fact, wrote gushing letters of this kind to all her friends.

A great many people expressed their disgust at Illiodor's attacks on the Empress and his dragging her young, innocent daughters' letters into it too; but others who hated Rasputin—a large and growing number among the nobility and the Church—relished the vile accusations and the sexual revelations. Most of the clergy, however, did not exult, for the great majority in the Holy Synod supported Grigori Rasputin: on the death of the Bishop Anthony of Tobolsk, who had found Grigori not guilty of being a member of the *Khlysty* sect or of indulging in sex orgies, the Holy Synod had appointed as his successor, despite the furious attack made by Bishop Hermogen on their choice, Grigori's nominee Varnava, a deeply religious man who had earned his living as a gardener.

Rasputin's enemies were resolved to keep up the attack; there was to be no let-up. A lecturer named Novoselov, attached to the Academy of the Trinity and St Sergiev Monastery at Zagorsk, near Moscow, where Rasputin had stayed and worshipped, had made a study of the illegal religious sects and now published a pamphlet which sought to prove that Rasputin was a member of the *Khlysty* sect. His descriptions of the *Khlysty* orgies may have been wholly accurate, but his book does not establish that Rasputin belonged to this or to any other sect: repeatedly Rasputin had denied it. Indeed, it would have been difficult to get the faithful to assemble by night in his chapel in the courtyard in Pokrovskoe and then to set out in a large group, carrying lighted tapers, and, by singing hymns and dancing, work themselves into an eroto-religious frenzy, the leader flogging those who did not keep up the pace. Eventually the tapers were put out and in the darkness the men and women coupled freely, often incestuously: Rasputin was accused on one occasion of having, while engaged in these rites, incestuous intercourse with his sisters; but he had only had one sister, the epileptic who died before the chapel was built. In any case, it would have been impossible to hide such practices from the villagers.

Following the publication of Novoselov's accusation, the Holy Synod was asked to deal with Rasputin. Some months earlier Lukianov, the Procurator of the Synod, who had prepared for Stolypin a report against Rasputin, many details in which were suspect, was dismissed. Similarly Novoselov's pamphlet was also suppressed, whereupon Guchkov published a condensed version of the pamphlet in his newspaper *Golos Moskvy*, which was read eagerly and passed round. Other newspapers, not to be outdone, took an even stronger line and denounced Rasputin as a 'fornicator of human souls and bodies'. Irritated by all this, the Tsar issued an order forbidding any newspaper to publish anything about Rasputin.

Kokovtsev, Stolypin's successor, a small dapper man, capable, but without Stolypin's shrewdness or skill, decided to have a personal talk with the Tsar about Rasputin. The Tsar granted him an audience in February 1912, but, after listening to what he had to say, told him to go and see Rasputin himself. Like Stolypin, Kokovtsev says an attempt was made to hypnotize him, but he remained firm and ordered Grigori, just as Stolypin had done, to leave the capital and never show his face there again. On hearing this echo out of the past, Grigori looked at him without a flicker of reaction. To encourage him to go Kokovtsev offered him 200,000 roubles—'a fortune beyond the dream of avarice to a Russian peasant', says Anna Vyroubova, 'but Rasputin declined it, saying that he was not to be bought by anybody. "If Their Majesties wish me to leave St Petersburg, I will go at once and for no money at all." '

Then, to Kokovtsev's surprise, Grigori told him that the food supply was quite critical. It was not being moved quickly enough from the farms to the cities. 'You had better give your attention to the railways too.' Sir Bernard Pares described these remarks as both apt and extremely important.

Guchkov's successor as President of the Duma, Michael Rodzianko, an enormous man, about twenty stone in weight and with a bellowing voice, decided, after listening to Kokovtsev's comment on his interview with Rasputin, to go and see the Tsar himself. He was granted an audience on 10 March, barely two weeks after Kokovtsev's visit to the Palace. With courage, frankness and tact, he told the Tsar that he wanted to speak about Rasputin 'and the inadmissible fact of his presence at Your Majesty's Court. I beseech you as Your Majesty's most loyal subject, will it be your pleasure to hear me to the end? If not, say but one word and I will remain silent.' With his head averted the Tsar said: 'Speak!' Rodzianko then released the usual avalanche of accusations about rape and sex orgies which the Tsar had already heard. 'Have you read Stolypin's report?' the Tsar asked. 'No, I have heard it spoken of, but I have not read it.' The Tsar then said bluntly: 'I rejected it.'

Nevertheless Rodzianko was asked to draw up his own report. He went to see a member of the Holy Synod named Damansky, who was most reluctant to help. After being told by Rodzianko that he knew about Stolypin's report, Damansky brought out the papers that Luckianov, the former Procurator of the Synod, had collected for Stolypin. The papers were passed on by Rodzianko to officials of the Duma for examination and report. But the next day Damansky came and asked Rodzianko for their return and explained that the demand for their return had been made by a very exalted person. 'Who was it? Sabler?' inquired Rodzianko, referring to the new procurator. 'No, someone much more highly placed.' Pressed further, Damansky revealed that the demand for their return was made by the Empress.

'If that is the case,' said Rodzianko, 'will you kindly inform Her Majesty that she is as much a subject of her august consort as I myself, and that it is the duty of us both to obey his command. I am not in a position to comply with her wishes.'

When the report was completed Rodzianko asked the Tsar for another interview. It was refused. He was told to send the report. It was never referred to again.

'God Has Seen Your Tears'

Shortly afterwards Grigori Rasputin left for Pokrovskoe. He liked spending the summer there. Forty years old now, his vigour, his intense interest in life and in people, his eagerness to help others, trying to heal those who were ailing, to dance and sing and laugh with sudden unexpected spontaneity, drew the villagers to him.

His son Mitia, light-blue-eyed like his mother, was in his twentieth year and had recently married a buxom, attractive young woman of the same age, fair-haired and very hard-working on the farm and in the house. Grigori's father Efim Andreievich had died in the preceding year a few months before Anna Vyroubova's visit. In his sixties, he had been drinking heavily and was often quarrelsome, but they missed him and often talked of him, his religious dedication, his untiring work on the farm, his amusing memory of his brief stay in St Petersburg. Grigori's elder daughter Maria, now aged sixteen, was living in St Petersburg with the Sazonoff family and attending school as a day pupil. The younger girl, Varvara, not quite thirteen, was at Pokrovskoe: Grigori was taking her with him to the capital so that she too could go to school there. He had been staying with the Sazonoffs, a few months at a time, for nearly nine years. It would be too crowded with the two girls there and the numerous callers who came every day to see him. Before leaving St Petersburg, he had begun to look for an apartment and found one with five rooms at 64 Gorokhovaya. They would need a servant, and he decided to take Katya back with him: she had been with the family for many years and knew exactly how things should be run.

Grigori was in Pokrovskoe when the centenary of Napoleon's fiercely fought Battle of Borodino and his retreat from Moscow was celebrated with pomp and pride. Rodzianko attended the Borodino celebrations and noted: 'The Emperor, who passed quite close to me on the field of Borodino, looked askance at me and did not acknowledge my salutation: I understood that the cause of his dissatisfaction with me was my report on Rasputin.' The Tsar having ignored the report, Guchkov, leader of the Octobrists, the biggest party in the Duma, decided to have an open debate on Rasputin in the Duma. Rodzianko did his best to prevent it. The debate was avoided, but Guchkov, who had published Novoselov's attack on Rasputin, made a wild, unbalanced condemnation of Rasputin in the Duma.

'We all know,' he said, 'what a dark drama is being enacted in Russia. With pangs in our hearts and horror in our minds, we anticipate all its stages; and in the middle act stands an enigmatical tragi-comical figure —a sort of ghost from another world or a survivor from the gloom of centuries, a weird shape in the light of the twentieth century. He is not alone. Is there not standing behind his back a whole crowd, a motley company worshipping both him and his sorcery? Unnoticed individuals greedy for distinction, bewailing the power that is slipping out of their hands, obscure trades people, shipwrecked pressmen, contractors. . . . It is they who prompt him. Confronted by this phenomenon, it is our duty to shout words of warning: "The Church is in danger, and the State too is in danger." '

The Third Duma, having run its full course, was dissolved at the end of June 1912 and the Fourth Duma was elected on an even more restricted franchise to reduce, or if possible eliminate, the election of candidates of independent and undesirable views. Despite this, some deputies with left-wing leanings did slip through: one of them was Alexander Kerensky, a young, slender, keenly intelligent lawyer and an ardent reformer. The Fourth Duma not only stayed the entire course, but continued after the Revolution broke out when Kerensky was elected to be head of the Provisional Government.

The Tsar received the new deputies, and was surprised to see one of them, Ivan Hvostov, brother of Alexei Hvostov, wearing a large, unfamiliar badge. The Emperor asked: 'What is this badge?' Hvostov replied: 'It is a sign of membership of the Union of the True Russians' —the same patriotic but extremely reactionary society of which Rasputin had been made a member by Bishops Hermogen and Theophan but which, disagreeing with their political prejudices, he had left. The Tsar apparently had not even heard of it.

Grigori was still in Pokrovskoe in the autumn of 1912 when the Tsarevich had his most critical illness of haemophilia. The Imperial family had gone to Poland, as the Tsar wanted to shoot aurochs, the European bison. Alexei, not allowed to go riding with his sisters, did some rowing on a lake. It was while jumping into the boat that he fell and injured his left thigh against an oarlock: the swelling and other symptoms that ensued were alarming, and the boy, now aged eight, was in great pain for some days. Then, as he seemed to get better, the family went to Spala, an ancient, isolated hunting-lodge of the Kings of Poland. The residence was just a small wooden villa, so dark that lights had to be used even on the brightest day. The Tsar enjoyed the hunting with the Polish nobles, who, on returning with their kill, joined the Imperial family for dinner.

A telegram was sent to Anna Vyroubova, and she hurried to Spala from her small house in Tsarskoe Selo.

By this time [says Anna] Alexei's illness was believed to have taken a favourable turn and he was beginning to walk a little about the house and gardens. Occasionally he complained of pain, but the doctors were unable to discover any actual injury. One day the Empress took the child for a drive and before we had gone very far we saw that indeed he was very ill. He cried out with pain in his back and stomach, and the Empress, terribly frightened, gave the order to return to the palace. The return drive stands out in my mind as an experience of horror. Every movement of the carriage, every rough place in the road, caused the child the most excruciating torture, and by the time we reached home he was almost unconscious with pain.

The next weeks were endless torment to the boy and to all of us who had to listen to his constant cries of pain. For fully eleven days these dreadful sounds filled the corridors outside his room. . . . During the entire time the Empress never undressed, never went to bed, rarely even lay down for an hour's rest. Hour after hour she sat beside the bed where the half-conscious child lay huddled on one side, his left leg drawn up so sharply that for nearly a year afterwards he could not straighten it out. His face was absolutely bloodless, drawn and seamed with suffering while his almost expressionless eyes rolled back in his head. Once when the Emperor came into the room, seeing his boy in agony and hearing his faint screams of pain, the poor father's courage completely gave way and he rushed, weeping bitterly, to his study. Both parents believed the child was dying, and Alexei himself, in one of his rare moments of consciousness, said to his mother: 'When I am dead build me a little monument of stones in the wood.' There was no church at Spala and during the illness of the Tsarevich a chapel was installed in a large green tent in the garden.

I

Meanwhile, having arranged long before the crisis to receive Polish nobles who wished to pay tribute to the Tsar, Nikolai could not avoid a certain amount of entertaining, though both he and the Empress were in a state of acute anxiety.

Life continued as before [says Pierre Gilliard, the Swiss tutor], one shooting party succeeded another, and the guests were more numerous than ever. One evening after dinner the Grand Duchesses Marie and Anastasia (the two youngest daughters) gave two short scenes from Molière's *Bourgeois Gentilhomme* in the dining-room for their Majesties and the guests. The Tsaritsa sat in the front row smiling and talking gaily to her neighbours. When the play was over . . . I suddenly noticed the Tsaritsa running up stairs, holding her long and awkward train in her two hands.

Eventually the three doctors attending to the child pronounced, after careful analysis and consultations, that his condition was hopeless. The haemorrhage in the stomach was liable to bring on an abscess and could be fatal. From the child's bedside the Tsaritsa sent a note to the Tsar to say she feared the worst was about to happen. It didn't, but the suffering of the child and the agony of the parents dragged on.

The Tsar had always refused to reveal to the public what was really the matter with the Tsarevich. In consequence the most fantastic things were being said about the child—he had been seriously injured by an anarchist's bomb, he was mentally retarded, an epileptic. . . . Now that it was clear the Tsarevich was unlikely to live, his critical condition was revealed to the public in bulletins, but the actual illness of the child was not mentioned. Prayers were said in all the churches throughout Russia: many crowded into the Cathedral of Our Lady of Kazan in St Petersburg and prayed before the hallowed ikon night and day.

The Tsaritsa's sister, Irene, wife of Prince Henry of Prussia, who had taken over the vigil by the child's bedside, rushed to the small boudoir where the Empress was resting, to tell her that nothing more could be done.

Still the Empress declared [states Anna Vyroubova] that she could not believe that God had abandoned them, and she asked me to telegraph Rasputin in his home in Siberia, to pray for the child. His reply came quickly. 'God has seen your tears and heard your prayers. Do not grieve. The little one will not die. Do not allow the doctors to bother him too much.' The Tsaritsa was tremendously relieved. 'I am not anxious now,' she said. A day later, the haemorrhage stopped, the pain subsided, the boy lay wasted and utterly spent, but it was obvious now that he was going to live.

What had brought Alexei back from the brink of death? Was it just chance? Was it a miracle that Rasputin was able to accomplish by prayer? Or was it a prophetic vision that prompted Rasputin to phrase his telegram in those reassuring words: 'God has seen your tears and heard your prayers. . . . The little one will not die.' The doctors were unable to offer any explanation. One of them, Dr Federov, told the Tsar's sister, the Grand Duchess Olga Alexandrovna: 'The recovery is wholly inexplicable from a medical point of view.' Whatever the cause of the heir's astonishing recovery after all hope had been abandoned, to the Tsaritsa it was once again Rasputin who had saved the child's life, it was Rasputin's prayers that God had answered.

The Imperial family firmly believed [says Anna Vyroubova] that they owed much of Alexei's improving health to the prayers of Rasputin. Alexei himself believed it. Several years earlier Rasputin had assured the Empress that when the boy was twelve years old [that is in the summer of 1916] he would begin to improve and that by the time he was a man he would be entirely well. The undeniable fact is that after the age of twelve Alexei did begin very materially to improve. His illnesses were farther and farther apart and before 1917 his appearance had changed marvellously for the better.

His New Apartment

Grigori returned to St Petersburg in November 1912. He had been away for the greater part of the year. The relentless attacks on him by a handful of members of the Church and a few politicians may have caused him to stay away. But neither the Tsar nor the Tsaritsa accepted any of the allegations. Why should he not be affectionate and loving towards others, the Tsaritsa said. 'Read the Apostles: they kissed everybody as a form of greeting.' To avoid further attacks on the Imperial family, the Tsar thought it better for the time being not to invite Grigori to the Palace, which may be why he stayed in Pokrovskoe for so long.

Many people seemed to believe, says Anna Vyroubova, that Rasputin was living in the Palace with the Tsar and Tsaritsa. Her own tiny house, practically a bungalow with a second storey built over a small central section, was only a few hundred yards from the Palace and she was able to assert emphatically: 'He never lived in the Palace, seldom visited it, saw the Emperor less frequently than the Empress, and had among the women of the Court more enemies than friends.' On his return to the capital at the end of 1912, following the false gossip and scandal, he was asked to use a side-entrance to the Palace instead of the main doorway.

> He went upstairs by a small staircase [says Anna], he was received in the private apartments and never in the public drawing-rooms. . . . More than once I pointed out to the Empress the futility of the course pursued. 'You know that before he even reaches the Palace, much less your boudoir, he has been observed and noted down by the police at least forty times?' The Empress always agreed. She knew the police were everywhere, inside and outside the Palace. She knew there could be no secrets in the Palace and the Emperor knew it as well as she did, yet they persisted in trying to shield Rasputin from the publicity they knew to be inevitable for everyone.

Referring to the new five-roomed apartment in 64 Gorokhovaya that Rasputin had moved into on his return, Anna describes it as 'rather humble lodgings in an unfashionable street': the street was narrow, badly paved and shut in by gloomy houses, occupied mostly by artisans. His daughter Maria supplies details of the apartment.

One entered a courtyard and went through an archway which led to a stairway. The apartment was on the third floor. One came first to a scantily furnished antechamber, on the right of which was the dining-room, followed by my father's room and a bathroom, which was used only by my sister and myself, my father preferring to go to the Turkish baths; and finally there was the room that I shared with my sister Varvara, who was still a child. There was another big room, furnished with chairs round the walls for the visitors who waited there to see my father. My father never had fixed 'reception' days. People came and went away or waited if Rasputin was not there, or else they telephoned beforehand to announce their visit. It was my father himself, or perhaps Katya, who opened the door. From early morning the samovar steamed on the dining-room table, and a cup of tea and a portion of the very simple food that we ourselves had, was offered to any visitor whether known to us or a stranger. My father sat among the people gathered there and talked to them, answered their questions, and sometimes let himself be drawn into giving impromptu lectures on religious matters—completely forgetting the time.

On the whole, there was very little difference between these meetings at St Petersburg and the old gatherings at Pokrovskoe. The audience was never the same; instead of being limited to a circle of peasants, faces changed; certain faithful ones attended regularly, but the majority came from the four corners of Russia to beg my father to heal them, to obtain a favour, or a conversion; an astonishing mixture of all classes of society, from the humblest to the most powerful. I must say that all my father's sympathy was given to the poor and humble. He received with the greatest demonstrations of joy the gifts that these humble ones brought him from their villages—cakes, fruit, chickens, ducks. It would seem that nothing could give him greater pleasure, and he always found a means of making the donors accept whatever fell to his hand: packets of bank-notes, ikons, or other presents that he himself had received. On the other hand, he accepted the sumptuous gifts of the rich almost with condescension, even with roughness. He never asked for money in return for his time. He has been reproached with demanding payment. . . . This is absolutely untrue. He had no idea of the value of money; important sums must have passed through his hands, but he distributed them in the most generous and fanciful manner.

No sooner had Grigori returned to the capital than a messenger arrived with an invitation to Tsarskoe Selo from the Tsar and Tsaritsa: it was their first opportunity to thank him personally for the prayers that had saved the life of the heir to the throne.

For the first time Grigori used the side-entrance to the Palace instead of the main doorway. The police let him in, guards at every doorway saw him go through, there was in fact no secrecy: he may not have been seen coming in by the Press and by photographers, but guards and police were also capable of talking.

It was a warm-hearted welcome. Alexei had not fully recovered and was still in bed. Grigori went to his bedside with the Tsar and Tsaritsa, talked to the child and made him laugh quite heartily. After leaving the nursery he had tea with their Majesties.

The Tsar had been facing another Balkan crisis. Bulgaria, Serbia, Montenegro and Greece had launched a war against Turkey. It was obvious that these small countries had little chance of winning, but they were in fact victorious and Turkey agreed to an armistice. But what concerned Russia was Austria's resolve not to allow Serbia, which had played her part in the victory, to obtain from Turkey a stretch of coastline on the Adriatic. Grigori had read about it in the newspapers. There was an outburst of indignation in Russia; even members of the Duma, led by the President Rodzianko, talked of going to war.

Once again Rasputin warned the Tsar, as he had done four years earlier, not to go to war. Sir Bernard Pares, who had first-hand knowledge of events in Russia at the time, records in his book *The Fall of the Russian Monarchy* that the Minister of Foreign Affairs 'Sazanov had great difficulty in keeping the country out of war. In this he had the firm support of his Sovereign; but it is also interesting to note that one of the chief contributing factors was the direct influence of Rasputin. . . . A reactionary paper, without naming him, even gave him publicly the credit for the preservation of the peace.'

Eighteen months later the same crisis involving Austria and Serbia arose for the third time. Rasputin was not in St Petersburg to warn the Tsar. The First World War might have been avoided if he had been.

Even while he was staying in only two rooms with the Sazonoffs and later having an additional small room for his daughter Maria, people kept coming all day long to see him and at times even late at night. Things were, of course, much easier in his new apartment. The concièrge had a lodge off the courtyard at the foot of the staircase, and he generally knew if the *staretz* was in or out. But even when they were told that Father Grigori was not in, visitors stood on the stairway one behind the other. Most of them were women, some of them old, wrinkled and frail; others were married women in their forties and fifties, some quite attractive. There were also a dozen or more men— members of the clergy and some officials: they did not, however, include Badmayev or Manuilov or Simanovich, who always telephoned beforehand. Of these Simanovich, who called himself Rasputin's secretary, visited him quite frequently. In his *Rasputin—the Almighty Peasant*, not all of it accurate, he states:

> In looks Rasputin was a real peasant, strong and stocky. His table manners were appalling and very rarely did he use knife and fork. One of the dishes most popular in his household was soup served with rusks. Rasputin dipped the rusks into the soup and passed them round to the others at the table. He never touched meat, cakes or sweets. His diet consisted mainly of fruit, potatoes and caviar, and he drank considerable quantities of wine. Most of his provisions were supplied by his numerous followers, particularly the ladies.
>
> After he had cured my son Joann of St Vitus's dance, I asked him if he would cure me too. I drank and gambled heavily and often I was away from home for three or more days engaged in these pursuits. One day Rasputin invited me to come and see him. When I arrived he decanted two different kinds of wine and then proceeded to mix them, pouring the wine into two glasses and then from one to the other and then back again. He then handed me his glass and we both drank. When we had drained our glasses he stared at me for some time: it gave me a most uncomfortable feeling. I never drank or gambled again for as long as he lived. Unfortunately I reverted to my old habits after his death. He cured the Tsar's drinking habits in the same way.

Badmayev used to come and see him often in his new quarters. Grigori's daughter Maria says he always needed her father's help to cure nervous diseases. The residents in the other apartments kept peeping to see who the visitors were. They saw a priest arrive with some fish for Father Grigori; and the wife of a doctor bringing a carpet for him; and some would come with bottles of wine. Many of the visitors were badly dressed, wearing threadbare workaday clothes.

Waking at six o'clock in the morning, Grigori would go to Mass at Afonskoe Podvorie and usually returned with a number of people whom he met there. Together they climbed up the stairs to his dining-room, where Katya, who had got breakfast ready, brought in tea and wholemeal rusks. Generally his daughters Maria and Varvara joined them. At eight o'clock the callers began to arrive. Maria says that at times they were so numerous that many waited in their carriages in the street, while the poorer men and women stood in queues.

One of the hardest tasks the Empress imposed on me [states Anna Vyroubova] was taking messages, usually about the health of Alexei, to these crowded lodgings of Rasputin. As often as I appeared the people overwhelmed me with demands for money, positions, advancement, pardons. . . . Sometimes I encountered a case of great distress which, if possible, I tried privately to relieve.

Grigori sometimes had his wife and two daughters with him in his apartment. The girls were in school all day; his wife went to the shops and the markets with Katya to buy groceries. Together they dusted and cleaned the apartment, prepared the food, brought the meals in for the visitors and generally one or other of them opened the door, though quite often it was Grigori who let callers in.

During that autumn of 1912 the two girls, who had seen the Tsar and Tsaritsa only from a distance as they drove by in one of a long line of carriages, were sent for by the headmistress during a morning lesson. Nervously they went through the corridors, wondering what rebuke or punishment awaited them. 'Your mother,' they were told, 'has sent for you.' Rushing out they saw their servant in the courtyard. 'Quick,' she said, 'Anna Vyroubova has telephoned to say that the Tsaritsa is visiting her this afternoon with her daughters and wants you to be presented.'

Wildly excited the girls rushed home. Maria put on a frock with a sailor collar and they set out with their mother by train for Tsarskoe

Selo. It was their first visit to Anna's house, though their mother had been there before and had met the Empress two or three times.

When we arrived [says Maria] the Empress was not yet there and Anna Vyroubova, noticing my excitement, asked me with a smile what I was afraid of. Just then the door opened and the Tsaritsa, imposing and dressed in black, entered the room. She was tall and dark, with something at once proud, very gentle and profoundly sad in her eyes. That rather fixed expression in which there was, in spite of her apparent friendliness, a sort of vague fear, uneasiness or shyness, is what has remained in my memory. I remember that this look so troubled me that day as to deprive me completely for several minutes of the use of my tongue.

Meanwhile the young princesses were surrounding me, plying me with a thousand questions which I answered falteringly. Strictly guarded as they were, more or less prisoners at Tsarskoe Selo ... the life of a girl who went to school with other children and once a week to the cinema, and sometimes to the circus, seemed to them the rarest and most enviable of wonders.

The Empress meanwhile conversed with Anna Vyroubova or asked questions of my mother, who answered her timidly in a tone of deep respect. Then came a silence during which she turned and looked at me with that affectionate interest which she always showed even after my father's death to the two daughters of her friend. At that moment I felt I must at all costs say something to her, that my silence must have surprised her, and that she would think me rude. I made a great effort to control myself, and, mustering all my courage, said: 'Is it true, Little Mother, that you have hundreds of servants?' I remembered my conversations with Marie Sazonoff and our talk of the luxury that must reign in the Imperial Palace, and before I could pull myself up, these words had escaped my lips. My question of course caused general laughter, and I blushed deeply at my stupidity; but the Empress answered very sweetly: 'Yes, my child, I have lots of servants, of course, but I could do without them if it was necessary.' And with a friendly hand she patted my cheek.

Once more the princesses clustered around me, and Anastasia questioned me teasingly. We chatted and laughed together in the little adjoining boudoir, sitting primly on the sofa like great ladies at a reception. When Anna Vyroubova came to remind us of the time and the carriage arrived to take the princesses for their drive, I seemed to have known them all my life and had to promise to come and see them again before long.

The princesses were not wholly cut off from normal life. They were allowed, Anna tells us, to have

their little preferences for this or that handsome young officer, with whom they danced, played tennis, walked or rode. These innocent romances were in fact a source of amusement to Their Majesties, who enjoyed teasing the young girls about any dashing young officer who seemed to attract them. The Empress discouraged association with cousins and near relatives, many of whom were unwholesomely precocious in their outlook on life.

| # 300 Years of Romanovs

Early in 1913 the 300th anniversary of the reign of the Romanovs was celebrated. It commemorated the historic moment when the Boyars of Moscow, led by the Patriarch, set out for Kostroma on the Volga, about 200 miles north-east of Moscow, to offer the crown to Mikhail, the young son of the two victims of Boris Godounov—the monk Philaret Romanov and his wife Martha, the nun. For the celebrations the Court moved from Tsarskoe Selo to the Winter Palace in St Petersburg, a residence which neither the Tsar nor the Tsaritsa liked. Despite its magnificence, they found it gloomy and disliked the tiny cramped garden.

The streets of the capital were gay with decorations and bunting and endless gifts were showered on the Tsar; but Prince Paul Vassili, an eyewitness, states: 'The festivities provoked no enthusiasm from the crowds. They were damped by the rain, which fell in torrents during the whole time they lasted. The illuminations in the town were splendid, the ball offered by the nobility of the province of St Petersburg to the sovereigns was like fairyland in its magnificence, but the nation remained indifferent.' An amnesty set free the thieves and common malefactors, 'but the political exiles,' Vassili adds, 'men of culture and the highest civic and private virtue, were left to their sad fate, with only their sorrow and despairing memories'.

The Jubilee thanksgiving service was held in the Cathedral of Our Lady of Kazan. Rodzianko, as President of the Duma, had arranged that a beautiful ancient tapestry, showing the first Tsar of the dynasty, Mikhail Feodorovich Romanov, with golden cupolas of the Moscow Kremlin in the background, should be bought and presented to the Tsar. He went early to the cathedral to make sure that members of the Duma had been given suitable seats. But, he found, they had been placed at the back of the cathedral, and he insisted that, since the first Romanov Tsar had been elected by the people, it was intolerable for officials to decide where the Duma's elected representatives should sit. After an angry and unpleasant argument, he had his way and seats well in front were reserved for Duma members.

Having achieved my object [says Rodzianko], I walked out into the cathedral porch for a rest as there was still plenty of time before the arrival of the members of the Duma. I must add that in order to 'fortify' our newly occupied positions, I surrounded them by a cordon of the available Duma sergeants-at-arms. I had not been in the porch ten minutes when Baron Fersen, the senior sergeant-at-arms, rushed out of the cathedral, looking very excited, and told me that an unknown man in peasant's dress and wearing a pectoral cross had placed himself in front of the space reserved for the Imperial Duma and refused to move. I guessed at once who it was, and hastening to our places found there the individual described by Baron Fersen. Sure enough, it was Rasputin. He was dressed in a magnificent Russian tunic of crimson silk, patent-leather top boots, black cloth full trousers and a peasant's overcoat. Over his dress he wore a pectoral cross on a finely-wrought gold chain. I drew quite close to him and said in an impressive whisper: 'What are you doing here?' He shot an insolent look at me and replied: 'What has that to do with thee?'

'If you address me as thou,' I said, 'I will drag you from the cathedral by the beard. Don't you know I am the President of the Duma?'

Rasputin faced me and seemed to run me over with his eyes. . . . Personally I had never yielded to hypnotic suggestion, of which I had had frequent experience. Yet here I felt myself confronted by an unknown power of tremendous force. I suddenly became possessed of an almost animal force, the blood rushed to my heart and I realized I was working myself into a fury.

Rodzianko said: 'Clear out at once, you vile heretic.'

'I was invited here at the wish of persons more highly placed than you.'

'Clear out at once, this is no place for you,' Rodzianko repeated.

Rasputin knelt and prayed. Rodzianko was about to have him thrown out when Rasputin, still on his knees, said: 'Oh Lord, forgive him such sin!' Then rose and left. 'I followed him to the western doors of the cathedral,' says Rodzianko. 'There a Court Cossack helped him on with his magnificent sable-lined coat and placed him in a car and Rasputin drove away,' unable to stay for the Jubilee celebrations to which he had been invited. Had he been there, he would have seen the brilliant display of embroidered uniforms and ladies dressed in pure white, glittering cuirasses and ikons flashing with diamonds and gems in the dim light of the vast cathedral. The Tsaritsa was robed in white, the blue ribbon of St Andrei across her shoulder, her beautiful face marked with sadness.

To the levee at the Winter Palace the entire Duma was invited. The historic tapestry which was to be presented was unfurled and displayed by the deputy presidents; then Rodzianko delivered his address and presented the Duma's gifts of an ikon and the tapestry.

There were deputations from all parts of Russia to pay homage, the women wearing the impressive and attractive national dress. As part of the celebrations, Glinka's opera *A Life for the Tsar* attracted a vast audience, but, says Anna Vyroubova, 'I felt that there was in the brilliant audience little real enthusiasm, little real loyalty. I saw a cloud over the whole celebration in St Petersburg.'

At Kostroma, the home of the first Romanov Tsar, there was genuine enthusiasm. The people waded knee-deep in the river to get nearer to the Imperial boat.

A Governess Complains

Before these festivities there had been trouble in the Palace at Tsarskoe Selo. For some years Mme Sophie Tyutcheva, the governess of the four young princesses, kept telling the Empress that the children should not be brought up as English girls, but as Slavs. She came of a good aristocratic family in Moscow, and had been a protégée of the Grand Duke Sergei, the Tsar's uncle, who had married the Tsaritsa's sister Elizabeth and been killed by a bomb thrown by an assassin in 1905.

Her relationship with the Imperial family, apart from her persistent criticism of the English form of their upbringing, had been very good: she was trusted and treated with affection. Brought up under the influence of a strict, bigoted priest and her cousin Bishop Vladimir Putiata, who had spent ten years in Rome, she resented the presence of Rasputin in the Palace: it was wrong, she said, for the princesses to catch even a fleeting glimpse of that common, untidy, bearded peasant. She was not prepared to accept that to a *staretz*, a man of God, one renders, as Dostoevsky has said, utter submission and full renunciation; a viewpoint which Leo Tolstoy endorsed specifically by saying that these men had freedoms that others lacked and were able to rebuke the exalted, even the Tsars themselves.

Mme Tyutcheva complained about it to the Tsaritsa, who told her that he came rarely to Tsarskoe Selo. When the heir was gravely ill and the doctors could do nothing, Father Grigori had been sent for and had saved his life again and again, as she knew. She said she didn't know. Sometimes, the Tsaritsa added, he came to spend an hour perhaps with the Tsar and with her, and Alexei came down to say goodnight and stayed to listen to Father Grigori's talk about Siberia and his wanderings. 'Alexei finds him delightfully amusing.'

'But the girls are there too,' said Mme Tyutcheva.

'Sometimes—yes.'

'As their governess I object strongly to their being with him.'

'They are not alone with him. The Emperor and I are always there. I cannot understand why you object. He is a man of God, deeply read in the Scriptures, and has made two pilgrimages to the Holy Land.'

But Mme Tyutcheva's ingrained hostility and contempt for him led to her 'spreading abroad a series of amazing falsehoods', states Anna Vyroubova, 'in which Rasputin figures as a constant visitor. She represented Rasputin as having the freedom of the nurseries and even the bedchambers of the young Grand Duchesses. According to her, Rasputin was in the habit of bathing the children and afterwards sitting on their beds and talking to them.'

When he heard of this the Tsar was furious. He sent for her and said: 'But you do not know him.' She agreed that she did not. 'Then don't you think,' the Tsar said, 'before you speak evil of him you should meet him?'

'Never will I meet him,' she said angrily. As she continued to spread these slanders the Tsar finally dismissed her.

She stirred up a lot of trouble when she returned to her home in Moscow and rallied her relatives to spread slanderous denunciations against the Empress. Next she went to see the Grand Duchess Elizabeth, the Tsaritsa's widowed sister, who had gone into religious retreat since the murder of her husband. Nevertheless, leaving the convent she went to the Empress at Tsarskoe Selo and urged her to get rid of Rasputin. It led to a complete break between her sister and herself.

Another accusation came from the Tsarevich's nurse Vishnyakova, who, on finding herself pregnant, declared that Rasputin had seduced her. The Tsar insisted on a full and thorough inquiry. It was discovered that one of the palace staff had been responsible for her pregnancy. Both were dismissed.

That Rasputin did have affairs with women cannot be denied. His daughter Maria thought he did. With his amazing physical fitness and his extraordinary vigour, it was natural, and indeed inevitable, that his reactions and desires would be normal and human. Again and again he said: 'We have been given human faculties and human attributes. They have been provided to be used; it would be wrong to pretend they do not exist and allow them through neglect to atrophy. That would be to reject God's gifts. How could it be sinful to use them? We sin in many ways—we all do. I have sinned many times and, recognizing it, I have been penitent. But I have wronged no one.'

Women sought his favours: often he rejected them. Sometimes the advances were made by him: if there was resistance, a sudden change would come over him, all lustful desire would drain away, and he would raise his hand and make the sign of the Cross, then kneel and pray for forgiveness. His wife apparently knew about it and was prepared to make allowances. 'He has enough for all,' she said. Despite what has been said so often by so many, there is no evidence either of sex orgies or rape.

Quoting from the Revelation of St John the Divine, Grigori said: 'Remember therefore from whence thou art fallen and repent. Notwithstanding I have a few things against thee, because thou sufferest that woman Jezebel, which calleth herself a prophetess, to teach and to seduce my servants to commit fornication. . . . And I gave her space to repent of her fornication; and she repented not.

'Behold, I will cast her into a bed, and them that commit adultery with her into great tribulation, except they repent of their deeds.'

While the tercentenary celebrations of the Romanov dynasty were in full swing, the unfrocked monk Illiodor was busy planning a revolution. 'It was my intention,' he wrote, 'to start a revolution on 6 October 1913. I planned the assassination that day of sixty lieutenant-governors and forty bishops throughout Russia. I chose a hundred men to carry out this plan.' But the police discovered it in time and Illiodor went into hiding. He embarked next on rounding up all the women and girls Rasputin was said to have raped, intending to castrate Rasputin after getting the facts from them. Apparently not many raped victims could be found, and the plan had to be abandoned. In his refuge, now in Finland, his brain was set to work on another way to injure, or if possible destroy, Rasputin. After much careful planning he chose murder.

While his thoughts were thus engaged, developments unconnected with Illiodor and Rasputin very nearly plunged the country into a crisis which could have led to a revolution.

In the Duma in the course of a debate on the national finances, a member named Markov pointed to the government ministers and shouted, 'You must not steal!' The House was not only horrified, but surprised, for Markov was known to be a reactionary and was regarded as a firm supporter of the government. The ministers walked out and refused to attend further meetings of the Duma.

Many believed that the incident had been deliberately planned and that Markov had been in collusion with the ministers. Ever since the election of the Fourth Duma, there had been a series of reactionary measures leading to widespread signs of public resentment and unrest.

A strike of miners in the Lena goldfields in Siberia was suppressed with horrifying and tragic severity. The miners, who were quite orderly and peaceful, were shot down. There was an uproar in the Duma. The opposition insisted on a full investigation and sent Kerensky, the brilliant young lawyer elected to the Duma a few months earlier, to conduct the inquiry. He had the co-operation of the local governor-general and archbishop. The report revealed that the order to fire had been given by a drunken, half-crazy police officer. Aware that the strikers had been shot down, the government had done nothing and now faced an angry wave of criticism. Labour unrest could no longer be checked or contained. The Lena goldfields incident has often been pointed to as the starting-point of the Revolution.

The Markov episode in the Duma could have brought the Revolution forward three or four years had the Tsar acted on the advice of his Minister of the Interior, Nikolai Maklakov. They had met some years earlier at Chernigov, near Kiev, where Maklakov was Governor. An ikon to which they were both attached drew them together and led to the Governor visiting the Tsar and his family: he used to play with the Tsar's children, jumping at them like an 'amorous panther'. Maklakov was ultra-Conservative and was wholeheartedly in support of the Tsar's autocracy, which doubtless helped to establish an even closer link between them. For the ordinary right-wing politicians he had nothing but contempt.

After the reactionary Markov had shouted, 'You must not steal,' and the government ministers had walked out of the Duma, Maklakov wrote to the Tsar, telling him that a *coup d'état* was necessary. He would himself as Minister of the Interior make a blunt, angry denunciation in the Duma and follow it up, if necessary, by abolishing all its legislation and dissolving the Duma. The Tsar was 'pleasurably surprised', but most of his ministers were against it. Had the Tsar acted on the advice of Maklakov and deprived the people of such limited powers as he had granted them eight years earlier, the coming of the Revolution could have been accelerated.

Kerensky had already begun to tour Russia, engaged, to use his own words, in 'strenuous political organizing and revolutionary work', which meant sounding the existing discontent and rallying the workers. Soon, Kerensky states, 'the whole of Russia was covered with a network of labour and liberal organizations—the co-operatives, trade unions, labour clubs'. He was at the same time proceeding fast with the

K

creation of a skeleton staff to take immediate advantage of the opportunity when it came.

To counter this Beletsky, Director of the Police Department, enrolled as one of his police-agents a leading Bolshevik named Malinovsky and had him elected to the Duma. There, prompted by the Police Department, Malinovsky made the most fiery, revolutionary speeches, calling on the workers to arm themselves and rise. The group within the Social Democratic party known as the Mensheviks, which means 'minority', in contrast to Bolshevik, which means 'majority', were astonished that no action was taken against Malinovsky by the government. Beletsky's reason for using him was to discover who the leaders of such an armed rising would be. It did not help very much. Lenin, who was in exile from Russia, living for a time in London, then in Switzerland, was furious when told of this. On taking over the government during the Revolution, Lenin summarily executed Malinovsky.

CHAPTER TWENTY-THREE

The Drums of War

Although war with Austria, and inevitably Germany too, had been avoided in the 1908–9 and 1912–13 crises, it was obvious to every discerning Russian that before long yet another threat would confront them. The menaces began even before the Balkan war against Turkey ended in the Spring of 1913. Austria increased her forces on the Russian frontier, bringing the three corps stationed in Galicia to full war strength. Russia immediately stopped the discharge of her own reservists. Germany at the same time, seeing that the Turks had been defeated by the Balkan countries, sent one of her finest army instructors, General Liman von Sanders, to take over the training of an important section of the Turkish army stationed at Constantinople. This was strongly resented by the Russians.

Kokovtsev, the Russian Prime Minister, while passing through Berlin, called on the German Kaiser, Wilhelm II, a cousin of the Tsar who had urged him to make war on Japan, fully aware that even if the Tsar won, the Russian army would for many years be in no condition to take on the armies of Germany and Austria. When Kokovtsev mentioned Russia's concern that the Germans were training Turkish soldiers, the Kaiser reacted with the utmost irritation. 'Are you issuing an ultimatum?' he inquired. Later at lunch the Kaiser said: 'I must tell you frankly that I fear there will be a clash between Slav and German. I feel it my duty to apprise you of this fact.' Feeling that war was inevitable in the very near future, Kokovtsev did not mince words when he saw the Tsar. Nikolai looked dreamily out of the window and said, 'It is the will of God.'

Early in 1914 the Russian Foreign Minister Sazonov called a conference on imperial defence. Russia already had an alliance with France. To rope Britain in too the Tsar saw the British Ambassador Sir George Buchanan. It would be a strong deterrent to war, he said, and added persuasively: 'Then we can sleep safe in our beds.' Sir Edward Grey, the British Foreign Secretary, refused: he felt that the British people would not agree to being drawn into a war between Russia and Germany.

It occurred to the Tsar that a marriage between his eldest daughter

Olga and Edward, Prince of Wales,* would establish a closer link between the two countries, but Edward did not decide to get married
for another twenty-two years. Prince Carol, heir to the Rumanian
throne, was the next choice: it would help to detach Rumania from the
alliance with Germany and Austria. Carol was eager, but Olga was
opposed to it: she would marry a Russian, she said. 'I don't want to
leave Russia.'

The millions of people living in Russia, Germany, Austria and France
had no suspicion that they, and Britain too, would within six months
be sucked into a devastating war that would spread across the world
and take an incalculable toll of human life.

Life in St Petersburg went on normally—gossiping, scandal-
mongering, dancing, drinking, going to the opera to hear Chaliapin
and to see Kschesinskaya dance in her latest ballet, card-playing, horse-
racing, clandestine assignations, fornicating, and also young boys and
girls flushed with happiness and hope as they were brought together by
romance.

Rasputin's daughters were growing up. Maria was already eighteen.
Grigori rejoiced in their numerous diversions: they had many friends,
chiefly school friends, and Marie Sazonoff went with them to the
cinema once a week or to Cinizelli's circus, or to Ostrova Island, known
as the Bois de Boulogne of St Petersburg. He did not object to their seeing boy-friends, but insisted on his meeting the boys and on his
daughters being home by ten o'clock in the evening. 'I will not have
people uttering the filth about you that they do about me,' he
said.

Vara, being some years younger, conformed. Maria, brimful of mis-
chief, occasionally stayed out after ten and used Marie as her alibi. It
was, one gathers, harmlessly innocent. Marie and she indulged at times
with schoolgirl delight in picking out names at random in the telephone
book and asking for the number. 'When a woman's voice replied from
the other end of the wire,' says Maria, 'the joke usually did not last
long. We would give some vague name or other, invent a vague excuse, or even put back the receiver without any further explanation.
But when the voice was a man's the game at once became much more
interesting. Whether it was M. Peterkin, barrister, M. Rochevsky,
rear-admiral, M. Chtcheglovitov, colonel of artillery, or M. Sablin,

---

* Later King Edward VIII, and after his abdication Duke of Windsor.

Procurator of the Synod, we never hesitated to recognize him, greet him warmly, call to his mind the delightful memory of our walks of the previous summer on Ostrova Island, and ask after Vassili or Sergei. And when our interlocutor in baffled astonishment protested, defended himself persuasively or, thinking he recognized our voice, answered in monosyllables because he was not alone, one of us would pass the receiver to the other and the bewilderment or uneasiness of the stranger would redouble until we finally put up the receiver, bursting with laughter, but only after arranging another rendezvous for the following evening, of course, without the least intention of turning up.'

But one day the tables were turned. She happened to be alone in the house when the phone rang and a man's voice asked for Maria Grigorievna. She was startled. He said he recognized her voice and had twice followed her on the Nevsky Prospekt; then added that he was in love with her and would very much like to meet her. She asked for his name, but he refused to give it until they met. She thought the police had got to know of the numerous phone calls to strangers. So she hung up. But a few days later he rang again and asked her once more to meet him, suggesting a visit to the opera or to the circus. But she didn't go. Nevertheless his phone calls went on . . . and they talked.

In June her father, her sister and she set out by train for Pokrovskoe. During the journey a young newspaper reporter, dark, short and amusing, talked to her and revealed that he had been phoning her. But when he added that he was going to Pokrovskoe, she became uneasy: she feared that he would tell her father about their talks on the telephone or invent some cock-and-bull story.

Towards the end of June

a considerable crowd was waiting as usual for the boat to come in, and while my mother, who had come to meet us, was embracing us and the peasant women were asking for my father's blessing, I lost sight of our travelling companion. The following morning we all went to Mass and again my father was greeted by large numbers of peasants. A woman in rags, of repulsive ugliness—her nose was crushed and misshapen—came up with them to my father and stared into his face: I remember that Dimitri called our attention rather loudly to her infirmity and brought down upon himself a rebuke from my father.

Grigori trotted the new-born colts in the courtyard. They talked of the hospital he was going to build in the village, and later on Maria went to show a friend some snapshots she had taken in St Petersburg.

I had not been in my friend's house five minutes when we saw my cousin Niura rush in breathless. 'Quick, quick, Maria,' she said, 'your father's been murdered. He's lying in the house dying.' We could already hear a muffled roar from the street. Men and women armed with cudgels and forks were running towards our house. 'She's killed the *staretz*,' they were shouting. 'Kill her! We'll drown her in the Tura!'

A strange procession came towards us. Some peasants were holding the horrible woman we had seen that morning at the church. Her clothes were hanging about her in rags and she was struggling with all her strength. 'Let me go! Let me go!' she said. 'I've killed the Antichrist!' Behind were children staring wide-eyed, women weeping and shaking their fists. In front of our house I saw in the dusk a large brownish pool of blood, and I all but fainted. In the doorway I saw the reporter who had travelled with us. 'Get away,' I shouted. 'It's you who have brought this on my father.' That was all I could say for my sobs were choking me.

She went in and saw her father stretched out on the bed. The lower part of his shirt was torn. Those who saw what had happened told her that he had just received a telegram and was about to open it when the beggar woman came up and stretched out her hand for alms. While Grigori was getting some money out of his pocket she drew a knife and plunged it into his stomach. He was injured by a deep thrust, his entrails were exposed. Placing his hand on the wound he turned to go into his house and saw the woman making a fresh thrust at him with the knife. He seized a piece of wood with his free hand and struck her sharply on the head, then dragged himself as far as the porch. Hearing him call, the servants rushed out and carried him in to his bed. The nearest doctor M. Vladimirov was at Tyumen, eighty versts away. It took him nearly eight hours to reach the patient.

Grigori, pale and almost lifeless in bed, heard the beggar woman's screams as she was dragged through the street by the villagers and sent a message to tell them to let her go. They handed her over to the police. At her trial it was revealed that her name was Khinya Gusseva and that she had been a prostitute at Tsaritsyn where Illiodor had his monastery; there was little doubt that she had been employed by Illiodor to murder Rasputin. She was found to be insane and was sent to an asylum. The journalist who had been phoning Maria knew of the plot and had come to Pokrovskoe to get an exclusive story of the murder.

The Tsar and Tsaritsa were at that time cruising on the Baltic Sea in their yacht the *Standart*; the telegram Grigori had received was from the Tsaritsa to tell him that Alexei had twisted his ankle while going on board. When they learned of the murderous attack, a telegram arrived every day to inquire how he was.

Grigori was moved to the hospital in Tyumen, where a specialist, sent by the Tsar, performed the operation. For two weeks it was uncertain whether he would live. He had to stay in bed for several weeks. He heard rumours of war, and then that partial mobilization had been ordered. Sitting up in bed he sent the Tsar this letter:

> My friend, I tell you once more: a terrible storm is threatening Russia—a disaster, suffering without end. It is dark. There is not one star left. A sea of tears. And how much blood! What more can I say? I cannot find words. Unbelievable horror!
>
> I know they all demand war from you, even the most loyal: they do not see that they are running towards the abyss. You are the Tsar. Do not let the fools triumph, do not let them hurl us with themselves into destruction. You may perhaps triumph over Germany, but what will become of Russia? When I think of it I realize that never was there a more terrible martyrdom. Russia will drown in her own blood . . . infinite suffering and mourning—Grigori.

Austria, or, to use its full title, Austria–Hungary, consisted of two separate independent states under one monarch, the Emperor Franz Josef I, who had been ruling the country since 1848 and was now eighty-four years old. The population, which numbered forty-six million, consisted not only of Austrians and Hungarians, but included an enormous number of Slavs—in fact more than half the population were Slavs, linked racially with Russia and looking on Russia as their powerful protector. There were also a large number of Poles, acquired in earlier high-handed partitions of Poland, as well as a considerable number of Czechs: most of these subject races struggled ceaselessly to attain their independence.

This vast sprawling country, with Russia to the north and east, Germany to the north and west, and Switzerland, Italy and the Adriatic Sea to the west and south, was referred to rather contemptuously as the 'Ramshackle Empire'. Financially it had been in debt for many years, but had an army of about 350,000 men, including cavalry and artillery. Its only hope of survival was by acquiring more and more territory in the Balkans, where the states, subject for centuries to Turkish rule, were too small and too weak to defy Austria–Hungary, knowing that Germany, whose vital southern flank was protected by Austria, would un-hesitatingly come to its aid. For six years, as we have seen, the Austrians had been busy nibbling at the Balkan states, confident that Germany would not allow Russia to intervene on behalf of the Slavs. Both the earlier endeavours could have led to war, to what might even have been a world war, had Rasputin not told the Tsar that the Balkans were not worth fighting for. Now a third danger presented itself. Doubtless the Austrians would have created one, but the tragic murder of the heir to the Austrian throne, the Archduke Franz Ferdinand, provided the excuse and led to the death of many millions of the human race, bringing immense anguish and far-flung destruction.

The Archduke Franz Ferdinand was not in sympathy with the policy of his uncle Franz Josef. He wanted the Slavs to participate in the government, but the Emperor and his Austrian and Hungarian minis-ters were totally opposed. To show his sympathy for the Slavs, the archduke, who had gone to Bosnia to watch Austrian army man-œuvres, arranged to visit Sarajevo, the Bosnian capital. The crowds, he insisted, should not be kept back by troops, but must be allowed free access to him as he and his wife (he was morganatically married to the Countess Sophie Chotek) drove through. Locally a small police guard was appointed as he went in an open car through gaily decorated streets with crowds waving their hands and cheering.

On the way to the city hall a bomb was hurled at his car. With im-mense presence of mind his chauffeur pressed hard on the accelerator and the bomb struck the car behind, injuring two officers. The Serb who threw the bomb was arrested.

After the reception at the hall the original route of the car was altered. The driver of the first car forgot this. The driver of the Arch-duke's car, about to follow him, recalled that a change had been made and began to turn his car round. At that moment a youth pointed his pistol at the car and fired twice, killing Sophie with the first shot and the Archduke with the second. As he collapsed Franz Ferdinand said: 'Sophie! Sophie! Don't die! Stay alive for the children!' There were three children, all of whom had been disinherited by the Emperor. The assassin was a nineteen-year-old Serbian named Gavrilo Princip. He died in an Austrian prison in 1918 of tuberculosis.

Obviously the murder of the heir to the throne could not be ignored. But few imagined it would lead to war. Even the German Kaiser Wilhelm II, who was, like the Tsar, away on a cruise, did not think it would. But the Austrian Emperor Franz Josef felt that punishment of the assassin was not enough. 'The policy to unite all Southern Slavs under the Serbian flag encourages such crimes and the continuation of this situation is a chronic peril for my house and my territories. Serbia must be eliminated.'

The Tsar's cruise in the *Standart* with his family began on 25 June, three days before the archduke's murder in Sarajevo. Alexei's injury, caused when he boarded the yacht, led to a haemorrhage flowing into his twisted ankle; the joint swelled and became rigid. The heir, now ten years old, wept, and when the pain became unbearable, he screamed. As Rasputin could not leave the hospital in Tyumen, he prayed there for the child's recovery. The news of the archduke's assassination reached them in the yacht, but the cruise went on. Not until 19 July, after cruising for twenty-four days, with Alexei's ankle still swollen, did they leave the *Standart*: they landed at Peterhof, for that was where the French President Raymond Poincaré was coming to see them the next day.

In the meantime the Austrians were busy drafting their ultimatum to Serbia. It was offensively phrased and contained demands which the Austrians hoped the Serbians would reject: all Serbian nationalist societies must be suppressed, insisted the ultimatum, all Serbian officers who were anti-Austrian must be dismissed. Acceptance was required within forty-eight hours: but what the Emperor Franz Josef wanted was not acceptance, but war. The ultimatum was not delivered until after Poincaré had left the Tsar, for Austria was well aware that the Serbs would appeal to Russia and that the Tsar would show the ultimatum to the president because of Russia's alliance with France. Sir Edward Grey, the British Foreign Secretary, said he had never seen one State send to another so formidable a document, and readily agreed to hold a conference of ambassadors in London to try to avert the outbreak of war. Germany brusquely refused to take part in it. Deeply humiliating though the terms were, the Serbs startled the Austrians by accepting them: that was not what the Austrians had expected and not what they were going to accept. Uncertain as to how their cards should be played, Austria waited until 28 July, then rejected the Serbs' acceptance and declared war. Early the next morning Austrian artillery began its attack on Belgrade, the Serbian capital. Only a few hours before the Kaiser had returned from his cruise in the Norwegian fjords.

The Tsar, despite urgent demands for a general mobilization by the Russian general staff, was convinced that the Kaiser would not want war and agreed only to partial mobilization. But reports from Count Pourtalès, the German ambassador in St Petersburg, had already informed Berlin that one and a half million Russian workers were on strike and that he had seen barricades being erected in the capital, telegraph poles being chopped up and tramcars being overturned in the streets. For these reasons, Pourtalès said, Russia would not be able to go to war. In a telegram to the Kaiser the Tsar said: 'The Austro–Serbian problem must be submitted to the Hague Conference. I trust your wisdom and friendship'; he added that in Russia he had ordered only partial mobilization 'for reasons of defence on account of Austrian preparations. I hope with all my heart that these measures won't interfere with your part as mediator which I greatly value.'

On receiving this the Kaiser went into a rage. 'For defence against Austria which is in no way attacking him. I cannot agree to any more mediation.' Sazonov, the Russian Foreign Minister, called on the Tsar and told him that general mobilization could not be delayed any longer: it took some time for Russia to mobilize; men had to travel from remote villages and railway transport was not as good in Russia as in Germany and Austria. With his face pale, his voice barely audible, the Tsar said: 'Think of the responsibility you are advising me to take. Remember, it would mean sending hundreds of thousands of Russian people to their deaths.'

Germany and Austria, said Sazonov, 'are determined to increase their power by enslaving our natural allies in the Balkans, destroying our influence there, and reducing Russia to a pitiful dependence on the arbitrary will of Germany and Austria'.

After a long silence the Tsar said: 'There is nothing left for us to do but to get ready for an attack on us.' Then, after pausing again, he gave the order for a general mobilization.

Pourtalès was instructed by the Kaiser, who had also ordered mobilization, to declare war on Russia on that same day, 1 August, at five o'clock in the afternoon. It was held back by Pourtalès for two hours, then, handing it to Sazonov, he leaned against the window and wept.

At Tsarskoe Selo, while the Tsaritsa and her four daughters were waiting at the table for the Tsar to join them at dinner, the news was brought to the Emperor. He arranged for his ministers to see him at nine o'clock and went in to dine with his family. On hearing that war had been declared, the Tsaritsa began to weep and soon the four girls wept too.

Is Russia Strong Enough?

On the next afternoon, after announcing that the country was at war, the Tsar and Tsaritsa and their family left for the capital. As they arrived at the Winter Palace they saw the vast square in front swarming with people carrying banners and ikons. The river Neva and the canals were choked with boats—steamers and yachts in the river, sailing boats, fishing smacks and dinghies in the canals. As the Tsar, in the simple khaki uniform of an infantry regiment, stepped out of his boat he was greeted with wild cheering by the excited crowds, who had waited in the sweltering sunshine. 'Lead us to victory, *Batiushka*!' they called. 'To victory!'

Even the Tsaritsa, wearing a white dress and with the brim of her hat raised off her face, found herself greeted with immense enthusiasm. Never before had they been so popular. During their visits to Moscow, Kiev, Kazan, Tomsk and other great cities the reception was equally rapturous. A little more than thirty months later the Tsar was forced to abdicate and the entire Imperial family were prisoners, not of the enemy, but of the Russian people.

On 2 August 1914 the barricades put up in the streets of the capital were taken down by the rebellious workers and their red flags were replaced by ikons and large portraits of the Tsar. Inside the Winter Palace the halls, staircases and corridors were lined with people, and as the Tsar walked towards the large white marble Salle de Nikolai, men and women got down on their knees to kiss his hand. In the marble hall where 5,000 people had gathered an altar had been erected with the ikon of the Vladimir Mother of God on it. It was believed to have miraculous powers and is said to have turned back Tamerlaine when he got within 150 miles of Moscow in 1395; and again in 1812 General Kutuzov prayed before that ikon and led the Russian army against Napoleon and forced his withdrawal from Moscow. Nikolai II now sought the ikon's aid and repeated the oath taken by Alexander I in 1812: 'I solemnly swear that I will never make peace so long as a single enemy remains on Russian soil.'

At the same time as the German ultimatum was delivered to Russia, another, also from Germany, was delivered to France. The neutrality of

Belgium, solemnly guaranteed by Germany, as well as by Britain and
other powers, was defiantly ignored by the Kaiser; as his troops marched
in, Britain, honouring her own assurance to this small nation, declared
war. In the four years that followed millions of lives were lost. Rasputin, who had sent a letter to the Tsar when there were rumours of war,
followed it up later with a telegram: 'Let Papa not plan war; for with
war will come the end of Russia and yourselves, and you will lose to the
last man.' The telegram was handed by Anna Vyroubova to the Tsar
who, after reading it, was furious and tore it into little pieces. He had
been drawn into the war. Could he have avoided it? Perhaps if he had
not ordered the full mobilization of his army . . . but it was the partial
mobilization of the Russian army that apparently infuriated the Kaiser.
Rasputin's telegram arrived after full mobilization was ordered, but
before the actual declaration of war. The Kaiser would doubtless have
found some other pretext for declaring war, or just have declared it, as
he did on France.

Just as much against the war as Rasputin was Count Sergei Witte, the
brilliant statesman inherited by Nikolai from his father Alexander III.
For eleven years he had served the Tsar and Russia, first as Minister of
Transport, then of Finance, when he put the economy of the country
on a sound basis; he built up an enormous gold reserve and encouraged
foreign enterprise, which led to many industrialists from abroad setting
up factories in Russia. It had been Witte who brought the disastrous
war with Japan to an end, and he was made the first Prime Minister
when the Duma was formed. Abroad when war broke out in 1914, he
hurried back to Russia to urge the Tsar to withdraw from the war, but
Nikolai was as irritated by his advice as by Rasputin's. 'This war is
madness,' Witte told the French ambassador Paléologue. 'Why should
Russia fight? What can we hope to get from it? An increase of territory?
Mon dieu! Isn't His Majesty's empire big enough already? Haven't we
Siberia, Turkestan, the Caucasus, Russia itself—enormous areas which
have not yet been opened up?'

But it was too late. There was no way of avoiding war now: Russia
had to meet the challenge or surrender. Stock was taken of their ability
to fight. The war with Japan, some felt now, had been in a way a
blessing: many additional military cadres had been formed, the training
of officers had been greatly improved and a twenty-five to thirty-five
per cent rise had been added to their pay. The navy too had been con-
siderably strengthened. In 1911, six years after the war with Japan, the

Tsar told Neklyudov, the new Russian ambassador to Bulgaria: 'It would be out of the question for us to face a war for five or six years—in fact until 1917—although if the most vital interests and the honour of Russia were at stake we might, if it were absolutely necessary, accept a challenge in 1915: but not a moment sooner in any circumstances or under any pretext whatsoever.' It had come, in fact, six months earlier.

Every day the tramp of marching men setting out for the Front could be heard along Nevsky Prospekt and all the way to the railway station, where they were packed into cattle-trucks. On the fringes of the capital long, impressive lines of cavalry and batteries of horse artillery were proceeding to one of the many Fronts Russia had to protect. Behind them were the ammunition wagons, ambulances, field kitchens and remount horses. Dust rose in great clouds behind them.

Russia's greatest asset was the enormous size of her army. There were 1,500,000 men in the standing army: with mobilization, the number reached 4,500,000; and behind them were millions more awaiting call-up. To get them to the Front generally took a long time. The average journey for Russian reserves from their call-up base to the Front was 800 miles: the Germans, much smaller and centrally situated, could get their reserves to any of their Fronts in less than one-fifth of that time. Russia's enormous distances were not the only cause of long delays; there was also the appalling inadequacy of the railways. These were serious disadvantages, and there were many more: a shortage of guns, a severe shortage of ammunition. Russian artillerymen were told, when the shortage became too acute, that they would be courtmartialled if they fired more than three rounds a day: one can imagine the demoralizing effect of the ceaseless attack by enemy shells, which could only be answered by three rounds every twenty-four hours.

The Commander-in-Chief of the army, the very tall, six-foot-six Grand Duke Nikolai Nikolaievich, a cousin of the Tsar, was magnificently impressive and widely admired by the army. Slender, with blue, blazing eyes and a neatly trimmed beard, he exuded tremendous energy: his wife Anastasia was one of the two Montenegrin princesses who had been the dedicated sponsors of Rasputin during his early years in St Petersburg, and the Grand Duke Nikolai Nikolaievich had been as attached to him as they were; but when they saw that Rasputin was not prepared to dabble in table-rapping and spiritualism they had turned away from him: the Grand Duke, who had once brought to St Petersburg Grigori's wife when she was suffering from a tumour, now so hated Rasputin that he threatened to hang him if he came within his reach.

The Minister of War, General Vladimir Sukhomlinov, who had held the office for more than five years, was nearly seventy now—a small man, plump, round-faced and completely bald. He was married to an attractive woman who was half his age, extremely extravagant and insistent that her husband should find the money somehow: it was believed that he got it from the sale of army contracts, some thought it came from the sale of information to the Germans. 'He enjoyed life and disliked work,' says Sazonov, the Foreign Minister. 'It was very difficult to make him work, but to get him to tell the truth was well-nigh impossible.' General Nikolai Golovin, who had served under him, states: 'Sukhomlinov believed that knowledge acquired by him in the seventies of the previous century and largely of no further practical importance, was permanent truth.' He believed in the bayonet not in machine-guns. Surprisingly the Tsar liked him very much, but when after ten months of war he discovered the appalling consequences of his neglect and incompetence, he dismissed Sukhomlinov, had him arrested, charged him with giving information to the traitor Myasoyedov, known to be an enemy agent; with criminally neglecting to supply the army with munitions; and with giving out contracts that benefited him. His sentence was penal servitude for life. General Polivanov, a younger, keenly intelligent man and a hard worker, succeeded him.

The Prime Minister, Kokovtsev, who had held that office since Stolypin's assassination in 1911, was suddenly dismissed in February 1914 and was succeeded by Ivan Goremykin, who had been Prime Minister for a very few months eight years earlier and was now more than eighty years old, senile and quite incapable of carrying out his duties. Nevertheless for two years he was retained in that all-important post.

TWENTY-FIVE

Rasputin Returns to Petrograd

On 31 August 1914 the German suffix 'burg' was removed from the name of the capital, which now became 'Petrograd'. Although the Revolution took place less than three years later, the name was not altered to Leningrad until 1924.

Grigori Efimovich Rasputin, after nearly three months in a hospital bed, came back to the capital late in September. It is said that he advised the Tsar to abolish the sale of vodka for the duration of the war: he pointed out that if vodka was available, the lonely wives of peasants who had been called up or had been killed would console themselves with vodka; it also had to be kept from factory workers if production was to go on. The Tsar agreed. From a financial point of view it was a costly sacrifice, because vodka was a state monopoly and brought the Government an enormous income. The ban was not observed for long: the rich had plenty of wine in their cellars, and in a twelve-month even the poor were able to get it.

Two Russian armies began the attack on Germany, one against East Prussia, the other striking north towards the Baltic. The purpose of these two armies was to squeeze the Germans to pulp with a pincer movement and come within reach of Berlin. Each Russian army was larger than the German force confronting it. The Russians were successful against East Prussia, but the army striking north ran into difficulties, yet managed to advance. It began well and the officers and men talked joyously of being in Berlin. But soon the tide turned and there was a shattering defeat in the Battle of Tannenberg. General Samsonov, seeing his army destroyed, committed suicide. It served, however, one important purpose; by drawing the German troops away from the Western Front the Russians saved Paris from falling into the hands of the enemy.

In Galicia, however, they triumphed gloriously against the Austrians. Four Austro-Hungarian armies were utterly routed, 200,000 men were taken prisoner and the capital Lemberg was captured. It was a notable victory, for Lemberg, the capital of Russian Galicia for centuries, had been annexed by Poland in the fourteenth century and captured by Austria in 1772. The Tsar, overjoyed at getting Lemberg back, discarded the name given it by the Austrians and called it Lvov again. To mark this notable victory the Tsar decided to make a public entry into Lvov. When told of this, Rasputin advised him to abandon the plan. The Tsar was intensely irritated: he had not yet got over Rasputin's letter and telegram from his sick-bed begging him to keep out of the war. He brushed aside the impertinent intervention. Shrugging his shoulders, Rasputin said: 'Before very long the enemy is likely to win it back. That would not be nice after the Emperor's impressive visit.'

The Tsar turned away, angrier than ever. By an odd coincidence Rodzianko, President of the Duma and a sworn enemy of Rasputin's, later made the same comment. He had gone to Lvov on behalf of the Duma and was greatly impressed by its beauty, its greenery and gaiety. 'The clean streets, the lively crowds, Russian soldiers, and even Russian policemen at the street corners—there was nothing to remind one of a conquered city. One might suppose we were at home in the midst of friends, with no trace of hostilities.' To his surprise he saw triumphal arches being erected and flags and bunting going up everywhere and was told that the Emperor was expected. 'Troops were lined up in the streets crowded with people and the hurrahs rolled and swelled as the cortège drew nearer.' After a service in the cathedral, the Tsar gave a large dinner for the local celebrities and those who were in his own entourage. After dinner the Tsar went up to Rodzianko and said: 'Did you ever think we should meet at Lvov?', to which Rodzianko replied: 'No, Your Majesty, I did not; and under the circumstances, Sire, I greatly regret that you have decided to pay a visit to Galicia.'

'Why?' the Tsar asked uneasily.

'Because in three weeks' time Lvov will probably be retaken by the Germans and our army will be forced to abandon the positions it now holds. . . . The soil on which the Russian monarch has once set foot cannot be lightly surrendered: torrents of blood will be shed upon it, but nevertheless we shall not be able to hold it.'

Unhappily the prophecy made by Rasputin and Rodzianko, obviously foreseen as a possibility by the military commanders, was fulfilled. Not long afterwards the Germans helped the Austrians to recapture Lvov and it was known once again as Lemberg.

The Russian army, with its varied picturesque uniforms and enormous mixture of nationalities, fought valiantly under brilliant commanders and achieved some remarkable victories, even Hindenburg

L

and Ludendorff at times had to retreat before the oncoming hordes. But the Russians were gravely handicapped because of their inferior rail transport with vile roads as the only alternative. There was no provision of feeding-points for the troops. More serious than all this was the appalling shortage of munitions and heavy artillery. When Rodzianko discussed this with the Commander-in-Chief, the Grand Duke Nikolai Nikolaievich, he was assured that it was only a temporary hitch and that quantities of ammunition would be forthcoming in a fortnight.

The men serving in the ranks of the Russian army were, unfortunately, treated appallingly. By the military hierarchy they were not regarded as ordinary human beings but as sub-human creatures. They were not allowed to ride in street cars or to enter public restaurants or even to read the newspapers unless special permission was given by their immediate officers. They obeyed orders without thought or question, and flung themselves against the enemy, relying mainly on the bayonet, which could hardly be expected to fend off shell-fire. Nevertheless sometimes amazing advances were made and vast stretches of territory were taken from the enemy. But for the most part they went to their death: one million Russian soldiers, one fourth of the entire Russian army, were killed, wounded or taken prisoner in the first five months of the war.

On the afternoon of 2 January 1915 Anna Vyroubova was travelling by train to visit her parents in Petrograd—a journey of only fifteen miles from Tsarskoe Selo. Suddenly there was a terrifying crash. She was hurled forward, her head hit the roof of the railway carriage and both her legs were caught in the coils of the steam heating apparatus. Almost simultaneously the carriage overturned and Anna felt the bones in her legs snap. Her pain was so intense that she lost consciousness.

When she came to she found herself firmly wedged in the wreckage. A heavy steel bar had fallen on her face and her mouth was full of blood. Someone brought a doctor to her. He looked at her and said: 'She is dying. Do not disturb her.' She was moved on the Tsaritsa's instructions to Princess Gedrioz's hospital at Tsarskoe Selo. Princess Gedrioz, who was the doctor in charge, told the Tsaritsa and the others gathered round Anna's bed to take leave of her. 'She cannot live till the morning.' Some hours later, in a fleeting glimmer of consciousness,

Anna thought she saw Rasputin standing by her bed. She had been saying repeatedly: 'Father Grigori! Father Grigori!' In her subconscious mind that seemed to be her only hope of survival.

Rasputin had not been told of the accident. Some hours after it happened he seemed to see her lying injured in a bed in a hospital. He borrowed a car from a friend and hurried to her bedside.

On arriving he brushed past the Tsar and Tsaritsa, who were standing beside her, made the sign of the Cross over Anna and took her hand in his. 'Annushka, look at me,' he said. She opened her eyes. 'Grigori! Grigori!' she said faintly. 'Thank God!' He held her hand as he said a long, silent prayer, then as he turned to go he said to the Tsar: 'She will live, but she will always be a cripple.' As he went through the door he collapsed and lay as if lifeless on the floor. This is confirmed by Anna Vyroubova and by A. A. Moslov, the Head of the Emperor's Civil Chancery, who says: 'He tottered from the room and fell outside in a faint, from which he awoke in a strong perspiration, feeling that all his strength had gone from him.' Apparently a Herculean effort was required to help Anna. She lived not only through the night, but for many years afterwards, dying in 1964 at the age of eighty, and there is no doubt that her recovery began when Rasputin visited her. The Tsaritsa always referred to it as a miracle and attributed Anna's cure to Rasputin; even the Tsar, despite the hostility he had nursed for months against Rasputin's attempt to advise him to keep out of the war, was deeply impressed by what he saw and said it was only too obvious that Grigori had extraordinary powers.

Although Anna had to rely on crutches, she was able to get about, travelling not only to Petrograd but to the Crimea, to Moscow and other towns, and quite often she climbed the three flights of stairs up to Rasputin's apartment at 64 Gorokhovaya. Anna, who had never looked forward to going there because the stairs were too crowded, found it less easy to climb them with her crutches. Her visits were confined now to taking messages from the Tsaritsa about once a month. A photograph published in the newspapers in Russia, various European countries and America, shows 'ladies of the aristocracy' seated round a table in his lodgings with Rasputin in their midst, suggesting that this was his harem. Anna, who is seen in that photograph, makes this comment:

> Rasputin had no harem at Court. In fact I cannot remotely imagine a woman of education and refinement being attracted to him in a

personal way. I never knew of one being so attracted, and although accusations of secret debauchery with women of the lower classes were made against him by agents of the Okhrana,* the special inquiry instituted by the Commission of the Provisional Government,† failed to produce any evidence in support of the charges. The police were never able to bring forward a single woman of any class whom they could accuse with Rasputin. The photograph is authentic, I figure in it myself and can explain it. It shows a group of women and men who, after attending early Mass, sometimes gathered round Rasputin for religious discourse, for advice on all manner of things, and probably on the part of some for the gratification of idle curiosity.

Many lovelorn women (and men too) used to go to those meetings to beg his prayers on their heart's behalf. He knew that unsatisfied love is a very real trouble and he was always gentle and patient with such people, that is if their souls were innocent. For irregular love affairs he had no patience whatsoever. Once at Kiev a government functionary approached Rasputin and asked for prayers for one lying very ill. Rasputin's amazing eyes gazed into the eyes of the other and he said calmly: 'I advise you to beseech not my prayers but those of St Xenia.' The functionary, completely taken aback, exclaimed: 'How could you know that her name was Xenia?'

The people who came to his lodgings included, she adds, petty officials, beggars, petitioners, grafting politicians who believed that, whether he was good or evil, his influence at Court was limitless, with secret police, spies and revolutionary agents haunting the place all the time. 'He kept telling all of them that it would be no good at all for him to present their papers. Often those who were sick and poor and those he thought deserving he would send to his rich and influential acquaintances with a note saying: "Please, dear friend, receive him." '

In the summer of the following year, barely eighteen months after her terrible accident, Anna made the long 1,600-mile journey to Rasputin's home, travelling by rail and steamer for seven or eight days. It was her second visit, and again she was sent there by the Tsaritsa.

---

* The secret police.
† Set up by Kerensky after the Revolution in 1917.

CHAPTER TWENTY-SIX

Fresh Attempts to Murder Him

Those who loathed Rasputin, and who had been inventing fresh stories, anecdotes and songs about him and had celebrated joyously when they heard that he had been stabbed by a woman and was unlikely to live, were horrified now to find that he had recovered and was back in Petrograd. Their detestation mounted. Fresh accusations had to be found or invented. With the country caught in the trials and tragic consequences of war, the obvious allegation was to accuse him of being a German spy, and they added that the Tsaritsa was his accomplice. Soon they revived the whispered, sniggering gossip that the Tsaritsa was Rasputin's mistress and knew that her daughters were having an affair with him too: 'She wouldn't mind. After all he is a man of God.' It was passed on from one to the other and, because they disliked the Tsaritsa, most of them believed it.

A fresh attempt to kill Rasputin was made four days after Anna Vyroubova's accident. It had been snowing heavily since Christmas, and by now the snow had begun to harden. Walking along the Kamenni–Ostrovsky Prospekt on the large central island north of the Neva, Rasputin heard horses' hoofs coming at him from behind at great speed. He swung aside, but was struck down by the sledge. Policemen rushed to his aid, others arrested the men in the sledge, who later, during their trial, admitted that they had come from Tsaritsyn, where Illiodor had lived and preached. But the men were allowed to go: General Dzhunkovsky, head of the police, detested Rasputin and was not prepared to offer any co-operation. Indeed all he was really interested in was to get Rasputin into as much trouble as he could, then prepare a condemnatory report and hand it to the Tsar: that, he felt, would be the end of any contact between this spiritual healer and the Imperial family.

An opportunity that could be used for this purpose presented itself a few months later. Grigori Efimovich was on his way to Pokrovskoe and was going down the Tura in a steamer. According to the police statement, all or some of which may have been true, he came out of his cabin drunk and presently went up and joined some soldiers. Taking a handful of money out of his pocket, he distributed it to the soldiers and asked them to sing; then, after a while, he went back to his cabin and brought some more money for the soldiers and joined them in the singing. When dinner was served he took the soldiers into the dining saloon, but the captain stated they were not allowed there and ordered them out. A row followed. Some passengers intervened and he is said to have been rough with them.

As Rasputin felt very strongly about the dreadful, contemptible treatment of soldiers, who were risking their lives for their country, he ignored the captain and the first-class passengers and joined the soldiers in what was obviously quite a harmless diversion. He denied that he was drunk and said that the passengers, who were hostile to the soldiers being brought into the dining saloon, had provoked him into telling them exactly what he thought of them.

General Dzhunkovsky, for whom the report had been prepared, went to the Palace and handed it personally to the Tsar, who just pushed it into his pocket and talked of other things.

There was another episode at about this time in which Dzhunkovsky once again played a role. Rasputin had gone to Moscow and was with a party of friends in a private *kabinet* at Yar, the most luxurious night-club in the city. On that lovely summer night the place was crowded. The music-hall performance in the main hall was watched by a delighted audience which included many English visitors. They were disturbed by shrieks, curses, the sound of broken glass and the banging of doors. It was caused apparently by Rasputin and his friends, all of whom were drunk. The manager sent for the police, who in turn telephoned to Dzhunkovsky, who was by now Assistant Minister of the Interior and happened to be in Moscow. He gave orders that Rasputin should be arrested. The police rushed in and dragged him to the nearest police-station. The Tsar must have been informed, for Rasputin was released the next morning and Dzhunkovsky was dismissed from his post.

Sir Robert Bruce Lockhart, the British Consul-General in Moscow, who was in the night-club that evening with some friends watching the music-hall performance, heard the distracting noises and saw the arrival of the police: he refers to it in his book *The Memoirs of a British Agent*. He admired Dzhunkovsky, but says this of the Russian police: 'I do not profess even to have mastered the psychology of the Tsarist police. I refuse, however, to believe either in its efficiency or in its honesty.'

In the first twelve months of the war much Russian territory had been lost to the enemy. A large section of Poland went, then the capital Warsaw was captured. The wild excitement of August 1914, the cheering, the flags and bunting, the bands playing in the streets, the devotion showed by millions to the Tsar and even the Tsaritsa, had by now vanished: there was disillusionment, anger and bitterness. Too many lives had been lost; too much of Russia had been lost. Was there any possibility now of winning the war? Scapegoats were sought. The smashing and looting of every shop with a German name belonged to the past: there were no more of them left. So they whipped up their frenzy against the Tsaritsa—she was born a German; her sister Irene was married to Prince Henry of Prussia, which made Russia's arch-enemy Kaiser Wilhelm II a member of her family; another sister, Elizabeth, whose husband the Grand Duke Sergei had been assassinated ten years earlier, was also a German, still living in Russia and said like her sister to be a German spy; their brother, Grand Duke Ernest of Hesse, was yet another German. It was a false, cruel accusation to brand the Empress as a German spy; her private letters to the Tsar, which were never meant for publication and were found after she, the Tsar and their entire family were murdered in Ekaterinburg, show clearly how much she loathed the Kaiser and how intensely she prayed for the utter defeat of the Germans.

From the very outset she dedicated herself to winning the war and helping those who were fighting to win it. The Ekaterina Palace at Tsarskoe Selo, the larger and more beautiful of the two palaces, was converted by her into a military hospital and she had under her wing eighty-five other hospitals in Petrograd quite apart from those in Moscow and other centres. An ambulance train, specially fitted out by her, was named the 'Alexandra Feodorovna' after her;★ and she undertook a rigorous course of nursing together with her two elder daughters Olga and Tatiana. 'To some,' she said, 'it may seem unnecessary my doing this, but help is much needed and every hand is useful.' Dressed in the grey uniform of the nurse, she visited the hospitals with her daughters and Anna Vyroubova, who says: 'I have seen the Empress of Russia in the operating room holding ether cones, handling sterilized instruments, assisting in the most difficult operations, taking from the hands of busy surgeons amputated legs and arms, removing bloody and even vermin-ridden field dressings, enduring all the sights and

★ Rasputin's son Dimitri served as an orderly in this train.

smells and agonies of the most dreadful of all places, a military hospital in the midst of war.' Writing to the Tsar, the Empress said: 'For the first time I shaved one of the soldier's legs near and around the wound . . . three operations, three fingers were taken off as blood-poisoning had set in and they were quite rotten.' She held the hand of a young frightened soldier who was afraid of an operation to amputate his leg; she sat for more than an hour beside one who was dying just to comfort him. Again and again she and her daughters made journeys to the Front in the ambulance train to help the nurses with the care of the wounded.

In Moscow an immense, angry crowd gathered in the Red Square and shouted insulting and obscene accusations against the Imperial family. The Tsaritsa should be locked up in a convent. The Tsar should be deposed and his cousin the Grand Duke Nikolai, Commander-in-Chief of the Russian army, should be made Tsar. The mob then marched on to the Convent of Mary and Martha, where the Tsaritsa's widowed sister the Grand Duchess Elizabeth was the Abbess. At the gates of the Convent they shouted 'Away with the German woman,' and as she came out, dressed in the grey and white robes of the order, they flung stones at her. 'You are hiding German spies here!' 'Bring out your German brother Ernest Duke of Hesse!' She invited them to come in and search the convent. Some soldiers came up and persuaded the angry mob to go.

To many Rasputin was another spy: there was no doubt about it in their minds. He didn't want the war, he didn't want the Russians to destroy the filthy Germans, and when the war started the Kaiser sent vast sums of money to Rasputin so that he could spy for the Germans— he and the Tsaritsa, they worked it out together. That he was against the war was well known: it was not denied; but his opposition was to *all* war, not only this one. That was clear in 1908 and again in 1912.

My father's aversion to war [his daughter Maria says] arose from two reasons: firstly the horror of war and its cruelties, his pity for its innumerable victims, and his doubts as to the outcome of such a massacre—in short, from all that is the very essence of true pacifism, comprehensible in 'a man of God'. In the second place, he saw things simply and clearly. He had the outlook of a peasant who understands the realities of an everyday life. He saw the internal upheaval that would inevitably be the result of a series of reverses, bringing in its wake a collapse all the more brutal from the dizzy heights to which the nation's illusions and enthusiasm had swept it.

It would be wrong, however, to assume that he wanted peace at any price. Talking to the Tsar on his return to Petrograd after his recovery from the severe knife wound in his stomach, he said that as they were involved in the war every effort *must* be made to obtain victory. 'Defeat will only bring in its wake the ruin of the dynasty, and in consequence the ruin of all Russia.'

In the Allied embassies in Petrograd there was constant talk of Rasputin being in the pay of Germany so that Russia would make a separate peace with the help of the Tsaritsa. The French Ambassador, M. Maurice Paléologue, had the opportunity during a personal confrontation with Rasputin of knowing exactly where he stood. In his *Memoirs* Paléologue records his reactions at their meeting:

Brown hair, long and ill-combed; a black, stiff beard; a high forehead; a large, jutting nose; a powerful mouth. But the whole expression of the face was concentrated in the eyes—flax-blue eyes, of a strange brilliance, depth and fascination. Their glance was at the same time piercing and caressing, ingenuous and astute, direct and remote. When his speech became animated, his pupils seemed to be charged with magnetism. In short, abrupt sentences, he sketched before me a pathetic picture of the sufferings that the war inflicted upon the Russian people: 'There are too many killed, too many wounded, too many widows, too many orphans, too many ruins, too many tears! Think of all the unfortunates who will never come back, and tell yourself that each one of them leaves behind him five, six, ten people who weep! I know villages, large villages, where everyone is in mourning. . . . And those who come back from the war, in what a state, dear Lord! Crippled, maimed, blind! . . . It is frightful! For a space of more than twenty years only pain will be harvested on Russian soil.'

'Yes, certainly,' I said, 'it is terrible; but it would be still worse if such sacrifices were to remain fruitless. An indecisive peace, a peace of exhaustion, would not only be a crime against our dead, but it would entail internal catastrophes from which our countries might never recover.'

'You are right,' Rasputin said. 'We must fight until we are victorious.'

'I am glad to hear you say that, for I know several persons in high places who count on you to persuade the Emperor not to continue the war.'

He stared at me with a suspicious eye and scratched his head, then bluntly said: 'There are fools everywhere.'

'The unfortunate thing is that these fools have found credit in Berlin. The Emperor Wilhelm is convinced that you and your friends are using all your influence to obtain peace.'

'The Emperor Wilhelm? But don't you know then that he is inspired by the Devil? Every word of his, every gesture, is ordered by the Devil. I know what I am talking about; I know all about such things. It is the Devil alone who upholds him. But one day, suddenly, the Devil will abandon him, for God will have decided thus. And Wilhelm will crumple up like an old shirt that one throws on the dung-heap.'

'Then our victory is certain. Obviously, the Devil cannot be the conqueror.'

'Yes, we will obtain the victory. But I don't know when. God chooses the hour of his miracles as it pleases Him. Therefore we have not come to the end of our troubles; we shall still see the shedding of much blood and many tears. . . . It will cost enormous sums, millions and millions of roubles. But we must not hesitate about the expense. For, do you see, when people suffer too much they become evil. They can be terrible; sometimes they even go so far as to talk of a republic.'

Just before leaving for Pokrovskoe to spend the summer with his wife and family, Rasputin was suddenly confronted by a Caucasian officer Maria wanted to marry. 'Simoniko Pehakadze,' she writes, 'was a Georgian by birth, virile, strong, with an olive complexion and dark eyes.' She was instantly smitten when she saw how magnificently elegant he looked in the uniform of a captain, with cavalry top boots and a greatcloak thrown over his shoulders.

Grigori was not impressed. He told Maria: 'He is only trying to get in with us to take advantage of my influence at Court.' But, realizing how deeply in love Maria was with him, he finally agreed and they got engaged. Some weeks later Grigori saw Pehakadze at a large party in the house of Count Tolstoy, the son of Leo Tolstoy, the famous author. Pehakadze did not come up to greet him, but quickly merged into the crowd. Surprisingly, some minutes later Pehakadze walked briskly up to him, drew his revolver and pointed it at Rasputin. Raising his eyebrows blandly, Rasputin said: 'You want to shoot me, but your hand is not responding to your will.' At this Pehakadze got flustered, turned the revolver on himself and fired. The bullet went into his chest, but the shot was not fatal.

Later that evening Pehakadze sent a message to Maria asking her to come and see him at once as it was urgent. She had not the faintest idea what the urgency was. She hurried to his house and was escorted to his bedroom, where she saw him lying pale and limp in bed, with a medical dressing in the region of his heart. She burst into tears. She kept asking what had happened and was told that he had been shot; she was not told by whom. Later she learned the truth. The engagement was broken off and Pehakadze was banished from Petrograd.

Not long afterwards an early caller arrived at Rasputin's apartment— a well-dressed, middle-aged woman wearing a smart hat, a fur stole and carrying a muff.

'Drop what you've got in your muff,' Grigori said sharply.

She was startled. As she drew her hand out a revolver fell on the floor.

'Now get out!' he told her. 'Get out!'

It was the fourth attempt to murder him in less than a year. There were to be more in the eighteen months that were left to him of life.

| # The Empress Rules

In the summer of 1915 Grigori spent some weeks, from 22 July to the middle of August, at his home in Pokrovskoe. During his absence from the capital developments were going on that were to involve him.

Following the dismissal of Dzhunkovsky for arresting him at the famous Yar night-club in Moscow, the former Chief of Police, Stefan Beletsky, was reappointed to that office. He was approached by Alexei Nikolaievich Hvostov, whom Rasputin had visited four years earlier on behalf of the Tsar at Nijni-Novgorod. Needing a new Minister of the Interior following the assassination of Stolypin, the Tsar wanted to know if Hvostov, who was then Governor of Nijni-Novgorod, would be a suitable successor. As we have seen, Rasputin was treated with contempt and sent away without being offered a cup of tea or a biscuit. Left with only three roubles, Rasputin used them to send a telegram to Anna Vyroubova saying that the grace of God was in Hvostov, but there was something lacking in him.

Since then Hvostov had been elected to the Duma, of which he was a right-wing reactionary member, and it seemed quite unlikely that he would ever be well disposed towards Rasputin. But, on learning from Beletsky of the close personal link that had been established between Rasputin and the Imperial family, he was driven by ambition to seek Rasputin's friendship and make him, if possible, a close ally. What, he wondered, would be the best approach? After deep reflection he decided to take two steps instead of one.

As a first step he went to see Prince Andronikov, a notorious homosexual and a cunning string-puller. The room in which he received his visitors was a curious combination of bedroom and chapel, in which a religious service was held before and sometimes after a deal was arranged. Andronikov's contact at Tsarskoe Selo was the Tsar's Groom of the Chamber, who was consequently talked of in whispers as also being a homosexual. It was through the groom that the Prince arranged the second step: Hvostov was received by the Tsaritsa, the Tsar being away at army headquarters. Nothing could have worked more favourably for Hvostov. Aware of the reverence with which the Tsaritsa regarded Rasputin, he began by telling her how much he admired

Rasputin and how deeply indebted he was to him. The Tsaritsa's face flushed with joy. 'I am yearning to see him,' she said; and wrote at once to the Tsar about the meeting and added: 'He calls our Friend "Grigori"!' The Tsar was impressed. Hvostov might make a good minister. With no loss of time a place was made available for him. The Tsaritsa, having insisted repeatedly that the severest form of censorship must be enforced to prevent the Press making further attacks on Rasputin, was furious on finding that nothing had been done by the Minister of the Interior, Prince Shcherbatov, and suggested to the Tsar that Hvostov should be his successor.

Before making up his mind the Tsar wrote to Alexei Hvostov's uncle, Alexander Hvostov, who was the Tsar's Minister of Justice, and asked for his opinion of his nephew. The uncle stated bluntly:

> This is a person absolutely inexpert in this work, one who by character is entirely unsuitable. I expect nothing good from it and in some ways I expect even harm. This is a man very far from stupid, but who cannot be critical of his own instincts and judgements. He is inclined to intrigue, and I think he won't content himself with this . . . and in all probability will try to become Premier; in any case all his activities in the office of Minister will not be devoted to the work, but to considerations which have nothing to do with it.

The doddery Prime Minister Goremykin was also opposed to the appointment.

Whatever the Tsar's reaction might have been, the Tsaritsa was determined that Hvostov should be appointed Minister of the Interior: Rasputin apparently was not consulted. She had been seeing quite a lot of Hvostov and was convinced that he would be able to control the Press. A closeness was established during their talks, and she began to use a pet name she had invented for him. The Russian word Hvost means 'tail' and in her letters to the Tsar she always referred to him as 'My Tail' and 'My honest Tail'. He got the job.

This gave him all the power he wanted. As Minister of the Interior he was in charge of the Police Department, and he brought in the Chief of Police Beletsky as his assistant minister. Together they spent some time working out how they should deal with Rasputin. Towards him, Hvostov explained, they would behave as close friends and dedicated supporters; but to Rodzianko, the President of the Duma, and to

others who hated Rasputin they would say with considerable emphasis
that they were going to ruin him: 'We shall compromise him,' Hvostov
told them, 'by taking him out in the evenings to restaurants and night-
clubs and the gipsy gatherings and get him drunk there.'

A few weeks earlier the Tsaritsa had been urging the Tsar to dismiss
the Commander-in-Chief, the Grand Duke Nikolai Nikolaievich, and
take over the High Command himself. She hated the Grand Duke because she felt he had become the focal point of popular adulation: she
even believed that he was going to depose the Tsar and rule Russia himself as Nikolai III and intern her in a convent. There does not seem to be
enough evidence to support this; but her persistence that the Tsar should
take full personal control of the army eventually made him give in. He
had always liked an open-air life and it was his duty, he felt, to be with
his army. He had wanted to do this during the Russo-Japanese War,
but had been persuaded not to. When he mentioned his decision to his
ministers the majority were overwhelmingly opposed to it, only the
very aged, cascading white moustached Prime Minister Goremykin
thought the Tsar's decision must be accepted. His Majesty, the others
said, was urgently needed for the direction of affairs at home, not at the
Front, where every reverse could be blamed on him wrongly and mis-
takenly: commanders-in-chief could be replaced, but the Tsar could
not. They tried to dissuade him, but failed. Following a meeting of the
council they sent this letter to the Tsar:

> Yesterday at the meeting of the council at which you presided, we
> unanimously begged you not to remove the Grand Duke Nikolai
> from the High Command of the Army. We fear that Your Majesty
> was not willing to grant our prayer, which is, we think, the prayer of
> all loyal Russians. We venture once more to tell you that to the best
> of our judgement your decision threatens with serious consequences
> Russia, your dynasty and your person. At the same meeting you
> could see for yourself the irreconcilable difference between our Chair-
> man [Goremykin] and us in our estimate of the situation in the coun-
> try and of the policy to be pursued by the Government. Such a state
> of things is inadmissible at all times, and at the present moment it is
> fatal. Under such conditions we do not believe we can be of real
> service to Your Majesty and our country.

It was signed by eight ministers: the Ministers of War and the Navy,
already committed by special military obligations to the sovereign,

could not add their signatures, but fully supported the statement. Goremykin and two others, one of whom was Alexander Hvostov, the Minister of Justice, and the other who was ill, did not sign.

Gossip suggested that the decision for the Tsar to take over the High Command was really made by Rasputin. It is, of course, possible that the Tsaritsa discussed it with him; for she had begun to seek the support of Rasputin for every decision she wanted the Tsar to make; it reassured her that through the *staretz* God was endorsing what she felt was the right course.

Ever since the Gusseva woman's murderous knife attack on Rasputin at Pokrovskoe there had been an indefinable yet perceptible change in him. Few were aware of it, but those who knew him well noticed the gradual deterioration in his personality. He still quoted the Scriptures as he had always done; he received the callers who sought his advice and guidance; he healed the sick; but his fibre seemed to have slackened; he took to drinking, not in the old, social, diversional way, but drinking without thought or control, for he was drunk almost every night and often became very noisy. The old restraint had gone, the controls no longer operated, and Hvostov and Beletsky made sure that he should be in that state night after night.

What had caused this decline? Had the very severe injuries in his stomach affected his personality? Or was it because the country had been drawn into a cruel, devastating war which he had tried through the years to prevent? Or was it the incessant volcanic hatred that he could see exploding in his face wherever he looked? Christ never answered accusations and he had no wish to depart from that hallowed example. We were in this world to suffer if the Lord wished it, even when the accusations were false, for often he was in Pokrovskoe when people said they had seen him rolling about drunk in Petrograd, raping every girl he saw and spending the night in the Tsaritsa's bed.

How he was to help the Tsaritsa with political guidance one finds it impossible to understand, for he knew little about politics, and of late his estimate of the people he met had become faulty. Earlier he had been a shrewd judge: as early as the Spring of 1911 he had urged the Tsar to bring back Witte as Prime Minister. 'Rasputin's views,' says Sir Bernard Pares, 'were very long-sighted and they coincided with Witte's.' But the old skill had left him now. Even his second sight was no longer reliable. He made mistakes, while the Tsaritsa, with her monumental and often unfortunate prejudices, made mistakes too and then sought, through Grigori, God's endorsement of her folly. He was forty-three now, and had little more than a year to live, and all through these remaining months of his life he slid downhill to his death.

In the Tsar's absence the Tsaritsa took over the running of the country, relying on Rasputin to obtain God's approval of all she was resolved to force the Tsar to do. She took from Rasputin the comb he used and gave it to the Tsar, saying: 'Comb your hair with it, lovey, before you make any important decision; and comb your hair with it several times before you see your Cabinet.' He left for army headquarters in the first week of September 1915 and the Tsaritsa sat down at once to write to him: she wrote every day, sometimes twice a day. In her first letter, a very long one, she said:*

> My very own beloved one—I cannot find words to express all I want to—my heart is far too full. I only long to hold you tight in my arms and whisper words of intense love, courage, strength and endless blessings. . . . You have fought this great fight for your country and throne—alone and with bravery and decision. Never have they seen such firmness in you before. . . . You are proving yourself the Autocrat without which Russia cannot exist. Being firm is the only saving—I know what it costs you. Don't laugh at silly old wify, but she has 'trousers' on unseen, and I can get the old man [Goremykin] to come and keep him energetic—whenever I can be of the smallest use, tell me what to do—use me—at such a time God will give me the strength to help you—because our souls are fighting for the right against evil. . . . Forgive me, I beseech you, my Angel, for having left you no peace and worried you so much—but I too well know your marvellously gentle character. Our Friend's prayers arise night and day for you to Heaven, and God will hear them. . . . Sleep well my sunshine, Russia's Saviour.

Since the outbreak of war the Tsar had visited all the Fronts, staying away at times for three weeks or a month, and during all these absences the Tsaritsa wrote to him regularly. Now, though no longer a visitor but in actual command of the army, he left practically all the decisions to his extremely able new Chief of Staff General Alexeyev. Much

---

* All her letters to the Tsar were written in English. The spelling and punctuation, it will be seen, were faulty.

ground and many men had been lost: the casualties were frightful. In ten
months from the outbreak of war to the end of June 1915 the total
Russian losses in killed, wounded and prisoners was 3,800,000.

Unlike the Tsar, the Tsaritsa kept interfering all the time. The ministers brought her their reports regularly. This gave her immense pride
and satisfaction and she referred to it in a letter to her husband in these
words: 'I am the first Russian Empress since Catherine the Great to receive the Ministers.' One wonders if her husband thought it tactful;
after all, *he* was the 'anointed by God'. To Goremykin she kept sending
the names of ministers whose dismissal she desired: they fell like nine-
pins—Samarin, Marshal of the Moscow nobility and Procurator of the
Holy Synod; Sazonov, the brilliant Foreign Minister; Polivanov, the
War Minister; and so on. On succeeding the lazy, incompetent Sukhomlinov, Polivanov had dealt with the shortage of heavy artillery
and ammunition with considerable energy and skill: the Empress disliked him because, she says, he was working very closely with Guchkov,
who had set up the Central Munitions Committee for the greater and
quicker production of munitions. The results were of immense advantage to the army and the survival of the country—but that she preferred
to ignore; all she remembered was that Guchkov had published in his
newspaper *Golos Moskvy* extracts from Professor Novoselov's offensive
pamphlet stating falsely that Rasputin was a member of the *Khlysty*
sect; and also for his attack on Rasputin in the Duma in March 1912.
The Tsar, however, refused to dismiss Polivanov: one of the very rare
occasions when he defied his wife. She, for her part, refused to give in
and by persistent nagging eventually got her way.

Guchkov was one of the most remarkable men in Russia. He was
leader of the Octobrists, the Conservative reform party, President of
the Third Duma, and amazingly active in a variety of fields. His path
had been strewn with adventure and drama. The grandson of a serf and
the son of a Moscow merchant, Alexander Guchkov kept dashing off
to remote corners of the earth to take part in a rising, a rebellion, or a
war. The Boxer Rebellion took him to China, the rising of the Boers
took him to South Africa to fight against Britain, the disorders in Mace-
donia saw him fighting with the Greek guerrillas; in Mukden he cared
for the wounded during the Japanese war, and he also fought many
duels. While being entertained by the Tsar and Tsaritsa in 1905, he told
them quite bluntly that the country needed a national assembly: eventually, despite the strong opposition of the Tsar and Tsaritsa, the Duma

M

was set up. His opportunity came when his party, by capturing one third of the seats, became the leading party in the Third Duma in 1907. Resolved, as so many were, to wipe out Russia's humiliation in the Japanese war, he lashed out at the grand dukes in the Duma, calling on them, in the name of patriotism, to resign their posts in the various defence organizations because, as members of the Imperial family, they were not subject to criticism, and consequently stood in the way of reform.

> If we consider ourselves [he said] entitled and even bound to turn to the people and to the country and demand from them heavy sacrifices for this work of defence, then we are entitled to address ourselves also to those few irresponsible persons from whom we have to demand no more than the renunciation of certain terrestrial advantages and of certain satisfactions of vainglory which are connected with those posts which they at present hold.

Though remarkably calm and quiet-voiced, he never dodged an issue or avoided dealing with an insult. Told by a member of the Duma that Stolypin, who was Prime Minister at the time, had spoken disparagingly of him, Guchkov sneered at Stolypin in a speech and, getting no reaction, said: 'Count, how long are you going to let me insult you?' That drew Stolypin's fire. A duel was fought. Guchkov wounded Stolypin slightly, and, as duels were illegal, he went to the Tsar and said he was prepared to take his punishment. Because of his insistence he was imprisoned for a fortnight and then freed.

One could go on about his activities. But only one other duel needs to be referred to. In the course of his investigations as Chairman of the Duma Commission of Imperial Defence, Guchkov developed the impression that Colonel Myasoyedov, an intimate friend of Sukhomlinov, who was then War Minister, was in fact spying for the Germans. He publicly accused him of spying, was challenged and fought a duel on one of the island suburbs. Guchkov waited until Myasoyedov had fired, then raised his revolver and fired into the air, turned and walked off without shaking hands. Not until some time later was Guchkov proved to be right. Meanwhile Myasoyedov had been made a high-ranking intelligence officer and was by aeroplane communicating information regularly to the enemy. On this being discovered he was arrested and hanged as a traitor.

CHAPTER
TWENTY-EIGHT

Still More Murder Attempts

Hvostov and Beletsky, his assistant at the Ministry of the Interior, plunged whole-heartedly and with tremendous energy into getting things done. Aware of the shortage of food and the constant rise in the cost of living, Beletsky directed his attention to opening new food shops and giving them a government subsidy. At the same time he began to deal with the problem of the refugees who came pouring in from the areas conquered by the enemy, and toured the provinces to raise money for them. He also paid out large sums of money to newspapers and magazines to induce them to keep the people constantly informed of the fine, unflagging war work of the Tsar and Tsaritsa.

The role of Hvostov was to rig the elections of the next Duma. His plan was to form a large shareholding company, nominally a public company, but directed by a large number of secret agents engaged specially for this purpose and, for some reason, paid in advance. As an extension of Beletsky's plan, the company was to start new newspapers, take over or subsidize those already in existence in the large towns and in the provinces, and control printing presses, bookstalls, advertisements, cinemas and even telephone communications. The subsidized newspapers were chiefly on the Left, with the exclusion only of the Bolshevik Press. Hvostov was convinced it was an unfailing way of getting the Press to do what you want. Enormous sums of money were paid out, but the plan did not work.

Hvostov's influence over the Tsaritsa was considerable: he advised her on the dismissal and replacement of some of the ministers. On the dismissal of the Minister of Religion, Samarin, by the Tsar, Hvostov supplied his successor, Volzhin, though not long afterwards the Empress began to complain about him also. When the Minister of Agriculture was dismissed, once again Hvostov found a successor, an honest *Zemstvo** worker named Naumov, who said he didn't want the job but was forced by the Tsar to accept it. And the homosexual Prince Andronikov kept popping up with the names of people who should be

---

* County council.

given office. The whole thing was madly chaotic. Two ministers, however, stayed on, though the Empress wanted their dismissal—Sazonov,
the Foreign Minister (she later changed her mind and decided he should
remain) and Bark, the Minister of Finance, for whom a successor,
Count Tatischev, was found by Hvostov, but the Cabinet then protested and Bark remained in office.

The time had now come, Hvostov and Beletsky felt, to get rid of
Rasputin. They planned to send him on a tour of the most famous
monasteries in Russia, get a number of smart, well-equipped carriages,
some priests as his companions and an ample supply of food and
madeira. When all was ready Rasputin refused to go. They tried to
get him into the impressive leading carriage prepared especially for
him, but, suspecting a plot of some kind, he forced open the door as it
was being shut and got out.

Hvostov and Beletsky were baffled. Something would have to be
done about Rasputin: he wasn't playing the game in the way they
wanted him to. After some reflection Beletsky decided that they should
get a man they could rely on to keep a watchful eye on him. Komissarov, who had been a General of Gendarmes, seemed to Beletsky to be
just the man for the job: he was reliable and faithful and accustomed to
doing the dirty work of other people. To make sure what Rasputin
was really up to, they assigned a squad of policemen with instructions
to prevent Rasputin seeing people they didn't want him to see. To the
Tsaritsa it was explained that no matter what Rasputin might say, they
were really trying to protect him from assassins as so many were out
for his blood.

Discovering that the Tsaritsa talked on the telephone to Rasputin
very early every morning, Komissarov was instructed to prompt Rasputin with what Hvostov and Beletsky wanted him to say to the Empress. It did not take long for Komissarov to be drawn to Rasputin: he
liked his child-like innocence, his kindness and charm, his deep feeling
for the poor, his complete indifference to the money given him by the
rich which he handed over to the first sad-faced man who came to see
him. What Komissarov did not like was the Scriptural quotations.
'Drop the theology, Grigori!' he would say. When he was drunk, as
Grigori often was during these last months of his life, Komissarov
would look after him like a nursemaid; and if that did not quieten him,
Grigori would be warned rather more sharply, like a child: 'If you
don't behave yourself I shall strangle you.'

The relationship became so warm and close that not only Komissarov but his entire police squad used to come into the apartment to spend hours talking, drinking, listening reluctantly to Grigori's religious talk, but more enthusiastically to the gipsy music on the gramophone, which they all joined in singing, and they watched Grigori with delight as he romped round the room dancing.

After spending a month at army headquarters, the Tsar returned to Tsarskoe Selo and took the Tsarevich back with him for the troops to see that he was there too. It was the first parting of the Tsaritsa from her son, and she missed him terribly. She did not argue, she did not complain, but those around her saw what she was going through. Quietly, without shedding any tears, she said good-bye to Alexei, who was now eleven years old, then turned to Pierre Gilliard, his Swiss tutor, and begged him to write to her every day giving details about the boy's health and how he was liking the life out there. That the Tsar needed the boy she was only too well aware, for he was alone, away from his family. Alexei would be of immense comfort to him.

Gilliard describes the beginning of the exciting adventure for him and for his pupil: 'We left for Mohilev* on 14 October and the Tsaritsa and the Grand Duchesses came to the station to see us off.' The Tsar reviewed some of the regiments that had been fighting the enemy in Galicia and the Carpathians,

but in spite of the terrible losses they had suffered they marched past the Tsar with a proud and defiant bearing. After the ceremony he mixed with the men and conversed personally with several of them, asking questions about the severe engagements in which they had taken part. Alexei Nikolaievich was at his father's heels, listening intently to the stories of these men. His features, which were always expressive, became quite strained in the effort not to miss a single word. . . . What made the greatest impression on the men was the fact that the Tsarevich was wearing the uniform of a private soldier, with nothing to distinguish it from that of a boy in the service.

On 16 October we arrived at Mohilev, a little White Russian town of a highly provincial appearance to which the Grand Duke Nikolai had transferred G.H.Q. during the great German offensive two

---

* Army headquarters.

months before. The Tsar occupied the house of the Governor which was situated on the summit of the steep bank of the Dneiper. He was on the first floor in two fairly large rooms, one of which was his study and the other his bedroom. Alexei Nikolaievich's camp-bed was accordingly placed next to his father's.

Alexei had his lessons in the study. After lunch, at which the Tsar had about thirty guests, the three of them went for a drive in the car, and left it for an hour's walk before returning to headquarters. Visits were made to various Fronts. At one of them, told that there was a casualty station quite near, the Tsar decided at once to go to it. It was tucked away in a dark forest with small torches giving a feeble light. 'His unexpected arrival at so late an hour at a spot so close to the Front was the cause of general astonishment, which could be read on every face.' As the Tsar went up to talk to each of the wounded, Alexei, standing by his father, was deeply moved by the suffering he saw and the moaning he heard.

Early in November a brief visit was made to Tsarskoe Selo. On returning to Mohilev, the Tsar set out for the frontier of Galicia.

On the morning of our departure, Thursday, 16 December [Gilliard records], Alexei Nikolaievich, who had caught cold the previous day and was suffering a heavy catarrh in the head, began to bleed at the nose as a result of sneezing violently. I summoned Professor Fedorov,* but he could not entirely stop the bleeding. In spite of this accident we started off, as all preparations had been made for the arrival of the Tsar.

During the night the boy got worse. His temperature had gone up and he was getting weaker. At three o'clock in the morning Professor Fedorov, alarmed at his responsibilities, decided to awaken the Tsar and ask him to return to Mohilev, where he could attend to the Tsarevich under more favourable conditions.

The next morning we were on our way back to G.H.Q., but the boy's state was so alarming that it was decided to take him back to Tsarskoe Selo. The Tsar called on the General Staff and spent two hours with General Alexeiv. Then he joined us and we started off at once. Our journey was particularly harrowing, as the patient's

---

* The doctor who accompanied the Tsar on all his journeys.

strength was failing rapidly. We had to have the train stopped several times to be able to change the nose plugs. Alexei Nikolaievich was supported in bed by the sailor Nagorny (he could not be allowed to lie full length), and twice in the night he swooned away and I thought the end had come.

Towards morning there was a slight improvement, however, and the haemorrhage lessened. At last we reached Tsarskoe Selo. It was eleven o'clock. The Tsaritsa, who had been torn with anguish and anxiety, was on the platform with the Grand Duchesses. With infinite care the invalid was taken to the Palace.

Rasputin was telephoned at once. He stood by the child's bed and prayed, and the bleeding stopped. Once again both the Tsaritsa and the Tsar saw that it was Grigori's prayers that had caused the child's recovery. 'Our Friend is our only hope of Alexei's survival—and our survival,' said the Tsaritsa.

The Tsar returned alone to G.H.Q., on 25 December. Alexei was not well enough to accompany him. 'It was a real sorrow to him,' says Gilliard, 'as he had been looking forward eagerly to presenting his heir to the Guard.'

A week or so later Grigori, attending a gala gipsy evening at the Villa Rode, was suddenly seized by a number of army officers. Savagely they began to attack him. A crowd gathered, the music and the singing stopped, and surprisingly the assault stopped too, the officers were no longer able to use their hands.

The eye-witnesses, describing the scene afterwards, stated that Rasputin's glaring mesmeric eyes completely paralysed the hands of the officers. Quite sober now, Rasputin smiled at them, returned to his seat, and clapping his hands, called on the gipsies to resume their singing and dancing.

It was his sixth escape.

The Tsar Surprises
the Duma

Since the election of the Fourth Duma in 1912 the political parties had been drawing together; they had become familiar with the details of the administration, and ever since the outbreak of the war there had been parliamentary co-operation. Even the revolutionary Mensheviks were patriotic, and the Labour party, led by Kerensky, was as wholeheartedly for the defence of the country as Guchkov's Cadets, many of whom were in uniform serving at the Front with the Red Cross. Only the Bolsheviks, not very numerous, stood apart.

Working in unison, the various groups repeatedly drew attention to the abuses of the Tsar's Government. The Prime Minister Goremykin's speech was coldly received, but the War Minister Polivanov was enthusiastically applauded when he assured the House that he meant to work with the Duma. Then came a demand from the Nationalist member, Count Vladimir Bobrinskoy, which the Tsar resented strongly when he was told about it: speaking, as it turned out, for almost the entire Duma, the Count asked for the setting up of a Ministry of Confidence. He indicated clearly that the Duma had no confidence in the Government, which was not elected by the votes of the people but nominated at the whim of the Tsar; and he demanded also that the Ministry of Confidence should be directly responsible to the Duma.

The acquiescence of the Tsar to this plan was not expected and was not granted. But the Duma, aware that it would take a little time, were resolved, now that they had got their teeth firmly into it, not to let it go. As a first step a Progressive Block was formed, representing pretty well all the parties, and a request was made for the granting of certain moderate reforms which were long overdue. The Tsar, on leaving for headquarters, issued instructions for the suspending of the Duma. Almost all the members were enraged and all the factory workers in Petrograd went on a two-day strike. The Civil Red Cross, meeting in Moscow, demanded the recall of the Duma and the appointment of a Ministry of Confidence: its representatives were sent to see the Tsar at headquarters but were not received. Rodzianko, the President of the Duma, asked for an audience, his request was also refused by the Tsar. A few days before this Sir Bernard Pares, who had kept in the closest

The Tsarevich Alexei, aged ten
(*Mansell Collection*)

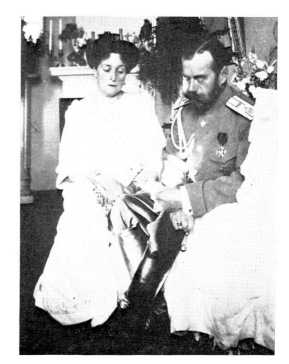

The Tsar and Tsaritsa at Spala in
1912 reading the telegram from
Rasputin which says: 'God has seen
your tears. . . . The little one will not
die' (*Mansell Collection*)

что завтре? ты наш
руководитель боже
сколько въ жизни
путей тернистыхъ

Rasputin in hospital after being stabbed in the stomach by Gusseva. His inscription states:'What will tomorrow bring? Thou art our leader, O God, how many thorny paths there are in life!' (*Mansell Collection*)

Tsar Nikolai II and the Tsaritsa Alexandra in the
three-centuries-old Imperial robes

The Tauride Palace where the Duma met (*Mansell Collection*)

The Yussupov Palace on the Moika canal in St Petersburg where Rasputin was murdered (*René Fülöp-Miller*)

Prince Felix Yussupov in sixteenth-century boyar costume

Maria, Rasputin's elder daughter (*Radio Times Hulton Picture Library*)

Kerensky standing up in a motor car
during the Revolution (*Mansell Collection*)

The ballerina Kschesinskaya's house
in St Petersburg. The house was
taken over by the Soviet; Lenin
made his speeches from the balcony
(*Larry Burrows/Time-Life*)

Lenin in disguise, with a forged passport which he used to escape to Finland (*Radio Times Hulton Picture Library*)

The Tsar and three of his daughters as prisoners in Tobolsk in Siberia (*Mansell Collection*)

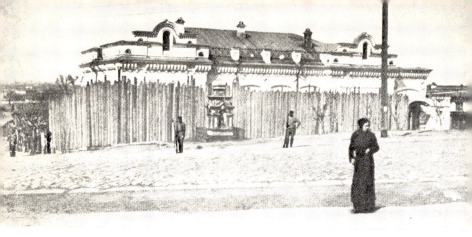

The palisaded Ipatyev house in Ekaterinburg where the Tsar and his family were murdered on the night of 16 July 1918 (*Radio Times Hulton Picture Library*)

Yurovsky, who led the murder squad and fired the first shot (*Mansell Collection*)

The room in which the Tsar and his family were murdered (*Mansell Collection*)

touch with all that was happening in Russia, saw Lloyd George, then Minister of Munitions, in London, and urgently warned him that if conditions were not changed in Russia, the war would inevitably bring about a revolution.

The Tsaritsa's contact with Rasputin during the Tsar's absence was not confined to talks on the telephone every morning: she went to Anna Vyroubova's house two or three times a week to see him and talk to him there. The changes she wanted to make in the Cabinet she discussed with him; generally he agreed with her, and sometimes he suggested some changes himself. But, as one can see from her letters to the Tsar, Grigori's thoughts were focused on far more serious matters than moving about the chessmen of the Ministry.

> Our Friend [she writes], whom we saw last night, is otherwise quiet about the war, now another subject worries him very much and he spoke scarcely about anything else for two hours. It is this that you must give an order that waggons with *flour*, butter and sugar should be obliged to pass. He saw the whole thing in the night like a vision, all the towns, railway lines etc. He says it is very serious and then we shall have no *strikes*. Only for such an organization somebody ought to be sent by you. He wishes me to speak to you about all this very earnestly, severely even . . . , therefore I already write about it beforehand for you to get accustomed to the idea.
>
> He would propose 3 days no other trains should go, except these with flour, butter and sugar—its even more necessary than meat or ammunition just now. He counts that with 40 old soldiers one could load in an hour a train, and one after the other—not all to one place, but to *Petrograd*—Moscow—and stop some waggons at different places, and have them by degrees brought on not all to one place, that also would be bad, but to different stations, different buildings— if passenger trains only very few would be allowed, and instead of all 4 classes these days, hang on waggons with flour and butter fr. Siberia. The lines are less filled there coming towards the west and the discontent will be intense if the things dont move. People will scream and say its impossible, frighten you, but its necessary and tho' a risk, essential. In three days one could bring enough for very many months. It may seem strange how I write, but if one goes into the thought—one sees the truth of it.

Despite the rather muddled phrasing of her letter, it is at any rate clear that Rasputin was giving some thought to the problems of the people—without food there would be acute discontent, strikes would follow as a protest, and ultimately it would lead to revolution.

The Tsar tried desperately not to give the country any form of parliamentary government. Against his will and against his resolve, the revolutionary events that followed the Russo-Japanese War in 1905 forced him to set up the Duma. He hated having to do it, and at no time was he prepared to visit it, even less address it. The Tsaritsa detested it and kept hoping that before long it would be abolished so that the Tsar could exercise his autocracy without any intervention from what the western world called 'democracy'; the Romanovs had ruled the country well for more than three centuries without its help. Yet, despite her intense antagonism, she passed on Rasputin's suggestion that the Tsar should 'turn up' at the Duma quite unexpectedly and say a few words, it 'might change everything and be a splendid deed'.

Rasputin played a much bigger part in the Tsar's visit than these few lines from the Tsaritsa would suggest. The new Metropolitan of Petrograd, Pitrim, a friend and supporter of Rasputin, also urged the Tsar to visit the Duma. One further suggestion made by Rasputin was that the Tsar should award a decoration to Rodzianko, the President of the Duma: it surprised the Tsar, for he knew how fiercely Rodzianko hated Rasputin and how angrily he turned him out of Kazan Cathedral where he had been invited for the Romanov tercentenary celebrations.

The visit of the Emperor to the Duma took place on 22 February 1916. Nervous, uneasy and very pale as he walked in, the Tsar was overwhelmed by the delighted and enthusiastic welcome of the surprised members, who at no time during the Duma's ten years had received a visit from the Emperor.

After a short prayer, Nikolai II, a remarkably good speaker, addressed the gathering as 'representatives' of his people—their hearts were warmed by the expression, for he had never regarded them as representatives. The Order of St Anne was conferred on Rodzianko, much to the annoyance of the Empress. Of the visit, Sir Bernard Pares comments: 'Rasputin was clever enough to mystify not only the Russian public but France and England, whose parliaments sent congratulations to the Duma on this first visit of its sovereign.'

CHAPTER THIRTY

Three More Murder Plots

Shortly before this visit, there was a celebration of Grigori's nameday on 23 January—the last he was to have. 'Warm and snowing again. Our Friend's Nameday,' the Empress reminded her husband in her daily letter. Anna was ill and was coughing. 'Grigori wanted her to come today,' she adds, 'but she really has not the strength to go and it would be utter folly fr. the human point of view.'

The day began for Rasputin with the traditional, religious practice observed by all Russian peasants on that anniversary—going to church and then to the baths. When he returned he found his apartment filled with gifts. Handsome and costly furniture, pictures, carpets and silver ornaments had been bought for him by Beletsky, who drew on official secret funds to pay for them; other gifts were sent by bankers and financiers who had sought prophetic guidance on what shares to buy. Some of the gifts he sent to his home at Pokrovskoe; others were given away to whoever admired them. Though ill and suffering from a bad cough, Anna got out of bed and travelled on that bitterly cold day from Tsarskoe Selo to Petrograd just to have lunch with him and convey the congratulations and good wishes of the Imperial family. As soon as lunch was over she left, for her doctor had warned her not to stay too long. But others kept arriving. The gipsies brought gifts for Grigori and sang and danced for him.

Among those who did not come were Hvostov, Beletsky and Pitrim the Metropolitan; only when alone with him did they show their friendship; to the world they always made it clear that they did not know Rasputin and had no contact with him whatsoever. Aware of this, Grigori, whenever one of them was entertaining, would telephone and tell the manservant to inform his master that he was required urgently on the telephone by Grigori Efimovich Rasputin. Sometimes he sent a messenger to Hvostov's house with strict instructions that he should walk boldly into the drawing-room and announce in a loud voice for the benefit of the guests that he had come from Rasputin.

Hvostov had been working to get rid of Goremykin, the aged Prime Minister, confident that the Tsaritsa would recommend him as the successor. She didn't; the office went to Stürmer, whom the Tsar had known and admired for some years. He was a hard-boiled reactionary who had served under Plehve in the Ministry of the Interior; then as Governor of Yaroslavl, a manufacturing town on the Upper Volga, where he was not liked. At Tver he had dismissed the entire legally elected *Zemstvo* because, being Liberal, it planned to build schools and hospitals and had appointed agricultural experts to advise the peasants on the sowing of their crops. The Duma was horrified when Stürmer's appointment was announced in February 1916.

So far as Hvostov was concerned, the opportunity for becoming Prime Minister had gone; and he blamed Rasputin for it, for Stürmer was a friend of Manasevich Manuilov, who knew Rasputin; but Manuilov had been closely associated with Prince Meschersky, a most intimate friend of the Tsar. In fact it had been Pitrim who made a special journey to see the Tsar at G.H.Q. to recommend Stürmer's appointment. But Hvostov still persisted in thinking that Rasputin was responsible.

He was resolved now to dispose of Rasputin finally, and the only way of achieving this was by murder. Both Beletsky and Komissarov were invited to discuss it and work out a plan. On leaving, the two men nodded knowingly to one another. 'The blame will be put on us,' said Beletsky. 'We must be careful not to fall into the trap.' So they decided to do nothing about it.

But Hvostov had no intention of letting it drop. The sooner it was done the better. He sent for them again and told them to present their plan without delay. Komissarov, possibly not very seriously—for he liked Rasputin—said: 'I could get some members of my police squad to dress as hooligans, waylay him, drag him into a side-street and strangle him. Then they could take his body to a point at the mouth of the River Neva and plunge it into the water.'

How, Hvostov asked, were they to get Rasputin into a dark side-street? Komissarov said they could arrange a dinner invitation at a restaurant, and Hvostov could come in a private car, wait in a side-street and see it being carried out. The dinner was arranged, but Rasputin did not go to it. Either Komissarov or Beletsky had tipped him off.

'A fresh plan,' Hvostov said, 'will have to be worked out. This time we must use poison.' Komissarov agreed. 'I dare not approach a local chemist,' he said. 'It would be dangerous—the details would certainly leak out. I know just the man for the job—a chemist at Saratov, where I used to be Prefect of Police.'

He was granted leave to go and get the poison.

Saratov, on the Volga, was 1,000 miles away from Petrograd. Once there, Komissarov decided to linger, but a sharp note from Hvostov ordered him to return at once.

Beletsky was present when Komissarov arrived with a number of bottles containing poison. He sat on the sofa beside Hvostov and explained the strength and effectiveness of each poison. He was asked which was the quickest and most violent. 'This one,' he said, raising the large dark bottle. 'I tried it on a stray tom cat which rolled over at once and died in agony.'

Hvostov's face glowed with joy. 'That is the one you must use.'

On leaving, Beletsky asked him about the poisons and was told that the bottles contained only various remedies from his wife's medicine chest. 'The poison labels were written and stuck on by me. I got the words out of a book I bought on dangerous drugs.'

A day or two later, while in Rasputin's apartment, Beletsky saw Komissarov pour out a drink for Rasputin, and then pour one from the same bottle for Beletsky and another for himself. Nothing happened to them. But the milk put out for the cat caused it to roll over and die. Rasputin was very upset and blamed the homosexual Prince Andronikov for poisoning his cat. Anna Vyroubova never spoke to Andronikov after that.

Every murderous plan of Hvostov's had gone wrong, and he decided now to handle it himself. He would not—in his position could not—commit the murder, but it would not be difficult to give someone enough money to carry it out. He found a rough, hardbitten Cossack who agreed to do it: he accepted the advance payment, but changed his mind afterwards and returned the money.

A day or two later Hvostov suddenly realized that the one man who could be relied on to murder Rasputin was Illiodor, who had tried it twice before. The first attempt, when the Gusseva woman plunged the knife into his entrails, very nearly succeeded; the second attempt was in the thick snow of January 1915 when Illiodor's men from Tsaritsyn tried to run Rasputin down in a sledge along the Kamenni–Ostrovsky Prospekt.

Illiodor was now living in Denmark, and as a first step Hvostov got in touch with a man named Rzhetsky, whom he had used for his dirty work while Governor of Nijni-Novgorod. He sent him to see Illiodor and work out a plan for murdering Rasputin. Beletsky was kept fully informed by Hvostov. At the Finnish frontier Rzhetsky was questioned by the passport authorities about his journey to Denmark and boastfully explained that the Minister of the Interior Hvostov had sent him on a mission. Questioned further, he lost his temper and hurled threats and insults at the officials, all of which was reported to Beletsky as Chief of the Police. On his return journey after seeing Illiodor, Rzhetsky was again challenged at the frontier and behaved vilely. He was held for an hour while the officials phoned Beletsky. Furious at the man's stupidity and anxious not to be personally involved in the plot, Beletsky told the frontier guards to arrest Rzhetsky. Telegrams kept arriving from Illiodor, all of which were intercepted by the police: one of them demanded money to provide Illiodor's men with funds to get to Petrograd from Tsaritsyn.

While the plot was being hatched by Illiodor and his murderous gang, Rzhetsky, to get even with Beletsky for arresting him, managed to contact a friend through a warder and got him to warn Rasputin that there was a plot to murder him. At the same time Beletsky, to wash his hands of the whole affair, also told Rasputin about the plot and advised him to stay at home. 'I shall tell you when the danger has passed,' Beletsky said. It seems to suggest that, but for the warnings given to Rasputin, any one of Hvostov's attempts to murder him might have succeeded; there is no indication that Rasputin's weakened second-sight gave him an inkling as to what was afoot or who were involved in these plots.

Hvostov's hostility towards Beletsky now became acute. He went to see the Tsar and asked for the dismissal of Beletsky; the Tsar agreed to do this and appointed Beletsky Governor-General of Siberia. Hvostov then called on Stürmer and took him to the Ministry of the Interior, where the two men, after locking the doors, produced all the records about Rasputin and burnt them. Why this was done is not clear. Hvostov then began to arrest a number of Rasputin's friends, including Simanovich, who had been the Tsaritsa's jeweller for years. Simanovich was sent to Narym in Siberia, but did not get further than Tver, where he was released. Next Hvostov began saying incriminating things against Beletsky to his friends in the Duma. Hearing of this the editor of a Petrograd newspaper *Bourse Gazette*, repeated it to Beletsky, who promptly gave him his version of what had really happened and the part Hvostov had played in it. It was for the record and not for publication. But the entire statement was printed in the *Bourse Gazette*.

Beletsky's appointment as Governor-General of Siberia was cancelled and Hvostov was sacked. Stürmer took over his job, and thus added the Ministry of the Interior to his work as Prime Minister.

During the Revolution, which began exactly a year later, the new Minister of Justice Alexander Kerensky set up an Investigating Commission of the Provisional Government. It was an entirely liberal and democratic inquiry into the activities of the Ministers of the Tsar. Both Hvostov and Beletsky gave evidence, and it is on their evidence that the above details of the attempts at murdering Rasputin have been based.

CHAPTER THIRTY-ONE

The Government
Disintegrates

Nobody seemed to like Stürmer. To all except the Tsar and the Tsaritsa, who chose him, and Manuilov, Pitrim the Metropolitan of Petrograd, and possibly to Rasputin, who sometimes shouted at him, he was a disaster. Rodzianko described him as an utter nonentity. Hvostov's uncle, still Minister of Justice, called him 'a false man, double-faced'; and, oddly enough, so did Pitrim, who added this further condemnation after the appointment had been made: 'Finished at fifty, constantly dozing.' But the Tsar stated that he had 'unlimited confidence in Stürmer' and was very glad the Empress had him to lean on.

Most of the ministers found him impossible to work with, and constantly had to appeal to the Tsar. Naumov, who against his will had been forced to take the post of Minister of Agriculture, insisted on working with the Duma: without the help of the Duma and the Zemstva, the local elected bodies, it would be impossible, he said, to cope with the food supplies. Trepov, the new Minister of Transport, also found it difficult to work with Stürmer. The Empress brushed aside their complaints. They were only there as specialists, she told the Tsar—Naumov was the gardener, Trepov was the coachman; each one had to do his own job, but in all other matters they had to take instructions from the butler, meaning Stürmer.

It was obvious as early as March and April 1916 that Stürmer was contributing unwittingly yet substantially to the coming of the Revolution. So was the Empress, who told him what to do: it had the endorsement of the Tsar, who wrote to her from army headquarters: 'It is a good thing you receive Stürmer—he likes your suggestions'; and again: 'He is an excellent man but irresolute'; and, somewhat irritably, 'The ministers persist in coming here and take up all my time.' However much one allows for the ill-health she certainly suffered—her heart had been affected since the birth of her son, she had to spend most of the morning in bed and often went about in a wheeled chair; and however much one admires her devotion of long wearisome hours to the running of the Empire, she had in fact no idea how to meet problems and overcome them: pushing ministers out of office at a whim and putting others in their place was no way to govern the country. Somebody had to govern it, and eventually the revolutionaries took it over.

Sazonov, the experienced and outstandingly able Minister of Foreign Affairs since 1910, quite suddenly, after a very pleasant discussion with the Tsar, who 'listened attentively and sympathetically to what I had to say about Poland', was dismissed because the Tsaritsa insisted on his dismissal. Discussions had gone on, and even promises been made, to grant Poland autonomy, but nothing had been done. Now not even a fragment of Poland remained in Russian hands. Sazonov's plan was to create a separate kingdom of Poland under the Tsar, with the possibility of adding the sections of Poland held by Austria and Germany before the outbreak of war. 'Gentle and good-natured,' Sazonov adds, 'he was pleased to meet any desires that seemed to him just.' Nikolai approved of the plan and gave instructions that it should be communicated to the Cabinet. Delighted at having 'won all along the line', Sazonov left for a short holiday in Finland.

The Tsaritsa was furious when she was told that the Tsar had accepted the plan. She immediately set out from Tsarskoe Selo with her four daughters (the Tsarevich was already there with his father) and Anna Vyroubova for army headquarters at Mohilev to tell the Emperor exactly what she thought of his folly in accepting Sazonov's plan. 'You are giving away Baby's future inheritance,' she said. Bullied by her and completely cowed, the Tsar withdrew his consent and sacked Sazonov while he was away on his very brief holiday in Finland. By doing this, just one of her many acts of folly, she did *not* secure the Tsarevich's inheritance, but lost not only Poland, which was lost already and might never have been recovered, but also the entire Russian Empire as well as the lives of the heir, her four daughters, the Tsar and herself.

The next change affected the Minister of Justice, Alexander Hvostov, uncle of Alexei Hvostov. Before Stürmer's appointment as Prime Minister the Tsar sent Rasputin to see if he thought the elder Hvostov would make a suitable Prime Minister. He was received coldly and was told that he only received petitioners on certain fixed days. Using Rasputin in this way, the Tsar and the Tsaritsa were obviously responsible for his involvement in political appointments. As Grigori had no opportunity of forming an impression, Alexander Hvostov did not get the premiership. Stürmer, who did get it, now wanted him moved from the Ministry of Justice to the Ministry of the Interior which Hvostov's nephew had occupied—the toughest ministry of all. 'I know

N

your health is not very good,' Stürmer told him, 'that is why I am going to give you a rest.'

Hvostov said: 'I am in critical need of rest.'

'Not from all office,' said Stürmer. 'I am just moving you to the ministry your nephew occupied.' Stürmer held that office himself and had found it too exacting, and yet he was pushing into it a man whose health was declining. Hvostov looked at Stürmer squarely, watched his shifty eyes for some moments, and said: 'How did you dare to do me this dirty trick?' He refused the offer, but was told by the Tsar that in time of war it was not an offer but an order. The pleading about his state of health, which the Tsar had known for some time and had only recently advised him to rest, was brusquely brushed aside. He took the office and Stürmer was free to be Minister of Foreign Affairs in succession to Sazonov.

Not many weeks later the elder Hvostov was dismissed for arresting Manuilov, who was charged with obtaining £1,000 for granting exemptions from military service. Rasputin was not in Petrograd when it happened. Aware of the various services Manuilov had rendered the country, and in particular the stealing of the Japanese secret code which was of immense service during the Russo-Japanese War (he was in fact decorated by the Tsar for it), the Tsaritsa also knew that he was a friend of Grigori: the man who made the arrest was dismissed at the same time.

CHAPTER THIRTY-TWO

Anna and Lili Go to Pokrovskoe

Bishop Varnava of Tobolsk, of humble origin, deeply religious and by occupation a gardener, was greatly admired by Rasputin and was, as we know, on his recommendation, appointed to take over the See on the death of the previous bishop. Some years later Bishop Varnava approached the Holy Synod with the request that one of his predecessors at Tobolsk should be canonized. After much opposition and argument, the canonization took place and a former Bishop John became St John of Tobolsk.

In the summer of 1916 the Empress wanted to visit the new saint's shrine, but unable to go herself, sent Lili Dehn and Anna Vyroubova.

When I arrived at Petrograd [says Lili] I discovered that Rasputin was to travel with us. I could not help thinking that, in view of popular feeling, it was most ill-advised to advertise the expedition, but I dared not suggest this. We left Petrograd in the greatest publicity. A special saloon carriage was attached to the train—it was a progress of publicity, wires were sent in advance all along the line to announce our advent, and crowds thronged the stations to catch a glimpse of us.

At last, late in the evening, we arrived at Tyumen and from there we took the steamer to Tobolsk. Little did I dream that in a year's time, the Imperial family were to make the same pilgrimage—of which the whole journey was to prove indeed a Via Dolorosa! They too were to see the black, swiftly flowing river, and the wild Tartar villages on its banks, and, like myself, they were to see the city on the mountain, with its churches and houses sharply silhouetted against the fast darkening sky.

We were received at Tobolsk by the Governor, the chief officials, and the Church dignitary, Varnava, and we were afterwards taken to our quarters in the Governor's house, where I slept in the little room which the Emperor, a year later, used as his study. The next day we visited the saint's grave and attended a very impressive service in the cathedral. Rasputin stayed with the priest, but unfortunately he quarrelled with Varnava, so matters became somewhat strained, and I was not sorry when our two days' visit came to an end.

On the way back to Tyumen Rasputin made a point of us stopping at his village and seeing his wife. I was rather intrigued at this as I had always wondered how and where he lived, and I felt quite interested when I saw the dark grey carved wooden house which was the home of Rasputin. The village consisted of a group of small wooden houses built on two floors. Rasputin's house was perhaps a little larger than the others, and he said that he hoped one day Their Majesties would visit him. 'But it's too far,' I said, aghast at the proposal. Rasputin was angry. 'They must,' he declared and a few minutes afterwards he added the prophetic words: 'Willing or unwilling, they will come to Tobolsk and they will see my village before they die.'

We remained one day at Rasputin's house. His wife was a charming, sensible woman and the peasants were a fine type—honest, simple folk who cultivated the fields belonging to Rasputin and accepted no payment—working absolutely in the spirit of holiness. Rasputin had three children—the two girls were being educated in Petrograd, but the boy was quite a peasant. Everyone was friendly but most of the villagers were strongly against Rasputin returning to Petrograd.

As we had decided to go on to Ekaterinburg and from there to Verkhoture, I thought it would be a good idea to persuade Rasputin to remain with his people. This he refused to do. I told Anna that there must be no more gossip and that she must persuade Rasputin to leave us. She promised to do so, but at the last moment he went with us to Ekaterinburg. I shall never forget my first impression of this fatal town. Directly we got out of the train I felt a sense of calamity. We were all affected: Rasputin was ill at ease, Anna perceptibly nervous and I was heartily glad when we reached the Convent of Verkhoture, which is situated on the left bank of the river Tura. We stayed a night in the guest-house attached to the Convent and then Rasputin asked us to go into the woods with him to visit a hermit who was locally supposed to be a very holy man.

The hermit in the heart of the forest and his hermitage might easily have been taken for a poultry farm. He was surrounded by fowls of all sizes and descriptions. He gave quantities of eggs to the Convent, but we supped frugally off cold water and black bread. The hermit had no use for beds, so we slept miserably on the hard, unyielding floor of dried mud, and I must confess that I was glad when we returned to Verkhoture and were able to sleep and bath in comfort.

They returned to Petrograd without Rasputin and found the town was filled with the most appalling gossip about Rasputin, and that the name of the Tsaritsa was drawn into every nasty, salacious remark made. Anna's name was drawn into it too. It was now being said that she too was Rasputin's mistress.

Rasputin returned to Petrograd a week or two later. Deeply concerned about the ceaseless, nauseating gossip, the Empress sent a telegram to Lili, who was in Reval, to return urgently. 'Why does Grigori stay in Petrograd?' she said. 'We can't possibly discard him. He has done no wrong.'

At the Empress's suggestion Lili went with Anna to Rasputin's apartment in the Gorokhovaya. He was not alone. It was tea time and he was surrounded by a small crowd of admirers. Among them was a Sister of Charity, Akilina Laptinsky, who, it was later discovered, was in fact a secret agent of the revolutionaries. With all his perceptive gifts, Grigori did not even suspect it, which merely confirms the belief that his extrasensory powers were failing. Lili, who knew her only as a Sister of Charity until the outbreak of the Revolution, felt that she had a great affection for Grigori.

On entering the room where the guests were having tea, she asked Grigori if she could speak to him privately. 'Certainly,' he said, but as he rose from the table, Akilina rose too and followed them into the next room.

Though annoyed, Lili said bluntly, 'Grigori, you must leave Petrograd at once. You can pray for Their Majesties equally well in Siberia. You know what is being said. For their sakes go.'

'Perhaps thou art right,' he said. 'I'm sick and tired of it all. I'll go.'

But Akilina, with rage in her eyes, banged her fist on the table and shouted: 'How *dare* you try and control the Father's spirit. I say that he *must* stay. Who are you? You are insignificant to judge what is best for anyone.'

Anna, who had come into the adjoining room with them, began to cry. Rasputin, surprisingly looking quite helpless, turned to Akilina and said: 'Perhaps thou art right. I shall stay.'

Lili, who had seen her quite often, felt that Akilina was occasionally ashamed of her Judas-like role. On one occasion, when Lili was at the railway station seeing Rasputin leave for Pokrovskoe, Akilina was there too and burst into tears as the train steamed out. 'Whatever is the matter?' Lili asked her. 'You will see the Father again.' But Akilina could not stop crying. 'Ah—you know *nothing*. If you only knew—if you only knew what I know.' It was mystifying. She apparently knew of something concerning Rasputin which terrified her.

CHAPTER THIRTY-THREE

Rasputin Tries to Stop Revolution

In Petrograd, Bernard Pares tells us, everything was growing fouler and more rotten every day, and at general headquarters, which he visited repeatedly, there was a nest of intrigues and jealousies. The morale at the Front at any rate was high, despite the very heavy losses —200,000 men lost in the summer fighting: 'Every shell it has lacked has been paid for in blood,' stated the senior British military attaché Major-General Sir Alfred Knox in his book *With the Russian Army*. The high morale at the Front was chiefly due to the work done by the War Minister Polivanov and by Guchkov through the War Industries Committees which Guchkov had organized. Knox regarded Polivanov as undoubtedly the ablest military organizer in Russia, and the formidable Hindenburg, one of the greatest leaders of the German army, declared that Polivanov had in fact restored the Russian army. Of course they had received most generous help from their allies, Britain and France; but to Polivanov was due the miraculous and speedy improvement in the supply of munitions and the training of the troops.

To the Empress none of this meant anything. 'Get rid of Polivanov,' she told the Tsar in a letter as early as October 1915. This the Tsar ignored, but other letters followed: 'Remember about Polivanov' and 'Lovy, don't dawdle', until at last the Tsar gave in. No letter of thanks was sent with his dismissal. The note the Tsar sent to Polivanov stated: 'The work of the War Industries Committees does not inspire one with confidence, and your supervision of them I find insufficiently authoritative.' The man recommended by the Empress, General Belaiyev, a subordinate in the office, had been exempting the protégés of the Empress and Anna Vyroubova from military service. The Tsar insisted on making his own choice and chose General Shuvayev, who was far better suited to the job. For Guchkov the Empress had an even greater hatred. Her letters to the Tsar are strewn with such phrases about him: 'Oh, could not one hang Guchkov?' 'Could not a strong railway accident be arranged in which he alone will suffer?' 'Guchkov is very ill— wish he would go—it's not a sinful wish.'

These frequent changes in the Government bewildered the public, weakened the authority of the ministers and made planning almost

impossible, for one did not know if he would be long enough in office
to carry them out.

> A bird of passage! Look around—
>   The gossip of the town is new;
> You'll see your Minister uncrowned
>   Within a month—or rarely two.
> By minutes now we count their term:
>   They go and leave a sulphurous smell. . . .*

The Empress was responsible for these continuous changes. In her
letters she kept up an hysterical assault on her husband and strangled
him with her love. At times he finds he can't take any more of it. 'I cannot keep on changing my mind once a fortnight,' he told her. Trepov,
whom he had made Minister of Transport, was appointed to succeed
Stürmer as Prime Minister: Stürmer had been summarily dismissed on
the advice of the Tsar's mother, the Dowager Empress Marie. Surprisingly the Tsaritsa had agreed, for she had grown tired of Stürmer: he
lacked courage, she said. Now a new Minister of the Interior was being
sought. Rasputin suggested Protopopov to the Tsaritsa because he had
an ikon, which he relied on to guide his decisions. 'I do nothing without Him,' Protopopov said. But others had already suggested Protopopov to the Empress. A member of the gentry, but deeply in debt,
Protopopov had studied law and been elected to the Duma, of which
he became vice-president. Guchkov thought well of him and regarded
him as a man who could get things done. In the summer of 1916 the
Duma was invited to send a deputation to England and France; Rodzianko, the President, unable to go himself, got Protopopov to lead it:
shortly after his return, Rodzianko told the Tsar that Protopopov
would make a good Minister of Commerce. The Tsar did not think
much of it. Protopopov's health was not good and, after a prolonged
course of treatment by Badmayev, he went to see Rasputin and asked
for his help.

Ever since Rasputin had mentioned Protopopov to the Empress the
bombardment of the Tsar had continued: 'Grigori begs you earnestly
to name Protopopov. . . . He likes our Friend since at least four years';

---

* Poem by Vladimir Purishkevich, a member of the Duma. Translated into English by
Bernard Pares.

and two days later: 'Please take Protopopov as Minister of the Interior. As he is one of the Duma, it will make a great effect and shut their mouths.' The Tsar was having too much of it and replied sharply: 'Our Friend's opinions of people are sometimes very strange, as you know yourself—therefore one must be careful.' The very next day she wrote again, and the Tsar, unable to take any more, replied by telegram: 'It shall be done.'

The Duma and even Rodzianko were enraged. Rodzianko spoke to Protopopov, who was servile in his manner and hinted that he could get Rodzianko made Prime Minister and Foreign Minister—which, of course, the Empress would never have tolerated.

Rodzianko said: 'Here are my terms. I shall choose my own colleagues. My term of office must be guaranteed for three years and the Empress must be sent to Livadia (the Imperial Palace in the Crimea) and kept there until the end of the war.'

Towards the end of the following month, October 1916, it became quite obvious that revolution could no longer be avoided. The most serious problems that faced the Government were food, transport and fuel. The Empress, who had for more than a year been running the country in the absence of the Tsar, tried to tackle these problems without understanding anything about them, continually moaning that her head went round and round while trying to take in the details given to her. Rasputin, with a clearer brain, and himself one of the masses, had a very thorough understanding of what *must* be done, and set out the essential means of tackling the problems:

Food—The rations should be weighed in advance to prevent the people having to wait for long hours in the queues, for it is during this wearying, distressing wait that their discontent develops and their minds become responsive to the calls of the revolutionists.

The Peasants—The Tsar must stand primarily for the peasants and should receive deputations from the peasants quite frequently.

Demobilization—Very serious problems will arise when demobilization comes. An enormous loan should be raised now to deal with it. This alone would not be enough; State and monastery lands should be appropriated for the demobilized men, and the manors of the nobility should be taken over and turned into schools.

Tolerance—There must be tolerance for all religions and races. The blood of the minorities is precious and the Tsar must give them all his fullest protection. Jew-baiting and the slaughter of men, women and children by *pogroms* has gone on for too long, it has always been popular with the Court and was used as a diversion at a time of national stress. This *must* be stopped.

A sound prescription, but it was not adopted and the hands of the clock moved on to the hour of twelve. On 29 October all the factories in the capital went on strike. The police were called to suppress the strike; two regiments of the Petrograd garrison, sent to support them, refused to shoot the strikers and turned their guns on the police. Four regiments of Cossacks were then brought up: they drove the Petrograd garrison mutineers back to their barracks, where 150 of them were shot. This led to another strike in the factories.

A police report on the period 14 October to 14 November states:

In the opinion of the spokesmen of the labour group of the Central War Industries Committee, the industrial proletariat of the capital is on the verge of despair, and it believes that the smallest outbreak, due to any pretext, will lead to uncontrollable riots, with thousands and tens of thousands of victims. Indeed, the stage for such outbreaks is more than set: the economic position of the masses, in spite of the immense increase in wages, is distressing. . . . Even if we assume that wages have increased 100 per cent, the cost of living has risen by an average of 300 per cent. The impossibility of obtaining, even for cash, many foodstuffs and articles of prime necessity, the waste of time involved in spending hours waiting in line in front of stores, the increasing morbidity due to inadequate diet and anti-sanitary lodgings (cold and dampness as a result of lack of coal and firewood), etc.—all these conditions have created such a situation that the mass of industrial workers are quite ready to let themselves go to the wildest excesses of a hunger riot. . . . The prohibition of all labour meetings, even those for the organization of co-operative stores and dining-rooms, the closing of trade unions, the prosecution of men taking an active part in the sick benefit funds, the suspension of labour newspapers, and so on, make the labouring masses, led by the more advanced and already revolutionary-minded elements, assume an openly hostile attitude towards the Government and protest with all the means at their disposal against the continuation of the war. Revolutionary circles have no doubts that a revolution will begin soon, that its unmistakable precursors are already here, and that the Government will prove incapable of fighting against the revolutionary masses, which are the more dangerous because they consist largely of soldiers or former soldiers.

The Tsar remained at headquarters instead of returning to tackle the crisis. The British ambassador, Sir George Buchanan, went there to impress upon him how serious the disorders in the capital were and, at the same time, to warn him against the dangerous consequences of repression. Grave warning was also given to the Tsar by his mother, the Dowager Empress, whom he went to see in Kiev. The warnings, unfortunately, had no effect. The new Prime Minister, Trepov, though a man of great ability, did not want the job, but he accepted it after being assured that drastic changes would be made in the Cabinet. The real trouble, he said, lay with Protopopov, and the Tsar agreed. Informing the Empress of this, the Tsar added: 'I am sorry for Prot.—he is a good, honest man, but he jumps from one side to another, and cannot make up his mind about anything. I noticed that from the beginning. It is risky to leave the Ministry of the Interior in such hands in these times.' On reading this the Empress got into a frenzy. 'Don't go and change Protopopov now. . . . It is for you and Baby I fight.' And the next day: 'I am but a woman fighting for her Master and her child. Darling, remember that it does not lie in the men, Protopopov and XYZ. I am fighting for your reign and Baby's future.' She set out for headquarters straightaway, and once again she won. Protopopov remained in office.

CHAPTER THIRTY-FOUR

The Murder of Rasputin

Some years earlier Prince Felix Yussupov, a childhood friend of Anna Vyroubova's—they used to attend ballet classes together—had been introduced by her to Rasputin. Through his mother the family was of Tartar origin and Moslem by religion, but later became Christian. By a fortunate marriage his grandfather (illegitimate and only a commoner) took his wife's title and became Count Soumarkov; then *his* son, on marrying Princess Yussupov adopted her title. The family were by now the richest in Russia. They had three palaces in Petrograd and others in Moscow and in the Crimea; young Felix, who declared with pride that he had his first sexual experience at the age of twelve, was sent to Oxford for his education, and on his return, just before the war, married the Tsar's niece Princess Irina. He was in the *Corps des Pages*, the training college for higher official posts in the army, but was not called up for military service.

Rasputin had met him again in the summer of 1916 through Maria Golovina and her pretty young daughter Mounia, both of whom were related to the Princess Paley and to Anna Vyroubova and were very close friends of Felix's. The meeting was sought by Felix, who said he had been unwell and would like Rasputin to cure him. They saw a lot of each other and a close friendship developed. Felix went often to his apartment and was affectionately addressed by Grigori as 'The Little One'.

Yussupov stated afterwards that he had contemplated murdering Rasputin for more than a year, and had established an intimate relationship with him so that he could get to know him well, receive his trust and possibly affection (both of which in fact he did receive), and not be suspected of involvement in any plot, for Rasputin, he felt, must have been aware that quite a number of people had plans to murder him.

On 16 November 1916 Purishkevich, a member of the Duma and an ardent monarchist, dined with the Tsar at army headquarters and likened the Government of Russia to that of Turkey and its various caliphs. It was obvious that he was boiling with indignation; and a fortnight later, on 1 December, Purishkevich launched in the Duma a powerful attack against the Government and denounced Rasputin as the destroyer of the dynasty. Felix Yussupov was present and was roused by the speech. Purishkevich said: 'As before there burns in me an endless love for my country and an unbounded and deeply loyal love for my sovereign.' But the time had come, he added, for the tocsin to be sounded from the belfry of Ivan the Great in the central tower of the Kremlin in Moscow. Contemptuous sneers were showered by him on the ministerial leapfrog and the dark forces that were behind it. Protopopov was reduced to a figure of jest and denounced as a contributor to the infamy of Russian life. 'If you are truly loyal,' he told the ministers, 'if the glory of Russia, her mighty future, which is closely and inseparably bound up with the brightness of the name of the Tsar, is dear to you, be off to headquarters, throw yourself at the feet of the Tsar and beg his leave to open his eyes to the awful reality.'

The Tsar spent a few days in Tsarskoe Selo from 8 to 17 December. The moment he returned to headquarters he received a letter from the Empress. 'Take no big steps without warning me,' she wrote. 'Not a responsible Cabinet, which all are mad about . . . Russia loves to feel the whip. How I wish I could pour my will into your veins.' She next sent him a list of the ministers and ex-ministers who should be sent to Siberia—Lvov, Milyukov, Guchkov and Polivanov. Her last letter to him, dated 17 December old style,* 30 December by modern reckoning, ends with the words: 'Felix came often to Him lately'—meaning Rasputin. She knew that much and suspected nothing.

Rasputin's daughter Maria says: 'Six months earlier Felix Yussupov came to the apartment, said he was suffering from a malady and asked Rasputin to cure him. He was lithe, elegant, rather affected in his manner. His nobility was of recent date: the title of Prince had been in the family for two generations only.' He showed Rasputin great affection, she adds, and came to the apartment at night in secrecy. Purishkevich also came to see her father, she says.

Particularly in the early part of 1916, when a change of Ministry was foreseen, Purishkevich sought my father's help to gain him his nomination as Minister of the Interior. He flattered my father and paid court to him after a fashion, hoping thus to gain his support and that of the Tsaritsa, the Tsar being at the Front at the time. My

---

* The Russian calendar was at that time thirteen days behind the Western calendar; it was not adjusted until 1924.

father's antipathy for Purishkevich increased with the frequency of their meetings. He had a horror of 'phrase-makers' in general and in particular of that health officer who made violent speeches glorifying the carnage of the war.★ So he refused to uphold the candidature of the Bessarabian representative and the latter's ambitions received a blow which provoked in him a veritable hatred of my father.

Anna Vyroubova states that for more than a month Rasputin had been thinking constantly of death. The last time the Tsar saw him was in November 1916 in Anna's house, and

> I heard every word of their conversation. The Emperor was de-
> pressed and pessimistic. Owing to heavy storms and lack of trans-
> portation facilities there had been difficulty in getting foodstuffs into
> Petrograd and even some army battalions were lacking certain neces-
> sities. Nature itself, said the Emperor, seemed to be working against
> Russia's success in the war, to which Rasputin replied, strongly ad-
> vising the Emperor never to give up the struggle. The country that
> held out the longest against adverse circumstances, he said, would
> certainly win the war. As Rasputin was leaving the house the Em-
> peror asked him, as usual, for his blessing, but Rasputin replied:
> 'This time it is for you to bless me, not I you.' Finally at parting he
> humbly begged the Emperor to do everything he could on behalf of
> the wounded and of war orphans, reminding him that all Russia was
> giving its nearest and dearest for his sake.

Yussupov, uncertain how to carry out his plan of murder, got in touch with Basil Maklakov, a lawyer, an outstanding member of the Duma and a brilliant orator. Maklakov dismissed the idea with 'He might easily be replaced by another Rasputin.' Felix disagreed. 'In a fortnight,' he said, 'the Empress will be in a mental home and the Tsar will become a good constitutional sovereign.' Felix discussed it next with Purishkevich, who revealed that he too was planning to murder Rasputin. Soon the two conspirators added a third—the Grand Duke Dimitri Povlovich, aged twenty-six, a first cousin of the Tsar, whom he called 'uncle' because of the big difference in their ages. He was constantly at the Palace and there was some thought that he might marry the Tsar's eldest daughter Olga. Two more conspirators were

---

★ Purishkevich had an ambulance train for the wounded and served on it himself.

added—a young army officer Captain Sukhotin, well-known in Petrograd society, and Dr Stanislas Lazovert, a friend of Purishkevich, who felt he would be helpful with the poisons. The five met in Purishkevich's ambulance train and in the cellar of Yussupov's magnificent palace on the Moika Canal, which Yussupov tells us, was being beautifully decorated and furnished to look like the rest of the house. Felix's parents were away, his wife Irina was in their palace in the Crimea, so the conspirators had the place entirely to themselves for the murder.

All agreed that they would not breathe a word about it to anyone, either before or after the crime had been committed. But a day or so later Purishkevich elbowed his way to Maklakov in the crowded lobby of the Duma and revealed to him the details of their plan and even gave him the date. Shortly afterwards Maklakov was approached by one of the Duma journalists, a woman named Becker, who gave him the full details of the plot, given to her, she said, by Purishkevich. Next, while being treated by his doctor, Purishkevich, unable to keep quiet, revealed the entire plot to him too. It is puzzling that, with so many in the know, not even a hint of it reached Rasputin or his friends.

The date chosen for the murder was 16 December 1916 by the Russian calendar, 29 December by the Western calendar.

Felix Yussupov invited Rasputin to his home to meet his wife, Irina, who was anxious, he said, to make his acquaintance. Rasputin accepted and was told by Felix that he would be calling for him at midnight. 'I would not like this to get about,' Felix added. 'I don't want my parents to know about it. I'll come up the back stairs for you.'

Rasputin's daughter Maria states that, for some time, the police had redoubled their watchfulness and it had annoyed her father. 'My sister Varvara and I had been warned that he was in danger and begged him not to go out too often. On this night, in order to force him to stay at home, my sister and I hid his boots before we went to bed.' When her father said goodnight, she saw that he had on his light blue blouse and the velvet breeches he wore for evening parties, and asked him if he was going out. Quite casually he replied that he had been invited to Yussupov's house.

A little earlier that evening Anna Vyroubova arrived with an ikon the Empress had brought back from Novgorod* for Rasputin. She was surprised when he told her that he was going to Felix's house. 'I knew

---

* The first capital of Russia, about 100 miles south of Petrograd. Not to be confused with Nijni-Novgorod.

that Felix had often visited Rasputin, but it struck me as odd that he should go to their house for the first time at such an unseemly hour.' When Anna mentioned it to the Tsaritsa, she said: 'There must be some mistake. Irina is in the Crimea.' Immediately after Anna left Rasputin's apartment, Protopopov arrived and was surprised to find that the triple police guard he had placed on it had been dismissed. He did his best to prevent Rasputin going to see Yussupov that night.

When the back-door bell was rung, Katya opened it and led Felix through the kitchen to the bedroom. Felix, who knew the apartment well, says the bedroom was very simply furnished. 'In the corner, close to the wall, was a narrow bed with a red-fox bedspread, a present from Anna Vyroubova. Near the bed was a chest of painted wood; in the opposite corner were ikons before which burned a small lamp. Portraits of the Tsar and Tsaritsa hung on the walls along with crude engravings representing Biblical scenes.' He noticed that Rasputin was wearing a silk blouse that night, with a thick raspberry-coloured cord as a belt. 'He had brushed his hair and carefully combed his beard. As he came close to me I smelt a strong odour of cheap soap.' Grigori, unable to find his boots, got Katya to look for them. 'The girls must have hidden them,' he told Felix. 'The study,' states Felix, 'was a small room with a sofa, a few leather armchairs and a large table littered with papers.' In the dining-room, the samovar was bubbling. There were glass bowls on the table with fruit and jam and biscuits and a large basket of flowers. The furniture here was of massive oak, the chairs had very high backs and there was a large dresser laden with crockery. By now Grigori and the maid Katya had found the boots. He put them on and was escorted by his murderer down the back stairs.

When they arrived at the large, attractive Yussupov palace facing the Moika Canal, Felix took him straightaway into the cellar with its low-vaulted ceiling, the walls of grey stone and the floor of granite. The furniture consisted of some carved wooden chairs, small tables covered with embroidery, a cabinet of inlaid ebony with a number of little mirrors, and an Italian sixteenth-century crucifix of rock crystal standing on it. On the floor an enormous Persian carpet had been laid for the evening, a white bearskin rug was placed in front of the cabinet, and right in the middle of the room was a table with a smoking samovar at which Rasputin was to sit. It was a bitterly cold night; snow lay thick on the ground outside and it was comforting to see a log fire scattering sparks on the hearthstones.

Before going out to fetch Rasputin, Felix had assembled his fellow conspirators in the cellar. They had decided to use poison, because, they felt, it would leave no trace of murder. 'The cakes and other dainties,' which Yussupov states 'Rasputin liked so much', were placed on the table. He ought to have known, as he had taken tea with Rasputin many times in the apartment and also at the home of the Golovinas, that Rasputin *never* ate cake. Everyone who knew him was well aware of that. Nevertheless Felix watched the doctor put on rubber gloves and grind the cyanide of potassium crystals into powder. Then he sliced the top of each cake, spread the powder thickly on it and replaced the top. They had agreed, while this was being done, to put a sufficient dose of cyanide in each cake to kill several men instantly. Poison was poured into the wine glasses selected for Rasputin's use.

As Rasputin entered the cellar he turned to Felix and said: 'You know* how I am being slandered. Remember how Christ was perse-cuted. He too suffered for the sake of truth.' He paused then. He could hear voices upstairs and a phonograph was playing *Yankee Doodle*.

'What's all this?' said Rasputin. 'Is someone giving a party?'

'No. Just my wife entertaining a few friends. They're going soon.'

Guided to the table, he was offered the poisoned cakes. Rasputin re-fused, then, according to Yussupov, changed his mind and ate two. Nothing happened. Felix was then asked for some madeira. It was handed to him in one of the glasses containing poison, and more was poured out for him in another of the poisoned glasses. Felix, waiting for him to fall off his chair, groan and toss with agony, was baffled. All Rasputin did was to ask for some tea. While sipping it, he asked Felix to play his guitar and sing some of the gipsy songs Felix loved. The other four conspirators, huddled at the top of the cellar stairs, wondered what was going on.

Rasputin's daughter Maria, does not accept that this is what hap-pened. It is Yussupov's version. Purishkevich, who also wrote about it, gives a somewhat different version. Maria, of course was not there. 'I'm positive,' she says, 'that my father did not eat the poisoned cakes, for he had a horror of sweet things.' As for the wine, 'doubtless the poison had not dissolved. . . . I am convinced that certain details given by the assassins were added partly to make the story more picturesque and partly to excuse the slaughter; for since it was a question of doing

---

* As stated in Yussupov's book. Rasputin would have said 'Thou knowest'.

away with a being whose devilish vitality resisted cyanide, it would be understandable that the five conspirators, in their terror, should riddle him with bullets.'

Now we come to Yussupov's account of the shooting. It was by now 2.30 a.m.: they had been two hours in the cellar. A noise upstairs made Rasputin turn and ask what it was. Glad to get away for a moment, Felix rushed up the stairs. Dimitri said he was tired and wanted to go home. Purishkevich said: 'We cannot leave him down there half dead.' Yussupov asked Dimitri for his revolver and returned to the cellar to complete the murder. He found Rasputin breathing heavily; slowly he turned and asked for more wine. After drinking it, he began staring at the cabinet. Leading him up to it, Felix said: 'Grigori Efimovich, look at the crucifix and say a prayer.' Rasputin glared at him, then as he turned to the crucifix, Felix fired. The bullet pierced his back in the region of his heart. With a terrifying scream Rasputin fell backwards on to the white bearskin.

On hearing this the other conspirators came rushing down the stairs. Rasputin's features, Felix states, kept twitching in spasms and bloodstains were spreading on his silk blouse. Then suddenly Rasputin's figure became quite still. Dr Lazovert examined the body and said he was dead. The army officer, Captain Sukhotin, put on Rasputin's heavy fur coat and drove off with Dimitri in Purishkevich's open car to give the impression that they were taking Rasputin home. Meanwhile Yussupov, relieved that the worst was over, had returned the revolver to Dimitri and was taking a last look at the corpse on the floor. He thought he saw an eyelid quiver . . . then there appeared to be slight tremors on the face. It *couldn't* be; it must be his own nervous imagination. He decided to see if there was any life left in Rasputin when, to his horror, he saw the corpse rise and leap at him with a wild roar. 'Trying to get my throat, he sank his fingers into my shoulder. I was powerless. By superhuman effort I succeeded in freeing myself. He fell on his back, gasping and still holding in his hand the epaulette torn from my shoulder.' He lay motionless for a while, then he moved again and Yussupov, terrified, rushed up the stairs, calling to Purishkevich.

As soon as he reached the top, he heard a sound behind him and, turning quickly, saw Rasputin climbing up the stairs on his hands and knees. Numbed with fear, Felix waited on the landing above, saw Rasputin open the door and crawl out into the courtyard.

Purishkevich rushed out after him, and now takes up the story.

What I saw would have been a dream if it hadn't been a terrible reality. Rasputin, who half an hour before lay dying in the cellar, was running quickly across the snow-covered courtyard towards the iron gate which led to the street. I couldn't believe my eyes. But a harsh cry which broke the silence of the night persuaded me. 'Felix! Felix! I will tell everything to the Empress,' the voice said. It was him all right—Rasputin. In a few seconds he would reach the iron gate. I fired. The night echoed with the shot. I missed. I fired again. Again I missed. Rasputin neared the gate. I bit with all my force the end of my left hand to force myself to concentrate and I fired a third time. The bullet hit him in the shoulders. He stopped. I fired a fourth time and hit him probably in the head. I ran up and kicked him as hard as I could with my boot in the temple. He fell into the snow, tried to rise, but he could only grind his teeth.

Yussupov then appeared with a rubber club and beat the dying *staretz* frantically with it, the snow becoming more and more crimson with his blood. The body was quite still by the time the beating stopped. A blue curtain was fetched from the house, the body was rolled into it and bound with a rope. The Moika quay in front of the Yussupov palace and the adjacent streets were quite deserted. A policeman approached the house and spoke to two of the servants. Felix agreed to see him. 'It was only horse-play,' he said, and added that one of them had shot a dog. Going back to the dead body after the policeman had left he found that Rasputin had changed his position.

A police constable now arrived. Purishkevich went up to him. The constable said they had heard the sound of the shots at the police station.

'Do you know who I am?' said Purishkevich, then with boastful pride he added: 'I am Vladimir Mitrophanovich Purishkevich, a member of the Duma. The shots you heard killed Rasputin. If you love your country and your Tsar, you'll keep your mouth shut.'

A few minutes later Dimitri, Sukhotin and Dr Lazovert returned in the open car, picked up the body wrapped and bound in the blue curtain, placed it in a closed car and drove off to Petrovsky Bridge, the place chosen for burying the body in the frozen river Neva. They spotted there a sentry box they had not noticed before. Not knowing that the sentry was asleep, they turned off the car engine, switched off the lights and, anxious to get away as quickly as possible, they hurled the body from the bridge into the river: it cracked the ice and disappeared. As they turned the car to leave, they noticed that in their panic they had forgotten to attach the weights to the body. Not wanting them to be found in their possession, they threw the weights out of the car, then noticed one of his snowboots, which was thrown out too. When they returned to Yussupov's palace, they noticed that the other snowboot was still in the car. They burned it. Apparently they did nothing about the blood-stains on the floor of the car.

Quite a different version of the murder, stating that some women were present at Yussupov's as well as two other grand dukes, was given by Aaron Simanovich, who had been closely associated with Rasputin for many years and saw him almost every day. In his book *Rasputin— the Almighty Peasant* he says:

At midnight I received a telephone call from Rasputin during which he told me he had been invited by Yussupov to his palace. I realized at once that Rasputin was in danger and I implored him not to go. He nevertheless insisted that he would and promised to telephone me again at 2 a.m. to set my mind at rest. When no call had come by 3 a.m., my son Joann and I set out to look for him. We enlisted the aid of Minister Protopopov, who organized a search-party. On arrival at the Yussupov palace, we were told by the night-watchman that he had heard shots in the house earlier and was almost certain that Rasputin had been murdered.

What actually happened we were told later by a cousin of Yussupov's, who herself had fired a shot at Rasputin. Those involved in the plot, among others, were Grand Duke Dimitri Pavlovich and two sons of Grand Duke Alexander Mikhailovich.* As Rasputin entered all assembled fired at him with the exception of Vera Koralli, a dancer and cousin of Yussupov's. Rasputin fell to the floor and, thinking him dead, the plotters bundled him into his coat and took him down to the cellar. Astonishingly Rasputin revived after a time, left the cellar and tried to climb out of the grounds over a high wall. This proved to be too much for him and he fell back unconscious. Dogs found him and their barking brought the household to the scene.

---

* He was the father of Princess Irina and had six sons who were brothers-in-law of Felix Yussupov. Felix states in his book that, being alone in Petrograd, he had been staying with his brothers-in-law and had dined at their house on the day of the murder.

That means that there was a party, which would have been normal in that house and would have attracted far less attention than the arrival of five solemn male conspirators. It also suggests that the cellar was not decorated and given a theatrical setting for the murder: that in itself would have attracted considerable attention and chatter among the household staff, and would have made it more difficult to keep secret: the way Purishkevich and Felix went about it, talking to Maklakov and others quite openly, even in the Duma foyer, before the murder, secrecy did not seem to matter. The barking of the dogs led to the shooting of one of them, which explains why the policeman was told about it.

Rasputin was forty-four years old.

'Rasputin is Missing'

Early the next morning Katya awakened Rasputin's daughters Maria and Varvara to tell them that their father had not come home. 'Some evil has overtaken your father,' she said. 'I feel that something has happened to him.'

Maria and her sister got down on their knees and prayed that he was safe and then tried to find out why he hadn't come home.

Maria phoned Yussupov. He said he knew nothing about him. 'I insisted,' says Maria, 'that Katya had opened the door to him and that she had seen her father go out with him. He then contradicted his first story and said that he had in fact come to fetch my father, but had only gone with him to the Villa Rode where they were going to join some friends and where he doubtless still was. At the Villa Rode they told me they had not seen my father the evening before.' She then phoned Mounia Golovina, but she had no news of him and came over immediately. A telephone call from Protopopov, the Minister of the Interior, inquired if her father had come home or if she knew where he had been the night before. Anna Vyroubova phoned next. At the same moment some police officers arrived and told Maria that shots had been fired at Yussupov's where a group of friends, including Purishkevich, had assembled.

Anna had informed the Empress that Rasputin was missing and she telephoned at once to the Tsar. Protopopov then phoned and said he had been informed by a constable that in the small hours he had heard a shot fired near the entrance to the Yussupov palace and Purishkevich, who was very drunk, said that it was 'nothing, nothing at all' and added that he had just killed Rasputin. 'I thought at first it was a joke,' said the constable. Yussupov and Dimitri Povlovich telephoned separately to ask to see the Empress. She refused to see them. Felix then wrote to her, 'swearing by the honour of his house' that they knew nothing about the disappearance of Rasputin and protesting against the unjust suspicions against them. 'He added,' says Anna, who had read the letter, 'that the rumour about Rasputin's visit to his house was without any foundation whatsoever. He had a party. All his guests got drunk and one, on leaving, shot a dog in the courtyard. The Empress passed the letter on to the Minister of Justice Makarov and ordered Protopopov to investigate the whole affair.'

Police were sent at once to Yussupov's house and found the body of a shot dog with a bullet hole in the head. This made the police even more suspicious, for the shooting of the dog could not account for 'the shambles of blood and disorder in the house', says Anna, or explain signs of 'a terrific struggle downstairs, on the stairs and in the upper room'.

An enormous number of detectives and police patrols were sent to scour all parts of the city within a radius centring on Yussupov's palace. Prince Dimitri's father, the Grand Duke Paul Alexandrovich, greatly disturbed by rumours that his son was involved in the murder, as it was now being called, of Rasputin, summoned his son and handed him a sacred family ikon and the photograph of his mother and asked him to swear that he was not involved. Holding in his hands the ikon and the photograph of his mother, Dimitri said: 'I swear it.'

Meanwhile Lili Dehn, who had arranged to visit Rasputin at five o'clock that afternoon, had a telephone call from the Empress. 'Don't go to Father Grigori's today, Lili,' she said. 'Something strange has happened. He disappeared last night—nothing has been heard of him since, but I'm sure it will be all right. Will you come to the Palace at once?'

On arriving she found the Empress lying on a couch in her mauve boudoir with her four daughters seated around her and Anna Vyroubova on a footstool. 'The Empress was very pale—her blue eyes were full of trouble, the young girls were silent and Anna had evidently been weeping. . . . She discountenanced any sinister conjectures, soothed the ever weeping Anna and told me to sleep in Anna's house tonight.' There had been threats that both Anna and the Empress would be murdered that night. Anna was given a room at the Palace and was kept well guarded.

The Tsaritsa then picked up her pen and resumed writing her letter of the 17/30 December to the Tsar.

My own beloved sweetheart—We are sitting together—you can imagine our feelings—thoughts—our Friend has disappeared. . . . I shall still trust in God's mercy that one has only driven Him off somewhere. Protopopov is doing all he can. I cannot and won't believe that he has been killed. God have mercy. . . . Come quickly.

Meanwhile both Dimitri and Felix were placed by the Tsaritsa under house arrest. The day passed without the police finding any revealing clue. The next day, 31 December by the Western calendar, was also fruitless. It was not until the following morning, 1 January 1917, that Joann, the son of Aaron Simanovich, the boy Rasputin had cured of St Vitus's dance and now aged twenty, noticed a snowboot lying on the ice and recognized it as Rasputin's. It was an important clue.

The police had begun by following the marks of motor-car tyres in the snow, leading out of the Yussupov palace. A number of tyre tracks were made by the cars used by some of the conspirators, before, during and after the murder. One led to the railway station, where Purish-kevich had his ambulance train; another track set out with a conspirator disguised as Rasputin in an open car—the cars went in different directions to take home Dimitri, Dr Lazovert, Captain Sukhotin and Purish-kevich, while Felix made his various trips to relatives and friends in different parts of the city all through the day after the murder. The journey from Felix's palace to the remote Petrovsky Bridge involved taking the Nikolai Bridge across the Bolshaya Neva, then going right across the Vassili Ostrov island and crossing the Malaya Neva, then travelling westward along an elongated island at the remote end of which was Petrovsky Bridge. So the tyre marks had been unproductive. Had the boot not been found the quest might have gone on for weeks without success.

In a few minutes [writes Maria], after breaking the ice, it was possible to liberate the body of my father; completely frozen, wrapped in his fur-lined coat and with his ankles bound by rope. An hour later Protopopov sent a car from the Ministry for my sister and me.

Nothing will ever efface my impressions of the moment when I saw it—the vision of horror is still as clear as ever before my eyes. The body was taken to the little chapel of the Chesmé hospital where it was laid on a whitewood table. The face was almost unrecogniz-able, clots of dark blood had coagulated in the beard and hair; one eye was almost out of its socket, and on the wrists were deep marks left by bonds that my father had succeeded in breaking in his death struggle, probably when, reanimated by the sudden shock of freezing water, he had made a supreme effort to escape from his prison of ice. His hand still lay beneath his chin, contracted in a last sign of the Cross.

In the warmth of a nearby stove streams of melted ice trickled and dripped from the body on to the flagstones. His garments, frozen stiff, crackled at the least touch. Varvara and I shivered without being able to utter a word, while our tears in that icy air burned our eyes and our cheeks.

We had telegraphed to our mother in Siberia to come to the bedside of our father, seriously ill. She immediately set out, accompanied by my brother Mitia; but she learned of the murder on the boat through the newspapers that published an account of the inquest. The autopsy of the body had been commenced without our having been notified beforehand. I learned later that it was thus ascertained that none of the wounds was actually mortal and that my father might very possibly have recovered had his murderers not taken the precaution of drowning him.

It was found that his lungs were full of water, indicating that he had been still alive when thrown into the river. The Tsaritsa had stopped the autopsy. She shuddered when she was told about it and gave orders that these gruesome activities must stop. 'Just leave the body of Grigori Efimovich Rasputin in peace.'

Maria adds:

When my brother Dimitri left Petrograd to return to Pokrovskoe at the beginning of November, my father blessed him, saying: 'Good-bye, Mitia, I shall never see you again.' The last letter my mother received in Siberia from him in St Petersburg was written in November 1916, one month before he was killed. It is his farewell to the family.

In it he says:

My hour is very near, but although it is bitter I do not fear it. I will take the suffering upon myself and so gain the Eternal Kingdom. It will not be hard for you and your children; you will see them often but not for very long. Pray and be strong in your affection and you will all be saved. Pray to God. Prayer brings salvation and joy to the world—Grigori.

Another letter, written by him on the day before his murder, was entrusted to Simanovich for delivery to the Tsar after his death. Headed

'The Spirit of Grigori Efimovich Rasputin of the village of Pokrov-skoe', it states:

> I write and leave behind me this letter at St Petersburg. I feel that I shall leave life before 1 January. I wish to make known to the Russian people, to Papa, to the Russian Mother and to the Children, to the land of Russia what they must understand. If I am killed by common assassins, especially by my brothers the Russian peasants you, Tsar of Russia, have nothing to fear, remain on your throne and govern, and you, Russian Tsar, will have nothing to fear for your children, they will reign for hundreds of years in Russia. But if I am murdered by boyars, nobles, and if they shed my blood, their hands will remain soiled with my blood, for twenty-five years they will not wash their hands from my blood. They will leave Russia. Brothers will kill brothers, and they will kill each other and hate each other, and for twenty-five years there will be no nobles in the country. Tsar of the land of Russia, if you hear the sound of the bell which will tell you that Grigori has been killed, you must know this: if it was your relations who have wrought my death then no one of your family, that is to say none of your children or relations, will remain alive for more than two years. They will be killed by the Russian people. I go and I feel in me the divine command to tell the Russian Tsar how he must live if I have disappeared. You must reflect and act prudently. Think of your safety and tell your relations that I have paid for them with my blood. I shall be killed. I am no longer among the living. Pray, pray, be strong, think of your blessed family— Grigori.

Simanovich states that on reading the letter the Tsar was deeply depressed and after that appeared to lose the will to live. Bernard Pares was told by Simanovich that this letter was conveyed by him to the Empress with an entreaty not to show it to the Tsar. He also claims that the letter and many other notes of Rasputin's were later returned to him by the Empress, 'and I have seen in his possession,' states Pares, 'her prayer-book with her favourite sign of the swastika, which she appears to have had with her at the time of her own death'.

The Funeral

As soon as news of Rasputin's death became known there was wild, hysterical rejoicing in Petrograd and elsewhere; and Protopopov felt that there would be angry demonstrations unless the funeral took place quickly and privately. Rasputin's family wanted the body to be sent to his birthplace Pokrovskoe in Siberia.

Akilina Laptinsky came hurrying to the Palace when she heard this and told the Empress that he should be buried in Tsarskoe Selo. 'He should be buried in his own village,' the Empress said, but after listening to what Protopopov had to say, she decided that the wisest move would be to have a temporary burial at Tsarskoe Selo and send the body to Siberia when the demonstrations had died down and things were quieter.

Anna Vyroubova, who was prostrated with grief, was having a church and a hospital built in Tsarskoe Selo and suggested that Grigori should be buried in the central aisle of the unfinished church.

The Emperor returned from headquarters early on the morning of the funeral.

As I attended the burial [says Lili Dehn], I may say with absolute conviction that mine is a true account of the proceedings. I have been told and I have read various wholly inaccurate reports—the most prevalent being that Rasputin was buried secretly at dead of night at Tsarskoe Selo. Nothing of the kind. Rasputin's burial took place at eight o'clock on the morning of 3 January. It was a glorious morning, the sky was deep blue, the sun was shining and the hard snow sparkled like masses of diamonds: everything spoke of peace and I could hardly believe that I was about to witness the closing scene of one of the greatest scandals and tragedies in history.

My carriage stopped on the road some distance from the Observatory and I was directed to walk across a frozen field towards the unfinished church. Planks had been placed on the snow to serve as a footpath, and when I arrived at the church I found a police motorvan was drawn up near the open grave. After waiting several moments I heard the sound of sleighbells and Anna Vyroubova came slowly across the field. Almost immediately afterwards a closed automobile stopped and the Imperial family joined us. They were dressed in mourning. The Empress, who carried some flowers, was very pale but quite composed, although I saw her tears fall when the oak coffin was taken out of the police van. The coffin was perfectly plain. It bore no inscription, and only a cross outside it testified to the faith of the departed.

The ceremony proceeded—the burial service was read by the chaplain to the hospital and, after the Emperor and Empress had thrown earth on the coffin, the Empress distributed her flowers among the Grand Duchesses and ourselves and we scattered them on the coffin. When the last solemn words had been uttered the Imperial family left the church. Anna and I followed them. Anna got into her sledge, I into my carriage. It was barely nine o'clock. I looked back at the snowy fields, the bare walls of the unfinished church and I thought of the murdered man who was sleeping there. I felt an immense pity for his fate, but above all I felt an immense pity and love for those who had believed in him and befriended him in defiance of the world, and on whose innocent shoulders the burden of his follies was destined to rest.

Rasputin was not the villain of the novel and the film. In my eyes he was an uneducated man with a mission; he spoke an almost incomprehensible Siberian dialect, he could hardly read, he wrote like a child of four, and his manners were unspeakable. But he possessed both hypnotic and spiritual forces, believed in himself and made others do so. I am not ignorant of what has been said concerning his abnormal animalism, his satyr-like sensualities, the nameless orgies in which young women and young girls gave themselves as willing victims to his lust. The reports about his dress and extravagance are also very much exaggerated. Rasputin lived and died a poor man. He usually wore the dress of a peasant and his wonderful jewelled cross only exists in the brains of novelists and journalists. At first he wore a simple copper cross, later he wore one of gold and sent it to the Emperor at Headquarters. This gift in Russia is usually unwelcome as it signifies that you present with it the sorrows and sufferings synonymous with the Cross. The Emperor thought Rasputin's cross was unlucky and gave it back to me and asked me to give it to Anna, who also refused to accept it—so I mislaid it.

Apart from his own feelings over the death of Rasputin, what the Tsar felt more deeply was the grief of his wife, who had relied so much on the guidance obtained from God through Father Grigori. He was handed a large file of evidence collected by the police against the chief conspirators—his young cousin the Grand Duke Dimitri and Felix Yussupov, who was married to his niece Irina. 'I am filled with shame,' he said, 'that the hands of my kinsmen are stained with the blood of a simple peasant.' The older generation of grand dukes, led by Dimitri's father Paul, the son of Alexander II, the Liberator Tsar and the only surviving uncle of Nikolai II; and Alexander Mikhailovich, Irina's father, objected strongly to the house arrest imposed by the Empress on her own authority on Dimitri and Felix. No legal action was taken against any of them. The Tsar ordered Dimitri to leave Petrograd and serve with the Russian forces in Persia, which saved his life as it was easy after the Revolution broke out to escape from there. Yussupov was banished to one of his own magnificent estates in the centre of Russia: a year later he and his wife Irina managed to escape from Revolutionary Russia. Purishkevich was, surprisingly, allowed to go free. Alexei, deeply moved by the death of Rasputin, who had so often eased his suffering, turned angrily to his father: 'Papa, is it possible that you will not punish them? The assassins of Stolypin were hanged.'

Basil Maklakov, the distinguished member of the Duma, to whom first Yussupov and then Purishkevich revealed that they were going to murder Rasputin, states in the Foreword he wrote for Purishkevich's book *Comment j'ai tué Raspoutine*:

The announcement of Rasputin's death in the theatres provoked great enthusiasm: everyone began to sing the national anthem. But the changes they expected were never realized: the Empress did not withdraw from her political activities, indeed she became even more active: the political measures taken at the beginning of 1917, the promotions and the dismissals showed a pronounced swing to the Right. The most dedicated enemies of the Duma returned to the scene. But there were other developments that were even more alarming. What were the feelings and thoughts of all those people who for three years had poured out their blood for a cause which they only half understood, who, silent and suspicious, had been searching for the cause of their unhappiness that was oppressing and menacing them still. One thing is certain: they never thought as we did. A woman of the aristocracy, a few days after the assassination of Rasputin, visited a military hospital where she found herself among a large number of wounded soldiers. Still full of her joy, she went up to the beds of some of the wounded men. She waited to see the joy in their faces: she saw only a hostile silence. She was surprised. 'Yes,' one of the soldiers told her, 'only one peasant managed to get as far as the throne, and it was him that the aristocracy assassinated.' The murder of Rasputin stopped nothing, changed nothing: it added a fresh uneasiness to the feelings of the people—it hastened the catastrophe. The inevitable drew nearer.

CHAPTER THIRTY-SEVEN

The Tsaritsa and
Rasputin's Children

The Empress's distress lingered long after the death of Grigori. She felt that her own life had been shattered, but she was too determined a woman to sit and mope over what had been lost and could never be recalled. Those around her could see that she had been weeping, but they never saw her weep. She felt that the future had to be faced and she faced it with courage and determination, without realizing that the things she was doing would not help Russia at all, but would destroy the monarchy and the Russia she was trying to save.

The French ambassador, Maurice Paléologue, after a private audience with the Tsar, wrote in his diary: 'Nikolai II feels himself overwhelmed and dominated by events . . . that he has lost all faith in his mission . . . that he has abdicated inwardly and is now resigned to disaster.'* It did not seem to matter, for the Empress had already taken over. The main telephone was moved from the Tsar's desk into her boudoir and placed, oddly enough, just below the portrait of Marie Antoinette. In addition she began to eavesdrop on all who came to talk to the Tsar. Kokovtsev, who had been Prime Minister from 1911 to 1914, came to see the Tsar to talk about the Alexander Lyceum (the Russian Eton), of which he was Provost. He had the uneasy feeling that someone was eavesdropping. 'I thought that the door leading from the Tsar's study to his dressing-room was half open, which had never occurred before, and that someone was standing just inside.' The Tsar knew what was going on and had a staircase and a concealed balcony built, where the Empress could lie on a couch and listen in comfort.

The change of ministers went on as before. Trepov who had replaced Stürmer as Prime Minister in November, left in January and was replaced by Prince Nikolai Golitsin, whom the Empress liked, but could not claim that he had been chosen because 'He likes our Friend'. Golitsin, being elderly, begged the Tsar to find someone else. Purges were also made by the Empress in the Council of State, the approximate equivalent of the British House of Lords. She continued to rule the

---

* This suggests that the acute depression of the Tsar after reading Rasputin's letter was still with him.

country without advice or help. The decisions had always been made by her, and she had used Rasputin merely to get God's approval, confident that God would agree. Suggestions made by Rasputin, such as raising a huge State loan to help the soldiers on demobilization and appropriating State and monastery lands for them, seizing the manor houses of the nobility and converting them into schools, tolerance for all creeds, insistence that the Tsar should receive representatives of peasants at frequent intervals—all of it sound, all of it of the utmost advantage to the country and the people, for *these* recommendations by Rasputin the approval of God was not sought.

For the Empress the only minister who counted was Protopopov: he did not always bother to attend the Cabinet meetings, and, when he did, one or other of the ministers asked the Emperor to dismiss him. Many were convinced that, in addition to being quite inefficient, he was half mad, and it was generally believed that he had taken to holding spiritualist seances to seek guidance from Rasputin.

Rasputin's family was not forgotten. The Empress took them under her wing. 'It was arranged,' states Maria, 'that my sister and I should go to spend the day with the Grand Duchesses in Tsarskoe Selo'; then, embracing Rasputin's daughters affectionately, the Empress said: 'You must look now on the Tsar as your father.'

> Those were the only bright moments [Maria says], so many of my father's friends, so many of the constant visitors to our house forgot us. Grigori Rasputin being dead, they had no hope of obtaining further favours.
>
> My father's resources were at all times exceedingly precarious. He never received the smallest pension from Their Majesties. Yet in the last years of his life he made a touching effort to accumulate a certain amount, setting a few notes aside in his desk when he thought of it. 'That's for Matriona's [Maria's] portion,' he would say. At his death his whole fortune was found to consist of 3,000 roubles [£300]. As for the sum accumulated in his desk—it had completely disappeared. During the two days of distraction that followed my father's disappearance, an army of people passed through our apartment; had somebody had the lack of delicacy to take advantage of the situation by searching the desk?

The Empress from her own privy purse sent 30,000 roubles (£3,000) for each of the three children of Rasputin.

Besides this [Maria adds] we still had our home in Pokrovskoe, which thanks to my mother's practical spirit and good judgement, was transformed and enlarged. The *isba*, cradle of the family, had been raised, rooms added to it and numerous gifts had given an appearance of comfort, if not luxury, to its interior decoration.

The last time we saw the Empress at Tsarkoe Selo, she said to us sadly: 'Go my children, leave us, leave us quickly—we are being imprisoned.'

The poor everywhere, and the peasants in Siberia especially, celebrated Mass and said special prayers in the churches in memory of their 'martyr son Grigori Rasputin'. In Pokrovskoe the villagers brought flowers to decorate the oratory Grigori had built in the courtyard of his home.

Two months later, when the Revolution began in March 1917, a group of revolutionary soldiers broke into Anna's new church in Tsarskoe Selo where Rasputin was buried, dug up his body and carried it to the Forest of Pargolovo. There they built a funeral pyre of logs, drenched his body in petrol and set fire to it. A crowd of peasants, seeing the flames rise from the snow-covered earth, came up and formed a circle round it in an all-night vigil.

P

The Revolution

While the Tsaritsa pulled the strings of her political puppets and the dazed Tsar looked out of the window at the grey sky and the loveliness of the snow-covered park, slowly, but not imperceptibly, the Revolution crept up and gradually gathered force. Rodzianko, President of the Duma, told the Tsar: 'Do not compel the people to choose between you and the good of the country.' Pressing his head between his hands the Tsar said: 'Is it possible that for twenty-two years I have tried to act for the best and that for twenty-two years it was all a mistake.' Rodzianko replied: 'Yes, your Majesty, for twenty-two years you have followed a wrong course.' The British Ambassador called to give him a similar warning and was received standing up so that the meeting should be brief. 'Your Majesty must remember,' said Sir George Buchanan, 'the people and the army are but one and in the event of a revolution only a small portion of the army can be counted on to defend the dynasty.'

The bitterly cold winter had brought the temperatures down to 40° below zero. The railways, on which the food supplies depended, were brought to a standstill. A run on the bakeries brought in bread rationing. Strikes broke out in the metal-works. Women began to demonstrate in the streets—they had suffered acute privation in the two and a half years of war, and most of them had lost a husband, or a father, or heaven knew how many sons.

Meanwhile the political parties in the country had begun to coalesce into larger groups: all the liberal and left-wing deputies in the Duma, except the Socialists, formed a single party called the Progressive Bloc; they numbered 240 out of a total of 402 deputies: Rodzianko and Guchkov were its leaders. The Socialists tried to merge, while the Bolsheviks and Mensheviks tried to do the same. The aristocrats formed their own separate group known as the Union of Nobles and planned a palace revolution to get rid of the Tsar and the Tsaritsa. A few days before Rasputin's death the Grand Duke Paul, the Tsar's only surviving uncle, advised the Tsar to give the country a constitution. The Empress shook her head and the suggestion was turned down. The Tsar, a heavy chain-smoker, just kept on smoking. Some weeks later, on 7 February, the Grand Duke Alexander Mikhailovich, cousin and brother-in-law of the Tsar and father of Felix Yussupov's wife, handed a long letter to the Tsar stating: 'The situation cannot last long. I again repeat one cannot govern a country without listening to the voice of the people. . . . In conclusion I will say this, strange as it may appear, it is the Government which is preparing the revolution, the people do not want it.'

Next the Grand Duchess Maria, widow of the Tsar's eldest uncle the Grand Duke Vladimir, telephoned Rodzianko at one o'clock in the morning, asking him to come round urgently. He felt it would suggest a conspiracy to meet at that hour and went for lunch the next day. All her sons were there. She launched a devastating attack on the Empress, spoke of her pernicious influence and her interference in everything. 'She is the cause of the danger which threatens the Emperor and the rest of the Imperial family. Such conditions can no longer be tolerated. Things must be changed, something must be done, removed, destroyed.'

'What do you mean by removed?' Rodzianko asked.

'She must be annihilated.'

'Who?'

'The Empress.'

A *coup d'état* was being worked out by Prince Georgei Zvov, President of the *Zemgor* (the Civil Red Cross), and others including General Alexeyev, the Tsar's Chief of Staff. Everyone felt something had to be done quickly: there was no time to lose.

The Grand Duke Michael Alexandrovich, a brother of the Emperor, informed the Tsar that he ought to return to army headquarters because there were grave threats of mutiny. At home for two months with nothing to do but mope and be miserable, he had no wish to give up his dazed idleness. Reluctantly he agreed to go, saying: 'I shall take up dominoes again in my spare time.'

He left Tsarskoe Selo on 8 March, and that was the day the Revolution began. But nobody seemed to take it seriously: thousands of workers were already on strike, and crowds wandered through the streets of Petrograd calling for bread and peace. The cobbled streets, the shops, the entire setting was unchanged: occasionally one heard shots fired, lorries went by laden with noisy youths and one saw a few dead bodies lying in the road or in the gutter. People came to their upper windows to see what was going on and went in again. But life for the upper classes continued as before. Paléologue, the French

Ambassador, had guests to dinner that night, discussing which of the ballerinas at the Maryinsky theatre they preferred—Kschesinskaya, Pavlova or Karsavina; and the next day, 9 March, Buchanan sent a report to London stating: 'Some disorders occurred today.'

Crowds began to attack the bakeries in the north of the city and the Cossacks were brought out to support the police. Voices from the crowd shouted, 'You are not going to shoot the hungry,' and the Cossacks shouted back, 'We won't shoot.'

On Saturday, 10 March, the crowds, much larger now, carried red flags through the streets and shouted 'Down with the German woman!' meaning the Tsaritsa. The police fired on them; about sixty people were killed and many more wounded. The Cabinet, realizing that they were unable to handle the crisis, decided to replace a number of ministers. A telephone call to inform the Tsar was answered with the command that they must all stay in office. They begged the Tsar to return and deal with the situation, but he had left forms for proroguing or dismissing the Duma, which was accordingly prorogued. Later that Saturday evening, in reply to a harassed message from General Habalov, who had some weeks earlier been placed in command of the army in Petrograd, the Tsar telephoned: 'I command that the disorders in the capital shall be stopped tomorrow, as they are inadmissable at the heavy time of war with Germany and Austria.'

The next day, Sunday, posters were displayed everywhere in Petrograd warning the people that the police would fire on them if they gathered. The notices were ignored, the crowds were larger than ever. The police fired several times and a great many people were killed. The Pavlovsky Regiment was then called out, but the men mutinied and killed their colonel. The crack regiment of the Guards, Peter the Great's famous Preobrazhensky, came and disarmed the mutineers. Later that day the Volynsky Regiment mutinied and killed one of its officers. The Duma, on receiving the Tsar's prorogation order, refused to disperse and set about forming its own Cabinet. The names of likely members were noted. Basil Shulgin, a prominent Conservative member of the Duma, recommended Alexander Kerensky, the brilliant young Labour leader. Rodzianko meanwhile, as President, sent a telegram to the Tsar telling him of the very serious developments in the capital, ending with the words, 'May the blame not fall on the wearer of the Crown.' The Tsar did nothing. He just pushed aside the telegram, saying: 'Some more rubbish from that fat Rodzianko.'

Events on the next day, Monday, the 12th, were decisive. The soldiers of the Volynsky Regiment, whose barracks were near the Duma, came out and were joined by men of other regiments. Kerensky, engaged in discussions with other groups of the Left, on hearing the news sent someone to invite all the regiments to come to the Duma. One by one they all came and were joined by the factory workers. The Assize Court was sacked and set on fire, and when firemen arrived they were driven off. All the prison gates were forced open and the prisoners set free. The Arsenal and the formidable fortress of St Peter and St Paul were seized next. By noon 25,000 armed men had joined the Revolution. By the evening almost all the troops, including the Guards, had gone over. Military headquarters were captured as well as twenty police stations—all were set on fire.

Soon news was brought that the workmen were, by a show of hands, holding elections in various parts of the city for a Soviet or Council of Workmen Delegates, just as in 1905. Then 80,000 of these workers, waving Red banners and singing the 'Marseillaise', began to march to the Tauride Palace, where the Duma was in session. There was great uneasiness: one of the few officers who had come over earlier with the mutineers rushed in and asked for help. Kerensky consulted other members of the Duma, but they said nothing: so he took it upon himself to give the orders. Urgent action, he said, was necessary if any control was to be maintained.

In a few moments the crowd arrived and filled the halls, leaving no room to move. It was a friendly crowd. 'Kerensky took charge,' writes Shulgin. 'He spoke decisively, authoritatively, as one who had not lost his head. The soldiers who had streamed in consulted him and took his orders without question.'

The Soviet executive took possession of one of the halls in the Duma chamber, while the Cabinet appointed by the Duma got busy in another. Protopopov was told to retire. No one said a word to him as he left.

The people of the city began to arm that night, and the Grand Duke Michael, brother of the Tsar, who had attended the meeting of the Duma Cabinet, telephoned headquarters. He suggested that a minister who had the confidence of the country must be appointed at once. The Tsar, after a long delay, said he would make his decision when he returned to Tsarskoe Selo.

As the Grand Duke Michael left the Duma building in the small hours of the Tuesday morning, he saw lorries dashing along the street carrying red flags and firing captured machine-guns wildly. Fires were blazing in every quarter of the city. The police and army officers who had escaped execution by the mutineers were being hunted down, and begged the Provisional Committee of the Duma to help them.

All was over now. The Revolution, not consciously launched by agitators, had erupted spontaneously: the discontent had been boiling for years and now bubbled over because of the lack of food and of fuel to keep warm.

There were no leaders. The rebels came to the Duma for help and the Provisional Government Committee took them under its wing.

CHAPTER THIRTY-NINE

'They Will See My Village Before They Die'

On Tuesday, 13 March, lorries laden with revolutionary troops arrived at Tsarskoe Selo. The garrison there had already left and the Palace was protected only by the guard which had assembled in the courtyard. The Tsar meanwhile was on his way home from headquarters, taking a round-about rail journey to avoid delaying the troop-trains.

The next day the Duma selected the ministers for the Provisional Government. Prince Lvov was appointed Prime Minister, Guchkov Minister for War, Kerensky Minister of Justice: he accepted because, as Vice-President of the Soviet, he felt it would establish a link between the two groups who occupied different wings of the Tauride Palace.

The Government decided that the Tsar must abdicate, and Guchkov and Shulgin, both prominent members of the Duma, left at five o'clock the next morning by train to see the Emperor. At headquarters General Alexeyev, the Tsar's Chief of Staff, had already, at Rodzianko's request, consulted all the generals commanding the various Fronts about the Tsar's abdication. All agreed that it was essential. The Emperor, when told, was surprised and deeply affected. A form of abdication was sent to him by Alexeyev and the Emperor began to deal with it.

Late that night, 15 March, Guchkov and Shulgin, after a long, bitterly cold journey, arrived at Pskov and were received by the Tsar in the drawing-room of his train. Despite the years of hostility shown by the Empress, Guchkov was gentle and filled with grief. Shulgin's distress was even more evident.

After reading the document they had brought and hearing from his doctor that his son would never be cured, the Emperor named his brother Michael as his successor. 'You will understand a father's feelings,' he said. That night, no longer Tsar, Nikolai wrote in his diary: 'All around treachery, cowardice and deceit.'

Crowds waiting at Petrograd station when the two Duma delegates returned, insisted on being told what had been arranged. On learning that Michael was to be Tsar, they angrily made it clear that they would not put up with another Romanov. It was with difficulty that Guchkov and Shulgin got away. Grand Duke Michael, approached about the succession, found that Guchkov and Paul Milyukov, Minister of

Foreign Affairs, were in favour of his accepting; Rodzianko, Lvov and Kerensky were totally opposed to it. Michael eventually refused the Crown.

Later that afternoon the Tsaritsa was told of her husband's abdication. Count Paul Benkendorff, Marshal of the Imperial Court, states: 'As we left her, I saw that she sat down at the table and burst into tears.' To one of her ladies-in-waiting she said: 'Abdicated! And he all alone down there!'

Nikolai, granted leave by Guchkov and Shulgin to return to head-quarters to say good-bye, spent five miserable days there, completely ignored by the men around him and shown only the meagrest ceremony. His mother, the Dowager Empress, came from Kiev to comfort him; and was followed by a group of men sent by the new Government to put him under arrest, partly for his own safety; at the same time the Tsaritsa and her family were placed under arrest at Tsarskoe Selo. The ex-Tsar arrived there on 21 March. In their rooms, during a long talk with his wife, he broke down completely.

They occupied the same section of the Palace as before, but were allowed to use only a very small part of the park, where Nikolai got busy sweeping away the snow and doing some gardening, always with an armed military escort in attendance, who dressed badly, slouched and smoked, turning away if the ex-Tsar extended his hand to greet one of them. They shot the deer in the park, and it was most distressing for young Alexei to hear Derevenko, the sailor who was in attendance on him and who had received so many favours from the family, shout at him and sharply order him about.

Kerensky, anxious to move the ex-Tsar and his family to another part of the country for their safety, was agreeably surprised to receive, through the British ambassador, a message from King George V, offer-ing a home for Nikolai, his wife and children. It was readily accepted by the fallen rulers, who hopefully began to get their luggage together for the journey. But Kerensky came up against tremendous opposition. Asked what the Provisional Government's plans were for the ex-Tsar and his family, he said he was going to take them himself to Murmansk from where they could board a ship for England. The Soviet group in the Tauride Palace were most indignant and gave orders to the rail-waymen not to let the train through.

The partnership between the Duma and the Soviet was most uneasy. The Provisional Government, run by experienced members of the

Duma, was allowed by the Soviet to carry on, while they strengthened their own ranks. To the Soviet of Workers' Delegates they now added the Soviet of Soldiers' Delegates, and posted an army order stating that in all political actions the military unit was under the Soviet of Workers' and Soldiers' Delegates. Within two months there were two million deserters from the fighting forces.

Despite recurrent clashes, the Provisional Government continued for eight months. Kerensky, as Minister of Justice, set up a Commission of Investigation to examine and interrogate the Ministers of the Tsarist régime as well as others prominently involved: these included Anna Vyroubova, Prince Andronikov and others. At the head of the Commission was the Procureur of the Court of Assizes at Ekaterinoslav, Vladimir Michaelovich Roudenev. The ex-Emperor and ex-Empress were examined by Kerensky himself, who during the weeks of examination separated Nikolai and Alexandra so that there should be no collusion over their answers; only at meals were they allowed to meet, with an official always present. Benkendorff states: 'The confidence which the Emperor felt in Kerensky increased and the Empress shared the confidence'; they felt now that Kerensky was their sole protector. The statements made by Beletsky and Hvostov to the commission were most revealing, especially about the attempts to murder Rasputin, which have been quoted earlier. Anna Vyroubova was asked if she was Rasputin's mistress: her reply was brief: 'You had better get a doctor to examine me: he will be able to confirm my denial.' She was found to be a virgin.

After a very thorough examination of witnesses and studying police and other reports on Rasputin, Vladimir Michaelovich Roudenev said:

As so much was bruited in the public Press about the immorality of Rasputin, the closest attention was given to this phase. From the reports of the secret police it was found that his love affairs consisted solely of night orgies with music-hall singers and an occasional petitioner. It is on record that when drunk he sometimes hinted at intimacies in higher circles, especially in those circles through which he had risen to power, but of his relations with women of high society nothing was established, either by the police records or by information acquired by the Commission.

As for the accusation that in Siberia Rasputin was accustomed to bathe in company with women, and that he was affiliated with the

Khlysty sect, the Extraordinary Commission referred these charges to Gramoglassov, Professor of the Ecclesiastical Academy of Moscow, who after examination of all the evidence, testified that among peasants of many parts of Siberia the common bath was the usual custom, and that he found no evidence in the writings or preachings of Rasputin of any affiliation with the *Khlysty* doctrines.

Rasputin was a man of large heart. He kept open house, and his lodgings were always crowded with a curiously mixed company living at his expense.

The investigation disclosed an immense amount of evidence concerning the petitions carried by Rasputin to Court, but all these, as has been said, referred merely to applications for positions, favours, railway concessions and the like. Notwithstanding his great influence at Court not a single indication of Rasputin's political activity was disclosed.

On 16 April, five weeks after the start of the Revolution, Lenin arrived in Petrograd from Switzerland, travelling in a sealed carriage across Germany. He commandeered the charming house the ex-Tsar had presented to his mistress, the pretty little dancer Mathilde Kschesinskaya, and made it the Bolshevik headquarters. From the small upper balcony, Lenin addressed the crowds every day, stressing the need for fraternization at the Front and the immediate ending of the war. The distressed dancer hurried to the Tauride Palace and begged the Soviet group there to take care of her furniture, carpets, curtains and pictures. They agreed and carefully packed her things and moved them to a safe place; but she discovered later that all her possessions were taken over. So she fled to Paris.

On 3 May soldiers and workmen, furious on hearing that Guchkov and Milyukov wanted the war to continue, demonstrated in the streets and demanded their dismissal. The rising was suppressed, but the two ministers sent in their resignations; and Guchkov, the valiant adventurer, went to the Front and joined the Cossacks. In July there was a far more serious clash. While Kerensky, now the dominant figure in the Provisional Government, was at the Front to rouse the patriotism of the troops, the Bolsheviks in the Soviet tried to seize control, but the Cossacks and the Preobrazhensky Regiment came out in support of the Provisional Government, and the Soviet, discarding the small number of Bolsheviks in its midst, rallied to support the

Government. Prince Lvov now resigned and Kerensky became Prime Minister.

Seeing how close the Provisional Government was to losing control, and how dangerous it would be for the ex-Tsar and his family if the Bolsheviks came to power, Kerensky decided to move them from the capital. He obtained through the Swedish ambassador a guarantee from Germany that the British cruiser taking the family to England would not be attacked. But Lloyd George, the British Prime Minister, conscious of the years of hostility towards the Tsar by certain sections of the Liberal and Labour parties, sent a message to the British ambassador for verbal delivery: Sir George Buchanan, with tears in his eyes, said that the offer of asylum to the fallen rulers and their family was no longer 'insisted on'. A safe part of Russia was now sought and Tobolsk was selected; on the night of 13 August, Nikolai and his family travelled in a train flying a Japanese flag. At every station the carriage curtains were drawn. At Tyumen the family boarded a steamer for Tobolsk and saw, as they passed Pokrovskoe, Rasputin's house by the bank of the river Tura.

The family were lodged in the Governor's house at Tobolsk, old-fashioned but comfortable, with a very small garden. Nuns from a convent often brought food for them. The Bishop there was Hermogen, whom they knew well. With the royal prisoners were some members of their household—Dr Botkin, Prince Dolgorouky, General Tatichtches, Countess Hendrikova, Pierre Gilliard the Swiss tutor, Sidney Gibbes the English tutor, Alexei's faithful sailor Nagorny, and a number of maids and other servants. Their life, though cramped and confined, was not unpleasant. They were able to correspond with friends.

To Anna Vyroubova the ex-Tsaritsa wrote on 21 December: 'Yes, the past is finished. I thank God for all that there has been, that I had; and I shall live on memories, which no one shall take from me.' And again on the next day: 'The Lord is so near, one feels his support. I have peace at heart, though often I suffer greatly, greatly, for the country and you, little daughter.' And, just before Christmas: 'He [Nikolai] is simply astonishing, such strength of spirit, though he suffers without end for the country.'

To Lili Dehn too she wrote often. 'Have you received my postcard of 28 October? Everybody is well—my heart is not up to much, fit at times, but on the whole it is better. I live very quietly and seldom go out as it is too difficult to breathe in frozen air. . . . I read a lot, embroider and draw (I have to do it all with my spectacles, I am so old). I think of you often, pray for you and love you tenderly.' And on 15 March 1918, when they had been at Tobolsk for seven months:

> Today we have 20 degrees of frost, but the sun is warm and we have already had real Spring days. Godmother [meaning herself] does all housekeeping now, looks through books and accounts—a lot to do, quite a real housewife. Everybody is well—only a few colds, and feet ached, not very badly, but enough to keep from walking. They have all grown. Marie is now much thinner, the fourth [Anastasia] is stout and small. Tatiana helps everyone and everywhere, as usual. Olga is lazy, but they are all well in spirit. They are already sunburnt, they work hard, sew and cut wood, or we should have none.

Meanwhile Kerensky faced another attempt by the Bolsheviks to overthrow the Provisional Government. On 6 November (by the old calendar 24 October—hence the 'October Revolution') the Bolsheviks in Petrograd, with almost all the troops on their side, struck, and on the next day the whole town was theirs. The Winter Palace, defended by a battalion of women soldiers, was captured by the Bolsheviks. Ministers of the Provisional Government were arrested and confined in the fortress of St Peter and St Paul. Kerensky, in Pskov to gain support from troops outside the capital, managed to escape. A Bolshevik Government was formed with Lenin as Prime Minister and Trotsky as Foreign Minister. All land was nationalized, private trade was made illegal, universal suffrage at the age of eighteen was granted to both sexes and negotiations were begun to end the war.

With the Bolsheviks in power the position of the ex-Tsar and his family was changed completely. On Christmas Day prayers were said in the church at Tobolsk for the Tsar and his family, and, as a result, they were not allowed to go to the church again. Then the expenses for the family were cut down to 600 roubles* a month for each person; shortly afterwards they were put on soldiers' rations. Orders were next given for the removal of epaulettes: the ex-Tsar removed his. From one week to the next the humiliation continued.

* Normally it would have been equal to £60 per month, but the rouble had greatly depreciated.

In April 1918 an official arrived from Moscow with instructions, he said, to escort the ex-Tsar to Moscow. Nikolai felt that the German ambassador wanted him to sign the Peace Treaty: 'I will sooner cut off my hand,' he said.

Nikolai got ready to leave. The ex-Tsaritsa, with her son very seriously ill, was confronted with a distressing decision: should she stay with her son or accompany her husband? After pacing the room restlessly for some time, she decided it was her duty to be with her husband. Their daughter Marie and Dr Botkin went with them, attended by an escort of eight soldiers.

Though late in April, the river Tura was still frozen and they had to travel in carts, stopping to change horses at various points. Their last stop was under the windows of Rasputin's house in Pokrovskoe. Grigori's widow, son and both daughters looked sadly at them. 'My mother,' says Maria, 'wanted to go to them while the horses were being changed, but the guards were watchful.' The Grand Duchess Marie made a quick sketch of the house and sent it to Maria later. 'Apart from that,' adds Maria, 'they could do no more than blow kisses to my mother from a distance. Alexandra Feodorovna was weeping.' Rasputin had always said to Lili Dehn and others: 'Willing or unwilling, they will come to Tobolsk and they will see my village before they die.' Nikolai made a note in his diary of their stop in front of Rasputin's house.

They boarded a train at Tyumen. The man who was to escort them to Moscow was ceaselessly watched by a group of men from Ekaterinburg in the Ural mountains. He tried to avoid them, for he knew that the Soviet at Ekaterinburg was ferociously hostile and was resolved to prevent the ex-Tsar and his family from escaping.

To protect them Yakovlev, who was escorting the ex-Tsar, telephoned Moscow and was told to take the prisoners to Ekaterinburg and hand them over to the local Soviet. A small, old-fashioned house there, belonging to a merchant named Ipatyev, was taken over for the prisoners. It stood on a slope so that part of the ground floor was below the level of the road. Three weeks later, young Alexei, still unwell, arrived with his three sisters, the two tutors and the retainers. The tutors on arriving at Ekaterinburg were officially ordered to leave.

The Soviet was now in charge. The meals were brought to the table in a large bowl into which everyone dipped their spoons, including Avdeyev, the new man in charge, who stretched across the shoulders of the ex-Tsar and his wife to help himself.

There were apparently attempts to rescue the imprisoned family. Thousands of Czech prisoners-of-war, on their way across Siberia for repatriation, had been formed into an army by Admiral Kolchak, a dedicated monarchist, and were advancing fast on Ekaterinburg. Captain Paul Bulygin, formerly on the staff of the Dowager Empress, fearing that the advance of the Czech troops might prompt the Soviet to murder the family, worked out a plan to take them by river steamer to the Arctic Ocean. A note signed by a 'White' officer reached the ex-Tsar asking him to open one of the windows as a signal. He did. In his diary, on 27 June, Nikolai made this entry: 'We spent an anxious night, and kept up our spirits, fully dressed. All this was because a few days ago we received two letters, one after the other, in which we were told to get ready to be rescued by some devoted people, but days passed and nothing happened, and the waiting and the uncertainty were very painful.'

As Kolchak and his troops approached, the Soviet began to act. A new military commandant arrived at the Ipatyev house. The Russian troops guarding the prisoners were dismissed and were replaced by German, Magyar and Lett prisoners-of-war. The ex-Tsaritsa in a letter to Anna Vyroubova said: 'Though the storm draws nearer, I am calm in spirit;' and in another letter 'Behold the bridegroom cometh!' All hope had by now departed. On the evening of 14 July the entire family got down on their knees and sang 'At rest with the Saints'. On the morning of 16 July, Yurovsky, who was now in charge, informed the commander of the guards that the entire family was going to be killed that night and ordered him to supply his men with revolvers. Around the house there was a double palisade, erected before the prisoners were moved in: a large truck was now concealed in the passage there.

Late that evening the ex-Tsar and his family were ordered to descend to the ground-floor room, which had small windows overlooking the garden, and, because of the slope, was a half-basement at the other end. Nikolai led the way, carrying his son in his arms. He asked for some chairs, and three were brought—in these the parents and their son sat.

Yurovsky and his men then entered. The Soviet's sentence of execution was read out by Yurovsky, who fired first and killed Nikolai. All the other men then raised their revolvers and fired at the rest, who included Dr Botkin and the retainers. Neither Alexei nor Anastasia were killed at once, further shots had to be fired and on Anastasia a bayonet was used.

The children's spaniel, Jimmy, in the room with them, had his head battered with the butt of a rifle. The ex-Empress and the girls must have got down on their knees, for the bullet marks were at a low level on the wall.

The bodies were carried out to the truck and taken to a mine shaft outside the village of Koptyaki, fourteen miles away, where fires were lit and vitriol used before the bodies were dropped into the mine.

On the walls of the room where the family was murdered one of the Germans in the shooting party wrote these words quoted from a poem by Heine: 'Belshazzar was that same night done to death by his servants.'

Nine days later Kolchak's army captured Ekaterinburg.

Further Reading

Nicholas II: *Journal Intime*. Translated by A. Pierre. Payot, Paris, 1925.
The Letters of the Tsar to the Tsaritsa 1914–1917. Bodley Head, 1929.
Letters of the Tsaritsa to the Tsar 1914–1916. Introduction by Sir Bernard Pares. Duckworth, 1923.
The Secret Letters of the Last Tsar: The Confidential Correspondence Between Nicholas II and His Mother, Dowager Empress Marie Feodorovna. Edited by Edward J. Bing. Nicholson & Watson, 1937.

Alexander, Grand Duke of Russia: *Once a Grand Duke*. Cassell, 1932.
Anonymous: *The Fall of the Romanoffs*. Herbert Jenkins, 1917.
Benkendorff, Count Paul: *Last Days at Tsarskoe Selo*. Heinemann, 1927.
Botkin, Gleb: *The Real Romanovs*. Revell, 1931.
Buchanan, Sir George: *My Mission to Russia*. 2 vols. Cassell, 1923.
Buchanan, Meriel: *The Dissolution of an Empire*. Murray, 1932.
Petrograd, The City of Trouble. Collins, 1918.
Bulygin, Paul, and Alexander Kerensky: *The Murder of the Romanovs*. Introduction by Sir Bernard Pares. Hutchinson, 1935.
Buxhoeveden, Baroness Sophie: *Left Behind: Fourteen Months in Siberia During the Revolution*. Longmans, 1929.
Before the Storm. Macmillan, 1938.
The Life and Tragedy of Alexandra Feodorovna, Empress of Russia. Longmans, 1928.
Bykov, P. M.: *The Last Days of Tsardom*. Martin Lawrence, 1934.
Dehn, Lili: *The Real Tsaritsa*. Thornton Butterworth, 1922.
Dillon, Dr E. J.: *Russia Today and Yesterday*. Dent, 1929.
Dukes, Sir Paul: *The Story of 'ST. 25'*. Cassell, 1938.
Florinksy, Michael T.: *The End of the Russian Empire*. Collier, 1961.
Fülöp-Miller, René: *Rasputin: the Holy Devil*. Putnam, 1928.
Gilliard, Pierre: *Thirteen Years at the Russian Court*. Hutchinson, 1921.
Huxley, Aldous: *Do What You Will* (Essays). Chatto, 1929.
Illiodor (Trufanov), Sergei: *The Mad Monk of Russia*. Century, 1918.
Kerensky, Alexander: *The Crucifixion of Liberty*. Barker, 1934.
Russia and History's Turning Point. Cassell, 1966.
The Catastrophe. Appleton, 1927.

Knox, Major-General Sir Alfred: *With the Russian Army (1914–17).* 2 vols. Hutchinson, 1921.

Kokovstsov, Count Vladimir N.: *Out of My Past: The Memoirs of Count Kokovtsov.* Stanford University Press, 1935.

Kschesinskaya, Mathilde: *Dancing in Petersburg.* Translated by Arnold Haskell. Doubleday, 1961.

Lockhart, Sir Robert Bruce: *Memoirs of a British Agent.* Putnam, 1932.

Liepman, Heinz: *Rasputin, A New Judgement.* Frederick Muller, 1958.

Massie, Robert K.: *Nicholas and Alexandra.* Gollancz, 1968.

Moorehead, Alan: *The Russian Revolution.* Collins, 1958.

Omessa, Charles: *Rasputin and the Russian Court.* Newnes, 1918.

Paléologue, Maurice: *An Ambassador's Memoirs.* 3 vols. Translated by F. A. Holt. Doran, 1925.

Pares, Sir Bernard: *The Fall of the Russian Monarchy.* Cape, 1939.

Preston, Thomas: *Before the Curtain.* John Murray, 1950.

Purishkevich, V. M.: *Comment j'ai tué Raspoutine.* Povolovsky, Paris, 1923.

   Nous avons tué Raspoutine. Povolovsky, Paris, 1953.

Radziwill, Princess Catherine: *Nicholas II: The Last of the Tsars.* Cassell, 1931.

   The Taint of the Romanovs. Cassell, 1931.

Rasputin, Maria: *My Father.* Cassell, 1934.

   The Real Rasputin. John Long, 1929.

Rodzianko, M. V.: *The Reign of Rasputin.* Philpot, 1927.

Robien, Louis de: *The Diary of a Diplomat.* Translated by Camilla Sykes. Michael Joseph, 1969.

Sava, George: *Rasputin Speaks.* Faber, 1941.

Simanovich, A.: *Rasputin, Der Allmächtige Bauer.* Hensel & Co. Verlag, Berlin, 1922.

Spiridovich, General Alexander: *Raspoutine.* Payot, Paris, 1935.

   Les Dernières Années a la cour de Tsarskoe Selo. Payot, Paris, 1928.

Vyroubova, Anna: *Memories of the Russian Court.* Macmillan, 1923.

Vassili, Count Paul: *Behind the Veil at the Russian Court.* Cassell, 1913.

Vögel-Jorgensen, T.: *Rasputin: Prophet, Libertine, Plotter.* Unwin, 1917.

Vorres, Ian: *The Last Grand Duchess.* Hutchinson, 1964.

Vulliamy, C. E. (editor): *Red Archives.* Translated A. L. Hynes. Bles, 1929.

Q

Wilton, Robert: *The Last Days of the Romanovs* (including depositions).
    Thornton Butterworth, 1920.
Wilson, Colin: *Rasputin and the Fall of the Romanovs*. Barker, 1964.
Yussupov, Prince Felix: *Lost Splendour*. Cape, 1953.
    La Fin de Raspoutine. Libraire Plon, Paris, 1927.

Index

Cassell & Co., Ltd, 1972